David Milner

Ward Lock Educational

ISBN 0 7062 4268 8

First published 1983

Set in 10 on 12 point Times New Roman
by Alan Sutton Publishing Ltd
and printed by Finland Printers Ltd
for Ward Lock Educational
47 Marylebone Lane
London W1M 6AX

A Ling Kee Company

Contents

For Rosmond, Daniel and Leah

Introduction

The first edition of this book was written nearly ten years ago; it was an attempt to provide an account of racial attitude development in young children and to describe some of the effects of racism on the development of black children. There was, at that time, no adequate single source of information on these processes that was accessible to teachers, social workers and others who, it was felt, would be assisted by more knowledge of this area. In some ways the book enjoyed an undeserved celebrity, precisely because it was the only contribution of its kind; but in a controversial and volatile field like race relations, writing has a more limited 'shelf-life' than elsewhere, and although the book has continued to appear in reading-lists, it has needed revision for some time.

Some of the first edition remains intact in these pages, principally the historical material; some has been discarded, for example the coverage of the West Indian and Asian cultural backgrounds. Despite many people's unwillingness to accept the fact, Britain's black population are no longer 'immigrants' and it is not helpful to treat them as such. The sending societies and the migration factor have receded in influence on the settlers, and as far as the children are concerned, may seem very remote indeed. In fact some 95 per cent of children of West Indian parentage now in the schools were born in Britain[310]. The very different perspectives of a native black population from an immigrant one are reflected in these pages; perhaps this also brings their experience rather closer to that of their American counterparts, from whom a good deal of the research material in this book is drawn.

The basic account of racial attitude development remains essentially the same, while taking note of recent developments in research and in the wider society. Through talking to a wide variety of audiences in the intervening period it was clear that the 'message' of the book had not penetrated far beyond a self-selected constituency of teachers committed to the principles of multiracial education. One of the imperatives that has emerged over the same period is the need to cultivate an awareness of these issues beyond multiracial areas and it is to this end that this basic account is directed.

The remainder of the book has been updated and some entirely new material and emphases have been introduced. The principal changes reflect (in order of appearance not importance) my wish to ground the account on a more thorough foundation of social psychology than before, and the need to take note of the radical changes in black identity that the past decade has seen, both in this country and abroad. My own views on this latter issue have changed significantly (and they have certainly 'changed' a great deal from how others have represented them), though, in response to changing *evidence*, not vogue, social pressure or wishful thinking. If there is another change of emphasis, it derives from a growing realization of the dangers in the psychologist's concern with 'prejudice'. Psychologists have reified 'prejudice' so that it is sometimes seen as a psychological phenomenon with a life of its own: something that people 'are' or 'are not', an affliction of their personality which determines whether they will feel and act favourably or unpleasantly towards minority groups and individuals. It can be that, but more often the racial prejudice with which this book is concerned is simply the individual manifestation of social, political and economic forces. This has been styled 'institutional racism' and refers to all those social processes, overt and covert, by which black people are (intentionally or effectively) devalued and disprivileged in a systematic way. This is not to say that we should solely restrict ourselves to a study of these wider forces of racism, excluding any psychological perspective in the process; in the final analysis, racism (even institutional racism) is mediated by and to *individuals*, alone and in groups. Individual and institutional racism should be seen as indivisible counterparts, mutually-reinforcing and regenerating each other. The term 'prejudice' has been retained, however, as a convenient shorthand for the psychological dimension of racism.

This book has no pretensions to being a handbook for multiracial education. Despite the recent proliferation of books with titles which sound as though they are precisely that, I rather doubt that such a book is possible, and certainly I am not the person to write it. I am writing as a social psychologist, who, while having spent many hours in classrooms, is not a classroom teacher in a school. I have been concerned rather to provide a theoretical and empirical background for those who are concerned about children's racial attitudes, and to try to spell out the principles on which, I believe, any ameliorative educational strategies should be based. These are not

2

issues and principles which are restricted to any one cultural context or period of time; just as evidence and insight from the United States and elsewhere constantly 'feeds in' to this discussion, so too can the contribution be reciprocated, it is hoped, by illumination of other problem areas 'in the light of' the British experience described here.

In the introduction to the first edition of this book I wrote: 'This book has been difficult to write through attempting to satisfy at least two different audiences; on the one hand, social psychologists and educationalists, and on the other, teachers, local education authorities, community workers and others, who have rather different needs through dealing with these issues at a practical rather than a theoretical level. Academic readers, therefore, should try to forgive the occasional intrusion of the real world, while other readers must try to bear with the anaesthetic prose style of the research reports from which so much of the material is drawn.' I can only say that the implicit apology applies with still more force to this edition.

It is a pleasure to be able to record in print my gratitude to a number of people who have helped me in various ways: my colleagues at the Polytechnic of Central London, particularly Stuart Menzies; the Commission for Racial Equality; the staff of the Research Centre for Human Relations, New York University, and Professor Thomas Pettigrew of the Department of Psychology and Social Relations, Harvard University for the facilities they provided for me; and a long list of people who have sustained me when I needed it, including Mollie Lloyd, Isidore Pushkin, Louise Derman-Sparks, Brad Chambers, Adrian Smith, and of course my family. Finally, I would like to acknowledge my enduring debt to my friend and teacher, Henri Tajfel, who died so tragically early this year. He will be remembered as a great scholar, but more important than that, as a *mensh*.

D.M.
London, October 1982

1
Prejudice: a pre-history

Prejudiced attitudes have almost certainly existed since groups of people first distinguished themselves from one another. Essentially, they are irrational, unjust or intolerant dispositions towards other groups, and they are often accompanied by stereotyping. This is the attribution of the supposed characteristics of the whole group to all its individual members. Stereotypes exaggerate the uniformity within a group and similarly exaggerate the differences between this group and others. The entire group is tarred with the same brush, obscuring individual differences. Of course, this process is made much easier when there are visible physical differences between groups; these can be persuasively depicted as signifying other, more profound differences and these differences of 'nature' can provide a reason for differential treatment. In this way prejudices and stereotypes have expedited the oppression of groups of people throughout history, and where there have been differences in skin colour, the most obvious and intractable of physical differences, the process has been facilitated.

This 'racial' prejudice is not essentially different from religious, political or other prejudices in its psychological dimension, as we shall show later; similar derogatory ideologies may develop between peoples who are visually indistinguishable but who differ according to other, more abstract criteria. Indeed, prejudiced attitudes need bear so little relation to real distinctions between groups that they can be fostered where no such differences exist. Walter Lippman[241] described how Aristotle understood this very well: 'to justify slavery he must teach the Greeks a way of seeing their slaves that comported with the continuance of slavery', for no obvious differences distinguished slaves and masters. Aristotle decreed that 'He is by nature formed a slave who is fitted to become the chattel of another person, and on that account is so.'[10] In this proclamation he was imputing certain constitutional characteristics to the slaves which predetermined their social role, thus justifying their exploitation as part of the natural order of things. As Lippmann puts it, 'Our slave must be a slave by nature if we are Athenians who wish to have no qualms.'

The essence of this is the recourse to quasi-scientific explanations of imaginary group differences to rationalize an exploitative social arrangement. It is a common feature of such social relationships, regularly repeated over the course of the following millenia and no doubt pre-dating this era also. The superstructure of group prejudice has invariably been supported by formal or informal theories of group differences, purporting to justify these attitudes.

It was not until the eighteenth and nineteenth centuries that 'scientific' theories of race became widespread, and only comparatively recently that race attitudes themselves came to be studied. This chapter will convey something of the climate of racial thought in the period leading up to the time when social psychology came to focus on these issues; we will show how the study of race and racial attitudes has been influenced by both academic and lay conceptions of racial groups, and by the prevailing context of social relations between them.

Hostile attitudes towards black people in Britain, for example, are not a new phenomenon. Queen Elizabeth I declared herself 'discontented at the great number of Negroes and blackamoors who had crept in since the troubles between Her Majesty and the King of Spain', a theme with which modern British politicians have been happy to associate themselves, despite the intervening centuries of civilization. The voyages of 'discovery' to the African continent and its subsequent colonization marked the first sustained contact between the 'white' peoples of Western Europe and the 'black' peoples of Africa and provided a great stimulus to popular attitudes towards these 'races'. Long before this, however, notions of dark and mystical beings were common in Western cultures and may have influenced the ways in which black people were later to be regarded. One of the earliest instances of this is found in the writings of John Cassian, a monk of Bethlehem around AD 400. He tells of his conversations ('Conferences') with the Egyptian hermits who directed their lives towards the attainment of a vision of God. The experience of one such ascetic is described in the following way:

> And when at last he sat down to eat, the devil came to him in the shape of a hideous negro, and fell at his feet saying: 'Forgive me for making you undertake this labour.'[63]

Another pilgrim to the desert, having had only palm leaves and dry bread to eat for twenty days,

> . . . saw the demon coming against him. There stood before
> him a person like a Negro woman, ill-smelling and ugly. He
> could not bear her smell and thrust her from him.

The hallucinogenic circumstances of these visions are less important
than the evidence they provide of an early association of 'the Negro'
with the Devil, with filth and with ugliness.

The association of blackness with evil is a common theme both
historically and cross-culturally. 'Black' had a highly pejorative
connotation in England in and before the sixteenth century. Its
meanings included 'deeply stained with dirt, soiled, dirty, foul . . .
having dark or deadly purposes, malignant; deadly, disastrous,
sinister'[204] and so on. White had a correspondingly pure connotation. The two colours, 'being coloures utterlye contrary'[204] denoted
the polarity of good and evil, virtue and baseness, God and the
Devil. The association of these colours can be seen in literature,
folklore and mythology for centuries before this time and indeed till
the present day. James I wrote a book on witchcraft called *The
Demonologie* in which many of the stories relate to the 'master of
the coven' who was not only the personification of the Devil but was
also always portrayed as black. Nor is this usage restricted to the
literature of the occult. Gergen[133] points out that in the mainstream
of English literature, 'a tendency to use white in expressing forms of
goodness and black in connoting evil is discernible in the works of
Chaucer, Milton, Shakespeare, Hawthorne, Poe and Melville'; and
Bastide[28] detects the same tendency in religious art and literature.

The same colour usage has been shown to exist in a variety of
different cultures. Gergen[133] cites anthropological evidence from
Tibet, Siberia, Mongolia, West Africa, Zimbabwe and from the
North American Creek Indians, for example, all of which provide
parallel instances of these same colour values. This evidence has
persuaded some writers that there may be universal cultural experiences which have given rise to these associations, and that both may
influence racial attitudes. The argument is a controversial one and it
is reviewed in Chapter 4; for the present, suffice to say that these
colour values have certainly helped to provide an evaluative context
within which black people have been accommodated, and which
may have influenced their evaluation.

It was not until the mid-sixteenth century that English travellers

7

landed in Africa although Portuguese exploration and trading in the continent had been under way for a hundred years. Shortly, the first accounts of these 'black soules' reached London, as did a sprinkling of the black people themselves, imported as manservants and indentured labour. This was a rather sudden introduction to a people whose existence had been virtually unacknowledged, save for mention of Ethiopia in the Bible, and reference to the 'sub-Sahara' in the literature of antiquity. Moreover, the colour of these persons was the antithesis of the contemporary ideal – of alabaster skin and cheeks like roses. Extending the highly negative connotations of blackness and black objects to black *people* was therefore a logical step. The equation of whiteness with goodness, purity and humanity defined these totally 'opposite' beings as somehow inhuman. In Hakluyt's *Principall Navigations, Voiages and Discoveries of the English Nation,* Robert Baker described the beings he encountered in Guinea in 1562, 'whose likeness *seem'd* men to be, but all as blacke as coles'[154]. From the unwittingly ethnocentric perspective of Europeans, this sub-human character was thoroughly confirmed by the black man's 'heathen' religions, 'savage' behaviour, his geographical proximity to the most human-like animals, the apes, and his libido. Interestingly, Bastide[28] detects a progressive change in the portrayal of Christ in religious painting dating from this time. Whereas previously unmistakeably Semitic features were depicted, these underwent a gradual Aryanization in an effort to avoid the stigma attaching to darker physical characteristics.

Curtin[79] argues that the travellers themselves were not unduly antagonistic towards black people and that the savage image of Africans was fostered less by them than by writers at home with a taste for the exotic; the public's curiosity and the 'libidinous fascination for descriptions of other people who break with impunity the taboos of one's own society' ensured that these aspects of African life were related in the greatest and most lurid detail. These writings inevitably affected popular conceptions of black people although they were not markedly hostile at that time. Jordan[204] suggests that 'It was not until the slave trade came to require justification in the eighteenth century that some Englishmen found special reason to lay emphasis on the Negro's savagery.' The colonization of the New World demanded an unlimited supply of cheap labour in order for its enterprises to survive. Native crops required labour-intensive cultivation and Africa contained unlimited amounts of the human commodity. From the fifteenth century onwards the Portuguese had captured Africans, 'put yrons upon their legges'[154], and carried them into slavery. Early in the sixteenth century black slaves were supplied to their settlements in America; later a few Englishmen supplied the Spanish with slaves, but the English did not enter significantly into the slave trade until the seventeenth century.

When they did, they did so with a vengeance. Some fifteen million slaves were landed in the Americas from the sixteenth to nineteenth centuries. As Segal[340] wrote:

> The slave trade was more than the hinge of colonial exploit-ation . . . it was the basis of British — as well as French and American — mercantile prosperity and the source of industrial expansion. . . . It was the huge profits from the slave and sugar trades which produced much of the capital for Britain's industrial revolution. . . . The technological achievements which were to give the West political and economic domin-ance over so wide an area of the world were made possible by the miseries of the middle passage.

The brutalities of slavery have been amply documented elsewhere and will not be reiterated here. Accompanying and rationalizing the system were certain racial ideologies which were quite as brutalizing as the material conditions of plantation life. These were largely a reflection of the uncomfortable contradiction between whites' actual treatment of the slaves, and the high moral tone of the puritan ethics they piously espoused. Explanations of the discrepancy had to be generated, and these were couched in terms of the inferiority of the slaves, and both their sub-human status and the social arrange-ments embodied in slavery were legitimized in law. The code of South Carolina portrayed Negroes as 'of barbarous, wild, savage natures' and many states passed laws which confined the slaves (and their offspring) to bondage for life, forbade marriage, education, religious practice and even social life for slaves.

Racial thought in the eighteenth and nineteenth centuries
Coincident with the period of slavery was the infancy of scientific thought about human types. This was not fortuitous, but the result of intellectual curiosity aroused by white Europeans' first prolonged contact with the apparently different variety of human beings they had found in Africa. Developments in biology and later in anthro-pology stimulated interest further. The earliest racial theorizing in Europe sought to explain the political ascendancy of particular European races by their superiority according to certain mental and

physical criteria. Boulainvilliers was a proponent of this type of view as early as the seventeenth century, eulogizing the Germanic race. Though this was not a new notion, it helped to refurbish the myth of Nordic superiority which in turn undoubtedly influenced the evaluation of the starkly contrasting dark peoples of the world.

As well as being politically expedient, theories which sought to classify and order human types reflected similar developments in biology. In 1735, Karl Linnaeus[233] published his *Systema Naturae*, a classificatory scheme for all plant and animal life, including humans. This attempted to make sense of the wealth of information about living things emerging from the scientific discoveries of the period. Later Linnaeus distinguished four varieties of human beings — black, yellow, red and white, but he did not order them in any way. At about the same time, an ancient equivalent, 'The Great Chain of Being', was resurrected. This was a conception of all living things as an ordered hierarchy, headed by humans (who had a special relationship with Heaven by way of the next link upwards, the angels). This notion reassured people that they were both superior to animals and nearly divine, and as Jordan[204] notes, served 'to satisfy the eighteenth century's ravenous appetite for hierarchical principles in the face of social upheaval'. Fairly soon a synthesis of the various systems emerged, and although few explicit references were made to the hierarchical ordering of the races, there was an automatic assumption that the white European race was the primary stock, a matter which was obvious from its civilization and cultural ascendancy. And, as Curtin[79] points out, 'If whiteness of skin was the mark of the highest race, then darker races would be inferior in increasing order of their darkness', assigning the Africans to the lowest human station, the nearest link with the apes.

The following 150 years, until the start of the twentieth century, was the most fertile period for the development of racial thought. Barzun[27], Curtin[79], Gossett[147], Stanton[357], Bolt[41], Walvin[413] and Kiernan[218] provide admirable histories of this scientific era. Two themes of the period are particularly relevant for our purposes: the implicit racism of so much racial theory, and the relation of that theory to wider social and political circumstances.

To take the second of these first, it is possible to relate particular currents of racial thought to their authors' declared positions on wider racial issues. This is not to suggest a simple cause-effect relationship between the two, in either direction. But it is equally wrong to deny the intercourse, conscious or otherwise, between these two kinds of beliefs. The teachings of science, then as now, *are* enlisted to justify social and political policy; similarly, existing social arrangements are adduced as the living proof of scientific theory. Thus in the debate over slavery some of the Polygenist theorists, (who believed in the separate — and inherently unequal — creation of the different races), were themselves pro-slavery in their writings, while the teachings of the Monogenists who adhered to the 'official' account of Adam and Eve's procreation of the human race spoke for (or were recruited by) the other side. When we set aside individual examples and look at the whole period it is impossible to ignore the clear correlation between scientific thought and its social context. Scientists are inevitably influenced by the social arrangements and climate of values around them, and their own ideologies; at the same time, scientific theory plays a role in sustaining those arrangements. It is, as they say, no coincidence that the period during which white people were most directly engaged in the exploitation of black people — through the slave trade, slavery itself, imperialism and colonialism — was the period which saw the zenith of racist scientific thinking. There is clearly a sense in which it was *necessary* for certain ideologies concerning black people to develop among the public at large, in order to reconcile humanitarian religious beliefs with the barbaric treatment meted out to black people, and the scientific community was not immune from this process of rationalization. This is the other theme which emerges clearly from this era: that whatever the individual persuasions of racial theorists on the origins of the races, or the significance of racial differences, the common thread that runs through virtually all racial theory of this time is the fundamental assumption of the inferiority of black people.

A small sample of the principal racial theorists is sufficient to illustrate this. Edward Long, a biologist resident in Jamaica in the eighteenth century, exemplified both currents. He maintained that Africans were 'brutish, ignorant, idle, crafty, treacherous, bloody, thievish, mistrustful and superstitious people'[247]. An avid pro-slavery campaigner, it seems that he was not above fabricating evidence from his Jamaican experiences to support his arguments. At a more scientific level, Robert Knox's *The Races of Men*[224] was the first systematic racist treatise, and according to Banton[24], 'one of the most articulate and lucid statements of racism ever to appear'. His writings were enormously influential and his ideas found their way into the speeches of politicians, Emerson and Disraeli amongst them. His predecessor in Edinburgh, James Pritchard, was far more enlightened, and in fact anticipated much of Darwin's evolutionary theory. But although, as Curtin[79] points out, he attempted 'to defend the racial equality of mankind through the theory of monogenesis', he shared the assumption that Africans were presently an inferior race.

In Europe the French Count Arthur de Gobineau was the most prominent of racist thinkers and was internationally influential. Barzun[27] discusses the complex relationship between his thought and the social and cultural climate of his time. Nietzsche and W.S. Chamberlain, for example, were to take up his theories, and if they 'were the visible agents of dissemination for the Count's ideas of race, it is also true that they were helped by others, anonymous and unconscious propagandists about whom we can talk only as the 'forces' and 'movements' of the century'. The political influence of Gobineau's writings survived him by many years; his belief in the supremacy of the Nordic-Aryan race, and in the degeneracy of 'semitized' and 'nigridized' races was resurrected to bolster the doctrines of National Socialism in pre-War Germany.

In the New World, racial theory had a more vital aspect: it spoke to the immediate domestic relations between black and white, slave and master. The polygenist teachings of Morton and the 'American School' (primarily Nott and Gliddon) underwrote Southern slavery in justifying Negro subordination through 'scientific' evidence of innate inferiority. In an obituary of Morton, Gibbes[134] stated the matter quite plainly:

> We can only say that we of the South should consider him as our benefactor, for aiding most materially in giving to the Negro his true position as an inferior race.

In retrospect it can be seen that the opposing monogenists, though more humanitarian in motive, abetted this process by conceding the central tenet of Negro inferiority. Some, like Bachman, were prevented from admitting the possibility of racial equality by their own ownership of slaves.

To assert that racial theory in this period was implicitly or explicitly racist is not to make a value judgment from a more informed contemporary perspective; perhaps with the exception of the out-and-out propagandists, 'these were the teachings of science at its best for its own time'[79], and we would do well to evaluate current theory in the same critical light.

The advent of Darwinism might have diverted racial thought into more enlightened avenues, having established the fundamental kinship of the human races. But it is a measure of the grip that racist thinking held on the scientific community and the public at large that Darwin's theories and their derivatives were interpreted to provide a framework which could encompass racial strife and the subjugation of one race by another. As Gossett[147] shows:

> Darwin provided a new rationale within which nearly all the old convictions about race superiority and inferiority could find a place. . . . The idea of natural selection was translated into a struggle between individual members of a society, between different nations and between different races. This conflict, far from being an evil thing, was nature's indispensable method for producing superior nations and superior races.

These interpretations were given added weight by Spencer's beliefs: 'the survival of the fittest' was his concept. Spencer and his contemporaries helped to lay the foundations of sociology in America, and their influence extended to neighbouring disciplines like psychology. Similar racial thinking prevailed in England too: Sir Francis Galton's Eugenics movement provided further allies and marked the beginning of an unfortunate association between some branches of psychology and implicitly racist social theories about human types, an association which has continued long into the present century.*

To Galton, heredity was all; inherited biological qualities determined a person's place in the world. Intelligence and motivation were transmitted from one generation to the next and indeed the distribution of these capacities through different social classes was the foundation of social structure: social class was nothing more than the natural expression of biological differences in ability. In this scheme of things the rich are ordained to be so because of their natural abilities; the poor are naturally disadvantaged by their congenitally inferior inheritance, and the incidence of poverty, insanity, crime and immorality are further evidence of a degenerate blood-stock.

Naturally, this hierarchy of inheritance and ability was extended to races as well as social classes. Galton considered that 'the average intellectual standard of the Negro race is some two grades below our own', and, as if to clinch the argument, reminds us that 'it is seldom we hear of a white traveller meeting with a black chief whom he feels to be a better man'[132].

While Spencer's concept of intelligence was somewhat different

13

from Galton's in detail, he added a further term to the biological equation with his supposition that there was an inverse relationship between intelligence and fertility. In his view, the nervous system and the reproductive system competed for the same supply of 'nutrient elements' in the body and therefore to the extent that one prevailed the other must suffer. The far-reaching social consequence of this would be that the promiscuous and fertile ignorant classes would eventually out-number their more intelligent but less fecund superiors. The natural order would change, the human biological stock would deteriorate and society would decline into amoral chaos.

The Eugenics movement, drawing upon both these sources of intellectual inspiration, gained another natural ally in the fast-growing science of genetics. It was a short step from peering into the social abyss which Spencer had outlined to proposing that the principles of selective breeding which were emerging from plant and animal studies be applied to human beings. The ideal of human improvement was unimpeachable, even if the means were bizarre, and so the movement gained wide support. It has to be understood in the context of the social conditions at the turn of the century, when social problems were generally increasing, poverty and crime were widespread, class conflict and labour militancy were becoming more extreme, and mass immigration was adding a further dimension to the general social upheaval taking place. There was clearly an appetite for an ideology which re-stated the claims of the old order, did so in terms which portrayed it as natural and inevitable, and grounded its case in evidence from the new sciences. The Eugenicist beliefs embodied all of these things and offered practical hope that the social 'decay' might be reversed.

The influence of Eugenicism should not be underestimated. It flourished in Britain and America in the early decades of the century, and on the continent of Europe. Its most extreme and obscene expression was in its contribution to the ideology of national Socialism in pre-war Germany; less well-known is that this was not a unique aberration. By 1931, thirty American states had passed compulsory sterilization laws for certain categories of criminals and mental defectives, and though it is nearly impossible to determine how far these principles were practised, they are a telling index of the movement's influence. While the early enthusiasts for eugenicism may not have envisaged such an active prosecution of the movement's principles as the Nazis attempted, Galton nevertheless espoused the ends if not the means: in 1883 he wrote that he regretted that 'there exists a sentiment, for the most part quite unreasonable, against the gradual extinction of an inferior race'.[131]

The role of psychology in abetting these movements was a significant one, though in their less extreme manifestations. In the early years of the discipline as well as later there was an enthusiasm for psychometrics, for mental measurement. The woolly and subjective introspectionism of the early psychologists had given way to the objectivity of a rigorous behaviourism, and thoughts and feelings had been displaced by numbers. Building on Binet's pioneering work, Terman and others developed intelligence tests (like the Stanford-Binet) yielding IQ scores which, surrounded by the aura of science, appeared to offer a source of objective evidence on human abilities. And indeed, in the early days these IQ tests confirmed the Eugenicists' view that intelligence was correlated with social class. Thus psychology contributed a technology to the movement, but also little criticism of its bio-psychological determinism; in fact several prominent psychometrists were enthusiastic supporters of the movement.

In time, the alternative environmentalist and interactionist explanations of the correlation between intelligence and social class undermined the hereditarian position: this will be discussed further in Chapter 7. For now it is sufficient to remind ourselves that the intellectual parents of the psychometric tradition in psychology were happy to align themselves with the proponents of an extremely conservative social theory and policy; and that the core beliefs of inherited intelligence and its social distribution are as much matters of political belief as they are scientific fact, yet it is in the latter guise that they have been presented to successive generations of psychology and education students — and the public at large — since the 1920s. Always implicit and often explicit in this teaching has been the assertion of genetically determined (and therefore inevitable) black intellectual inferiority.

Social psychology and racial attitudes
It is clear that the nineteenth century saw little respite from racist thinking throughout the scientific community. However, in the surfeit of theory about race, racial *attitudes* were not studied at all. There are several reasons for this. The most obvious is that the social sciences were still very young, even in the last decades of the century. And if sociology and psychology were in their infancy, social psychology (whose natural province this study would be) was still a twinkle in the Founding Fathers' eyes. Very few social

phenomena had been scientifically studied, and social attitudes fell somewhere between the interests of sociologists and the concern of psychologists with the individual. Social scientists had not yet fostered the degree of objectivity necessary to consider racial attitudes *per se,* apart from their referents. There were two other related reasons, namely current racial attitudes amongst the public at large, and the state of scientific knowledge about race. Simply, prejudiced racial attitudes did not present themselves as an obvious candidate for study because they appeared to be legitimate. The staunch belief in the innate inferiority of 'the Negro', now supported by scientific findings, was reason enough for feelings of prejudice; what could be less remarkable?

Social psychology, in many respects linking psychology and sociology, did not emerge until the first two decades of this century. It was slow to turn its attention to racial attitudes and not until the mid-twenties did it seriously do so. We can trace the development of thought about race and racial attitudes through the very early textbooks of social psychology; like their predecessors in other disciplines, they closely mirror current scientific and public opinion.

One exception to this rule was a paper by a sociologist of the Chicago School, W.I. Thomas, who attempted to explain the psychology of race prejudice. In 1904[384] Thomas pointed to the mechanisms of discrimination in the smallest micro-organisms which make sense of the environment, serving 'to choose between the beneficial and the prejudicial'. Emotional states become associated with these distinctions which then may be aroused in other circumstances by suggestion and association. The vicissitudes of food-gathering and reproduction insist that individuals 'single out characteristic signs of personality in others and attach an emotional value to them'. Associations are formed with fellows of common interest and feuds struck against enemies. Distinctive characteristics are fostered for solidarity within the group, in contrast to others. Design, and later habit ensure that 'the usual is felt as comfortable and safe, and a sinister view is taken of the unknown'. A group, like an individual 'has a feeling of intimacy with itself' and 'signs of unlikeness in another group are regarded with prejudice'. Thomas argued that *race* prejudice,

> . . . is in one sense a superficial matter. It is called out primarily by the physical habits of an unfamiliar people — their colour, form and feature, and dress — and by their activities and habits in only a secondary way. . . . [But] this

16

prejudice is intense and immediate, sharing in this respect the character of the instinctive reactions in general.

However, when race prejudice is complicated by caste-feeling,

> The antipathy of a group for an alien group is reinforced by the contempt of the higher caste for the lower. . . . Under these conditions it is psychologically important to the higher caste to maintain the feeling and show of superiority . . . *signs* of superiority and inferiority (like racial characteristics) being thus aids to the manipulation of one class by another, acquire a new significance and become more ineradicable.

This early contribution is a strange mixture of the naive and the sophisticated. However, it appears not to have been acknowledged in the early textbooks of social psychology, which are much less enlightened about these issues where they mention them at all. Another sociologist, Edward Ross, actually produced the first book entitled *Social Psychology,* in 1908[325], in which prejudice is only briefly discussed. His own racial stereotypes, however, suggest a less informed and objective stance than Thomas's. He cites 'Negro volubility, Singhalese treachery, Magyar passion for music' as 'arising directly or indirectly out of race endowment'. Although he cautions that 'probably they are much less congenital than we love to imagine', he goes on to claim that social attitudes towards these groups have an innate aspect too: both 'class antipathy and race prejudice [are] inherited venoms [which] no force of logic can kill'. His own social attitudes were far from progressive and frequently intruded into his writings.

William McDougall, benignly remembered as the first real social psychologist was similarly uncritical of popular ideas. 'The Negro' merits only one mention in his textbook, *Social Psychology,* which first appeared in 1908[256]. In discussing the sex instinct, he stressed the deleterious consequences of 'unrestrained and excessive indulgence of the sexual appetite', and adds this footnote:

> It has often been maintained, and not improbably with justice, that the backward condition of so many branches of the negro race is in the main determined by this state of affairs.[256]

The book contains no reference to either attitudes or behaviour towards black people; race relations, it seems, were not yet

17

legitimate objects of research for social psychology.

Floyd Allport[4], another of the 'fathers' of the discipline, at first appeared to be not very much more enlightened some sixteen years later. He also emphasized the Negro's backwardness and cited evidence which quantified this in a quasi-scientific fashion. He said:

> Various investigators rate the intelligence of the full-blooded Negro as roughly between two-thirds and three-fourths of that of the white race . . . it is fairly well established however, that the intelligence of the white race is of a more versatile and complex order than that of the black races. It is probably superior also to that of the red and yellow races.

However he later referred to white people's behaviour towards black people, apparently the first social psychologist to do so; he even indicated that such behaviour might not be entirely justified:

> This discrepancy in mental ability is not great enough to account for the problem which centers around the American Negro or to explain fully *the ostracism to which he is subjected.* [italics added]

This seems to contain the rudiments of a value judgment, the slightest implication that this state of affairs is to be regretted. This is some advance over previous views which accepted the situation as entirely natural. Although Allport submits evidence for physical differences between blacks and whites — differences in blood pressure, emotionality and inhibition — he attributes differences in behaviour primarily to *social* causes. He maintains that 'The reason why the Negro tends to be asocial is that, growing up in an environment of poverty and ignorance, where stealth and depredation are often the accepted means of livelihood, he has had no opportunity for developing socialized traits.' He goes on to argue for 'organized supervision of the moral influences brought to bear on Negro children'.

However moralistic and patronizing this position now appears, it did at least acknowledge the importance of social and cultural influences on black character and abilities, as opposed to innate, biological influences. This was not solely Allport's insight, but it reflected a very important development, for in questioning the doctrine of innate inferiority, it introduced the idea of potential equality. It took black 'inferiority' out of the realm of innate, predetermined racial characteristics, and, *ipso facto*, introduced the possibility of change. If 'the Negro' was more a product of his environment than his race, and his environment was a product of the white man, then it was quite clear where the responsibility for the Negro's degraded position lay. Not only were white people vulnerable to this moral censure, but, in the context of this idea of potential equiality, their prejudice against black people could be seen as totally unjust. With their 'scientific' support crumbling, prejudiced attitudes began to appear to be irrational and unfair; from the mid-twenties onwards, prejudiced racial attitudes *per se* became a more urgent object of study by social scientists.

Clearly, this was a highly significant change of attitude on the part of the social scientific community. An entirely new perspective on an old and troubling problem had been attained, and one which had revolutionary implications for social science — and more importantly, for the society itself. If we look at the first twenty years of the century, the period during which this change came about, or crystallized, we can see a number of contributory causes. In social science itself the development of anthropology was breaking down the old ethnocentric ideas of foreign peoples. The wealth of information from studies of primitive societies all over the world showed that there could be infinite varieties of civilization, all equally satisfying to their peoples, so questioning the monolithic superiority of Western cultures. Alien peoples could no longer be caricatured and dismissed as inferior, nor could the 'alien' peoples at home, the American blacks.

During this period also, the elements of a sociology of black life came to be written. Du Bois and Booker T. Washington wrote powerfully of black people's predicament, from within the black community, and one of the single most influential contributions was made by a white journalist, Ray Stannard Baker, who travelled in both North and South, 'following the color line'. His writings[14] were serialized in the press in 1908 and caused a tremendous stir in the white community; without sociological tools of enquiry he nevertheless provided a systematic and disciplined account of black people's disadvantagement, and the discrimination they suffered in all areas of life. His assessment of the total situation was particularly acute: 'It keeps coming to me that this is more a white man's problem than it is a Negro problem.' This detachment is more remarkable when considered against the hysterical anti-Negro attitudes current in the South at that time, where some of his researches were carried out. This climate is very powerfully conveyed, unwittingly, in the title of one section of his work, which refers to the 'Difficulty of breaking the lynching habit', almost as though it were a mild addiction like smoking.

Studies of black life in several major cities were also conducted, among them Ohio, Boston, New York and Chicago. In some cases these were the result of the issues forcing themselves to the attention of social scientists and politicians through race riots. These were the local symptoms of a general movement, the emergence of black people from slavery and its aftermath to demand full citizenship. The movement was led by the black intellectuals aided by the Northern liberals; the moderate wing was represented by Booker T. Washington, who argued for black education, industrial training and business institutions. He sought to advance black people without offending white society, which led to him being viewed by many as an 'Uncle Tom'. He wrote:

> . . . the Negro is fast learning the lesson that he cannot afford to act in a manner that will alienate his Southern white neighbours from him. . . . The wisest among my race understand that the agitation of questions of social equality is the extremest folly.[414]

W.E.B. Du Bois was identified with a much more militant position, arguing that blacks must stand up against segregation and discrimination, and emphasizing the need to discover talent and leadership within the race. During this time black organizations proliferated; the first decade of the century saw the founding of the National Negro Business League, the Niagara Movement, and the National Association for the Advancement of Colored People, followed by the National Urban League. With them flourished campaigning periodicals like the NAACP's *Crisis* and black politics and literature came to prominence.

Two events more than any others accelerated these developments. The First World War saw discrimination in the armed services replaced by greater equality than some blacks had ever experienced before; it also gave thousands of whites their first experience of black men with equal or occasionally even superior status. Many blacks distinguished themselves in war service, and the contribution of the race as a whole underlined their right to citizenship in peacetime. The other factor was the exodus from the South. From wartime onwards a massive migration took place, encouraged by the prospect of high wages and less segregation:

Increasing numbers in the North meant more coloured voters, more coloured factory-workers, and potentially better-educated Negroes ready to assume leadership in every area of American life, racial and non-racial.[116]

And whereas the 'colour problem' had been previously restricted to the South, the migration ensured that prejudice and discrimination against black people became a nation-wide issue. Over and above this, the huge immigration of Europeans during these years made the issues of nationality, race and citizenship very controversial.

In the twenties, social psychology's enduring concern with racial attitudes began. While the 'founding fathers' of the discipline had speculated about the problem, this had been haphazard and unproductive, for in the absence of reliable evidence they had leant too heavily on 'common knowledge' with all the biases that entails. The mid-twenties saw the first empirical studies of racial attitudes, an attempt to ground explanations on a firm foundation of scientific evidence; though their methods were unsophisticated, these studies mark the progression of the discipline out of its 'alchemical' period.

Emory Bogardus was a pioneer in this early work. Initially he asked large numbers of people simply to assign a variety of race, nationality and language groups to particular categories, according to whether the individual had a 'friendly feeling' towards each, a 'feeling of neutrality' or 'feelings of antipathy'. Rather surprisingly, Turks had the most antipathy directed against them by the student subjects involved; the categories 'Negro' and 'Mulatto' came close behind them and their combined scores exceeded that of the Turks.[38] Bogardus then went on to ask each subject to 'select the race for which he felt the greatest antipathy and describe in detail the circumstances as nearly as he could recall them under which his dislike originated and developed'. He found that an important source of attitudes was 'traditions and accepted opinions' — hearsay evidence picked up from adults, literature and news items, and this accounted for nearly all the antipathy felt against the Turks, for few students had ever met one. Another source was direct experience of particular groups in childhood, usually involving fear or disgust; finally, experiences in adulthood with individuals were also generalized to the whole group, and fear and disgust figured in these, too. In another study,[39] Bogardus encouraged his subjects to make their antipathies more specific and at the same time bring them into the realm of everyday experience. He asked them to indicate to which of a number of social groupings and relationships each would admit the various nationalities, from 'to close kinship by marriage' at one extreme, through 'to employment in my occupation', to 'would exclude from my country'. Averaged over one hundred and ten raters, the English were admitted to the most and the closest social categories, the Turks to the fewest, with Negroes and Mulattoes close to the latter group.

The subject matter of these studies reflected the public concern with immigration from Europe and the rights of aliens, quite as much as any concern with racial prejudice towards the indigenous minority, the black Americans. In 1928 Bogardus[40] wrote a book entitled *Immigration and Race Attitudes* in which this emphasis continued. He reported the results of a great number of 'social distance' tests like those described, and further accounts of racial experiences. He re-asserted that the origins of racial prejudice lay in 'direct' and 'derivative' personal experiences. Direct experiences involved either physical repulsion due to appearance, smell, habits, living environment or social behaviour, while derivative experiences were the second-hand experience and attitudes culled from friends, relations, public speakers, newspapers and the like. Thus:

antipathy against the Negro is due to differences in biological appearances and forms, variations in cultural levels, and to widespread propaganda . . . [it] often begins with prejudice *caught by* children from their parents. [*italics added*]

This was perhaps the first acknowledgment of childhood prejudices, and one of the earliest descriptions of prejudice as a kind of social disease entity.

During this period, then, the study of racial attitudes developed a methodology. The idea of measurement of attitudes, of locating a person's sympathies and antipathies on a numerical scale of intensity brought an atmosphere of objectivity to a very personal and subjective issue. The new attitude-scaling techniques of Thurstone[387] and others encouraged these developments. But not all research relied on these methods: for the first time children were studied in the search for the roots of prejudice. The strength and pervasiveness of prejudice suggested that it might be innate and some people argued that racial antagonism was instinctive (an argument which had the additional advantage of making prejudice somehow legitimate). Others held that this could not be so, for children, bless them, were entirely free of prejudice. It turned out to be otherwise, as we shall see, but in any event it was clear that prejudice could not appear suddenly in adulthood, so that some kind of earlier learning must be involved.

Bruno Lasker[236] directed the first ever study of the development of racial attitudes through childhood, in the late twenties. He collected adult opinions on these issues by circulating questionnaires to discussion groups, social and religious organizations and the like, rather than eliciting attitudes directly from children. In the light of what we know about coercive pressures to conformity in group discussions, and 'second-hand' accounts of childhood behaviour, this circuitous method now seems rather questionable. Nevertheless, Lasker made a very acute distillation of hundreds of adult opinions which anticipates the findings of many of the later studies of children themselves. He describes how the child is:

> certain to have his mind canalized, even before he starts going to school, into habitual acceptance of the prevailing (racial) attitudes of the group within which he lives . . . the average child is made to notice outer differences and to accept them as signs of inner differences in value.

Lasker correctly identified the role of the parents in transmitting attitudes, by accident or design, and the importance of the school, church and other social institutions in reinforcing them.

As important as the findings of this study are the assumptions which lay behind it. It portrayed racial prejudice, unequivocally, as a social evil. And so in the space of thirty years the tacit acceptance of white attitudes towards blacks was replaced by a quite opposite perspective. The emergence of black people to demand equality with whites pinpointed the injustices of racial prejudice, and this notion itself became one of the assumptions of many social scientists working on prejudice. This was to be called the 'social problems' approach to the study of prejudice. It was a remarkable development in some ways, for it involved a value judgment — that prejudice was bad — and thus an element of subjectivity. And although, as we have seen, it was not the first perspective on the issue to be highly influenced by the investigators' own values, it did come at the time when American psychology was dominated by the hyper-objective Behaviourist school.

★

In the history of racial thought, then, we see a gradual change of

23

emphasis. Initially only the objects of racial attitudes were considered: the 'dark peoples'. The causes of relations between the races, and accompanying attitudes, were seen to be located firmly in the people themselves, in their innate character and abilities. As ideas of human equality came to be reinforced with scientific evidence, emphasis shifted to the social and cultural factors that might determine racial differences. This was a very crucial step, for it admitted that black people's deprivations and 'inadequacies' stemmed not from immutable genetic characteristics, but from the environment in which they found themselves — which could, in theory, be changed. The fact that this environment was largely a creation of white people placed the moral responsibility for its history and its future with them. The notion of potential equality carried with it the implication that white attitudes towards blacks were unjust and insisted they be examined. In this way, racial attitudes *per se* became the object of study. Attention was directed away from the targets, black people, and towards white people, the perpetrators of these attitudes. The nature of prejudice, its determinants and even potential 'cures', were all studied in an attempt to understand and perhaps even solve this 'social problem'.

* See Blum[37] for a more detailed account of Eugenicism.

2
Psychology and prejudice

In the 1930s the recognition of prejudice as a 'social problem' worthy of study led to the first attempts to *explain* the phenomenon, to identify its root causes in the individual and in society. During this era we encounter the first 'Grand Theories' of prejudice, attempts to account for it *in toto* from within the discipline of psychology. Whether or not the authors intended their theories to be so all-embracing, this is how they have been viewed and evaluated by subsequent generations of psychologists. Once again these early ideas now have a naive quality about them, not least because they tried to get to grips with social phenomena which were well beyond their scope. In other words, they tried to reduce complex *social* processes to very simple explanations in terms of *individual* psychological processes. This was a reflection of the mainstream of social psychology at that time which was hardly social at all. That is, social behaviour was largely seen as a simple aggregate of individual behaviours, rather than a qualitatively different sphere of action requiring different kinds of explanation.

The Frustration-Aggression Hypothesis, and the Scapegoat Theory of prejudice which derives from it are a case in point. The hypothesis drew on both Psychoanalytic Theory and Learning Theory, neither of which had previously engaged with the explanation of social behaviour to any great extent (nor indeed shown much affinity with each other). Its central proposition was that 'the occurrence of aggressive behaviour always presupposes the existence of frustration and, contrariwise, that the existence of frustration always leads to some form of aggression'.[97] Immediately we can see the influence of Freud's 'hydraulic' conception of the human psyche; the notion of a flow of psychic energy directed to the fulfilment of some desire, prevented or frustrated from expression, resulting in a 'head of steam' accumulating, which must somehow find release; and for Freud, aggression was the 'primordial reaction' to frustration. Implicit in this is the idea that the expression of aggression is cathartic. That is, aggression allows this dammed-up energy to be released and to dissipate, bringing relief from psychic pressure for the individual.

Naturally, the appropriate target for this aggression is the person or thing which caused the frustration. However, it may not be feasible for the individual to aggress against the source of frustration. The target may not be accessible, it may be some distant bureaucrat taking decisions affecting the individual's life who can never be identified, let alone confronted face-to-face. Or the frustrator may be too powerful so that aggression would be inexpedient or counter-productive — with further injury to the individual or even greater frustration. Or, regardless of the agent of frustration, aggression may simply be inappropriate in the situation in which the frustration occurs, so that the individual is constrained from aggression by social norms and etiquette.

The authors of the hypothesis, Dollard *et al.*[97], allowed for these circumstances by suggesting that frustration simply produces an instigation to aggression — a state of anger — which, while it must find release, will not necessarily be expressed in direct aggression against the appropriate target. It is the way in which the individual transforms the impulse to aggression against the appropriate target into a form of aggression against an inappropriate one which is the crux of the theory for our purposes. Two avenues for this substitution process can be followed, 'generalization' and 'displacement'. The idea of generalization is a simple one which comes from Learning Theory. In Pavlov's classical conditioning experiments, a dog which had been conditioned to salivate to the sound of a musical tone (by pairing that tone with the presentation of food, so that they had come to be associated) would then salivate to similar tones in direct proportion to their similarity with the original tone: the greater the similarity the greater the salivation. Just as the dog is generalizing a response associated with one stimulus to others like it, so it is argued that people will generalize aggressive responses from appropriate (but inadvisable) targets to inappropriate (but similar) ones. Billig[32] illustrates this as follows:

An example might be a man who believes that he is being frustrated by a particular group of persons, say policemen, generalizing his aggression to traffic-wardens and then to all forms of uniformed authority. The theory predicts that he should show maximum aggression to policemen, and aggression towards other uniformed authority-figures in direct

26

proportion to their similarity with policemen (i.e. more to traffic-wardens than bus-conductors).

Of course there are strong inhibitions against attacking policemen, and it is in this realm where the alternative method of 'displacement' may operate. Here the individual's anger is totally displaced and expressed against targets which may be quite dissimilar to the original frustrator. This is the essence of the Scapegoat Theory which says that, for example, race prejudice may arise from accumulated economic, political and social frustrations being expressed through the displacement of aggression onto minority groups who have not actually caused these frustrations (and are therefore inappropriate targets) but who may be convincingly depicted as having done so. Even this perception of the minority as a source of frustration is unnecessary if we accept Miller and Bugelski's findings in their study of a boys' summer camp[261]. The boys were promised an evening at the theatre in town, but first they had to take a long, dull examination composed of questions which were generally too difficult to answer. The examination was arranged to take longer than it should so that there was insufficient time left for the night out in town. When the boys were then asked to fill out rating scales assessing their attitudes towards Mexicans and Japanese, it emerged that their attitudes were considerably more unfavourable now than they had been before the frustrating experience.

The notion that we may vent our frustration-induced aggression on minority-groups who serve as scapegoats, is a persuasive one. At the level of individual behaviour it is easy to recall examples of innocent parties or inanimate objects being made the butt of some hostility generated in quite other circumstances. Beyond that kind of simple situation, though, the theory is beset with problems, particularly when it tries to explain the behaviour of masses of individuals acting in concert towards specific social targets over a long period of time, as in the case of racial prejudice. Firstly, there is the issue of masses of people experiencing similar frustrations at the same time. Secondly, there is the question of identifying both appropriate and inappropriate targets, as Tajfel has argued:[370]

The notion of displacement of aggression inescapably implies that there is some kind of identification by the aggressor of the original frustrating agent — and that the difficulty, internally or externally caused, of retaliating directly against this frustrating agent causes the aggression to be directed against another target . . . we would have to assume that, in very complex social situations, people know that their difficulties are caused by a certain social group and that in turn this group is immune from aggressive retaliation . . . and therefore another group is chosen as a target. No doubt, in some cases such an identification of the original frustrating agent is easily achieved as, for example, in the case of the foreign occupation of a country. But these are special cases. Much more frequent are the social situations in which there is neither an easy identification of, nor consensus about, those who are supposed to be responsible for the frustrations. Who is causing inflation?

So while we can look at say, pre-war Germany and acknowledge Dollard *et al.*'s contention that the accumulated frustrations of the German people since the Treaty of Versailles and the rise of anti-Semitism were coincident, we cannot admit a causal relationship between the two without explaining how the National Socialists articulated the country's ills and encouraged hostility against the Jewish minority. In other words, the overwhelmingly important feature of this era was the active political mobilization of discontent and its translation into a hostile ideology concerning a particular minority-group. The role of those socio-political processes was clearly just as important as the hypothesized accumulation of frustrations in achieving the end result. Yet there is nothing in the theory which speaks to these vital intermediate processes. The German people did not happen to be feeling frustrated *en masse,* for the same reasons, to the same extent and at the same point in time, and happen to feel they should take it out on the Jews with the same uncanny synchrony. Their grievances were voiced, ideologized and focused, and their behaviour towards the target group was encouraged and legitimized.

By the same token, while it is true (as Dollard *et al.* point out) that there was a close correlation between decreases in cotton profits in the American South during the 1930s and increases in lynchings of blacks, we have to insist once again that correlation is not causation. Unless we can show that cotton farmers always lynched blacks on the way home from a frustrating day at market, we have to come up with some intervening social phenomena to make the link between the two. For example, the expression of *collective* frustration, anti-black ideology, and the established normative persecution of black people through discrimination and violence are all social factors which would help to make the Scapegoat Theory fit the facts, but there is no mention of these social behaviours in the theory.

The frustration-aggression hypothesis identified a variety of individual reactions to frustration — the instigation to aggression, generalization and displacement — which give us insight into individual behaviour. These things may well provide some of the motive force behind some people's hostility towards minorities. Beyond this level, the theory is perhaps best regarded as a kind of analogue or metaphor when it is enlisted in the explanation of wider social behaviour. While the Scapegoat Theory can help to account for individual prejudices against racial minorities and how they are exacerbated, it requires the assistance of a variety of social and cognitive factors — such as ideology and conformity to social norms — if it is to explain how these individual reactions are translated into collective, coherent social actions.

Prejudice and authoritarianism
The Second World War stimulated an intense interest in the dynamics of prejudice. This was less a concern with the conventional 'prejudices' between warring nations than an urgent need to understand what was arguably the most extreme, obscene manifestation of racism yet encountered, namely the extermination of the European Jews. The realization that thousands of members of an apparently civilized nation had assisted or acquiesced in the systematic murder of millions of innocent people, demanded explanation. Inevitably, the climate surrounding these events influenced the direction of theory: the very obscenity of the Holocaust suggested a kind of mass pathology, a collective madness. Explanations for this ultimate prejudice were therefore sought in the 'disturbed' personality, for it was hardly conceivable that these were the actions of normal people. Theodor Adorno and his colleagues[3] set out to identify the characteristics of the fascist (or potential fascist) person in their monolithic Authoritarian Personality study. They reasoned that people who are prejudiced against Jews are likely to be similarly prejudiced against other racial or cultural minorities; that it is no coincidence that these attitudes tend to hang together, rather that they do because they are outward manifestations of a basic personality type, the authoritarian personality. The authors drew upon the Freudian perspective to account for the origin of this personality type in childhood experience. They tested their theory by the administration of attitude scales and personality tests to a

29

sample of over two thousand white, non-Jewish, middle-class Americans. Their scales and questionnaires were supplemented by in-depth interviews and projective personality tests with a sub-sample of their subjects. In attempting to relate ideology to personality the study was truly innovative both in its methods and its underlying theory.

Three attitude scales were given to the subjects, an anti-Semitism (A-S) scale, an ethnocentrism (E) scale measuring attitudes towards the racially or culturally different, and a Political and Economic Conservatism (PEC) scale. The fourth scale involved was a personality scale measuring 'potentiality for fascism or implicit anti-democratic trends'. It was meant to elicit evidence of personality patterns of an authoritarian kind which might make the individual particularly susceptible to fascist propaganda and beliefs. This, the F-scale, was the major measure of authoritarianism, as it came to be known. The title of the scale speaks volumes about the value-position of the authors and it is a striking indicator of the post-war climate; it also, however, gave hostages to fortune when a different national mood prevailed and the study came under fire for being less than objective.

Simply stated, substantial correlations between the subjects' responses to the four scales emerged from the study (though the PEC scale correlated less well with the other three). In other words, the authors seemed to have identified a constellation of different attitudes which did indeed hang together, and which was also related to certain personality characteristics as they had suggested. They then went on to look at this personality syndrome in greater depth by interviewing the highest and lowest scorers on the E-scale. In fact the construction and administration of the F-scale took place *after* these interviews had been conducted, and took account of some of the insights the investigators had gained in the process.

The interviews showed up many marked differences between the prejudiced and unprejudiced subjects; we will concentrate on the former. These people had a highly favourable conception of themselves and an apparently idealized picture of their parents, but beneath this favourable picture there was evidence of ambivalence. This, it seems, was quite fundamental, and psychologically uncomfortable, and was therefore glossed over with an elaborate glorification of self and parents. The authors felt that in fact, the upbringing of the prejudiced person was somewhat harsh and restrictive, and marked by parents securing emotional dependence and obedience from their children by the manipulation of love or its withdrawal. This regime would engender a kind of love-hate relationship with authority, which in adult life would be expressed in rigid obedience to power-figures, while the negative aspect of the ambivalence would be displaced onto weaker targets who could be hated without danger. It is essential to prejudiced people to maintain a favourable image of themselves and their parents, and clearly feelings of hatred and aggression are incompatible with that; therefore they must be repressed and denied and only positive feelings admitted to the self and the outside world. The negative feelings can surface in connection with minority-groups, particularly where there is social support for these feelings, giving them a legitimacy (and again avoiding conflict with the idealized image of the self); such is the appeal of fascist propaganda, giving the person a reference group which also identifies a target group and sanctions prejudice against it.

This need to resolve ambivalence is apparently something which distinguishes the prejudiced from the unprejudiced person in the study. The latter seems far more able to cope with both positive and negative feelings, whether about the self or the parents. Less threatened by the negative aspects, there is therefore less need to project these feelings onto others. It was Freud who originally coined the term 'projection' to describe a basic psychological defence mechanism which protects the ego. In that context it is interesting that the unfavourable characteristics most frequently projected onto minority-groups by the prejudiced subjects concerned sex and aggression, the basic drives central to Freudian Theory.

Adorno and colleagues generalized from this intolerance of ambivalence to suggest a broader trait, a whole style of cognitive functioning which they called 'intolerance of ambiguity': the need to see the world in rigidly defined black and white terms, to assign objects and events to quite distinct categories, and by implication, to over-simplify a complex reality. Although this was not adequately established in their data, some experiments with children by Frenkel-Brunswik[124], using stimuli that had nothing to do with racial attitudes, showed prejudiced children to be developing just such a cognitive style in their interpretation of ambiguous stimuli on perceptual tasks. Certainly this syndrome would seem to go hand-in-hand with the prejudiced person's impermeability to argument, and the very extremity of his/her attitudes, admitting no half-measures that would threaten these beliefs.

Subsequently, the Authoritarian Personality study came in for fierce criticism which continued well into the 1950s (for reviews of this literature, see Titus and Hollander[389], Christie and Cook,[67] and Kirscht and Dillehay[221]). While this was principally methodological criticism, its inspiration was at least partly ideological: post-war liberalism had given way to McCarthyism and Cold War politics, and some people took exception to Adorno's explicitly anti-Right wing stance. Nevertheless, there were serious methodological short-comings to the study which had to be conceded. Although the authors' primary concern was the interrelation of attitudes and personality, and not the incidence of this personality type in the population as a whole, it was argued that their sample was not a representative one. In gathering large numbers of subjects econo-mically, they had contacted a variety of institutions, organizations, clubs and social groups, and in a general way, 'organization-joiners' may well have some special characteristics not typical of the re-mainder of the population. More serious criticisms pertained to the construction and administration of the measures they used. We have already mentioned that the F-scale was constructed after the inter-views with the highly-prejudiced subjects, so it could be argued that the authors 'knew what they were looking for' in framing the F-scale questions — and therefore hardly surprising that they found it.

In all the scales the items were worded in such a way that, for example, the prejudiced person would consistently be answering 'yes' to the questions while the unprejudiced person would answer 'no'. Other work has shown that respondents can fall into an 'acquiescence response set', whereby a kind of snowball effect operates; the more they answer questions in the same way, the more they are likely to continue doing so. This has the effect of increasing the score on any one scale, and in this case, where all the scales were similarly framed, increasing the correlation between them. The criticism is a fair one and follow-up studies using more hetero-geneous items have resulted in lower correlations, though not markedly so.

Two criticisms of the in-depth interviews with the highest and lowest scorers on the E-scale deserve mention. Firstly, the inter-viewers were thoroughly conversant with their interviewees' responses to the attitude questionnaires before the interviews, so in no sense could they be considered 'blind' and objective assessors. Again there is the obvious implication that they knew what they were looking for, and found it. Secondly, they were relying on their subjects' recollections of childhood experiences, and particularly their parents' child-rearing methods. Testimony of this kind is notoriously unreliable, the events of twenty or even fifty years ago being filtered through all the biases and distortions of time, experience, memory and above all, selective perception and recall. Given that the prejudiced subjects were supposed to be more prone than most to idealizing their parents, this is a serious source of inaccuracy.

Broadly speaking, whilst criticisms of the Authoritarian Personality study were damaging to the theory, the correlations it had established and their partial replication in other studies, were too strong to be completely overturned. If the critiques detracted a little from the force of the theory, the authors could nevertheless claim to have identified a personality type who was particularly prone to develop hostile and rejecting attitudes to various racial and cultural minorities. Their account of the origins of this personality in particular childhood experience is plausible but less conclusively supported by the data.

It is when we go further than these simple statements that the theory becomes less sure of itself. The authors did not set out to develop a theory of prejudice in society as a whole, but it has often been enlisted in that enterprise; it is hardly surprising that the theory is inadequate to the task. It is simply not plausible to attribute, for example, race prejudice in the United States to the mass expression of personality dispositions towards authoritarianism and ethnocentrism, occasioned by a nation-wide pattern of harsh child-rearing practices. The very notion that this syndrome is in some sense 'abnormal' logically cuts across such an idea.

There is clearly a whole realm of human social activity which is excluded from the picture when we make this kind of explanatory leap from personality to society-wide prejudice. As with the Frustration-Aggression Hypothesis, we need to examine the mechanisms whereby individual impulses are channelled and brought to bear in unison on a target; even if we were able to do this within the theory, we have still begged many questions. What are the social, economic, political and historical reasons why the ideologies and norms of behaviour (to which we believe the authoritarian is particularly susceptible) have arisen in a particular society at a particular time? As Billig[32] points out:

Nazism cannot be explained by saying that its rise in the 1930s was due to the existence of large numbers of people who were unable to resolve their intra-psychic conflicts without projecting hostility onto convenient scapegoats. Similarly the decline of Nazism as a social movement cannot be attributed to the resolution of these . . . conflicts. . . . Nazism did not just affect those Germans who had highly authoritarian personalities; non-authoritarians who were not even members of the Nazi party also fought for the Third Reich and failed to register any protest against the persecution of the Jews.

The explanation of prejudice in terms of individual motivations and conflicts not only flies in the face of social facts, it carries with it dangerous implications for social action against racism. If we can conveniently locate prejudice in the 'disturbed' personalities of individuals, we may mistakenly believe that the resolution of their personal problems solves the issue. If, however, we acknowledge that socio-historical factors create a climate of attitudes and behaviour which permeates the society as a whole (and affects some individuals who are highly frustrated or authoritarian, more than others) then we will properly direct our efforts to social action, not individual therapy.

These different emphases on individual and social determinants of prejudice should not be seen as mutually exclusive or competing explanations. Unfortunately, they have often been seen in this way, probably because they originate in neighbouring disciplines, psychology and sociology, which have each claimed a monopoly of wisdom on the matter. Pettigrew[296] has shown that this opposition can be resolved. He depicts theories of prejudice as lying along a continuum, at one extreme of which lie the 'individual' theories which view prejudice as the *externalization* of inner needs and conflicts within the personality; at the other end are socio-cultural theories which 'view intolerance as a mere reflection of cultural norms and neglect individual differences'.

Pettigrew cites Minard's[268] study of a West Virginian coal-mining community which illustrates well how the pressure of socio-cultural norms may or may not prevail over individual dispositions towards or against prejudice. In this community the norms required almost total racial segregation in the everyday life of the citizens, *above ground*. In the mines, however, an equality based on common work-roles, achievement and common danger, made racial integration a necessary norm. Minard estimated that about 60 per cent of the white miners conformed to social expectations in both settings: that is, they segregated themselves from blacks above ground, but integrated below. Of the remaining 40 per cent, roughly half segregated themselves in both situations, while the other 20 per cent attempted social integration both above and below ground. Clearly, it would be difficult to explain the behaviour of the 'inconsistent' majority in terms of enduring personality dispositions to behave in a positive or negative way towards blacks, while these factors may well underlie the ability to withstand social pressure of the 'consistent' minorities.

Pettigrew's own studies in America and South Africa[295] throw some light on the relationship between individual and socio-cultural factors. In a comparison of Northern and Southern communities in the US, he was able to show that the more pronounced anti-black attitudes in the Southern sample were not generally accompanied by the heightened anti-Semitism and authoritarianism that the Authoritarian Personality theory would predict. The gross differences clearly reflected different social norms, but some of the Southerners — mainly the women — were found to be more anti-black and more authoritarian than the men, suggesting that some personality factors were operating. Then, comparing the attitudes of South African undergraduate students with their American counterparts, he found higher levels of anti-black attitudes amongst the South Africans without their being higher levels of authoritarianism overall. But again, the different social pressures toward prejudice in South Africa were not the whole story for, within the sample, higher levels of prejudice went along with greater authoritarianism, individual by individual. The picture was complicated further by various subgroups within the sample, such as Nationalist Party members who were clearly influenced by specific group norms towards greater prejudice, but who were not neccessarily more authoritarian. Pettigrew inevitably concluded that:

> In areas with historically embedded traditions of racial intolerance, externalizing personality factors underlying prejudice remain important, but socio-cultural factors are unusually crucial and account for the heightened racial hostility.

The social psychological perspective
Psychology's contribution to the explanation of prejudice is not restricted to the 'individual' theories so far discussed; there are further theories which take greater account of social processes. More recently, Tajfel[369] summarized much of what we have argued to date, and indicated the proper focus of these theories:

> Many of the 'individual' theories start from general descriptions of psychological processes which are assumed to operate in individuals in a way which is independent of the effects of

social interaction and social context. The social context and interaction are assumed to affect these processes, but only in the sense that society provides a variety of settings in which 'basic' individual laws of motivation or cognition are uniformly displayed. In contrast, 'social psychological' theories tend to start from individuals in groups rather than 'preliminary' individual laws, such as those, for example, applying to frustration and aggression or to cognitive dissonance. But they stress the need to take into account the fact that group behaviour — and even more so inter-group behaviour — is displayed in situations in which we are not dealing with random collections of individuals who somehow come to act in unison because they all happen to be in a similar psychological state.

At this social psychological level of explanation there is a body of theory which comes from both experimental investigations of small group relations, and from consideration of larger scale, real-life groups occupying different positions in the socio-economic structure. One cardinal principal concerning the fundamental influence of social structure, and the consequences for attitudes and behaviour of the relations between the groups within it was suggested by Secord and Backman:[338]

> The character of the existing relations between in-group and out-group generates attitudes towards the out-group which are consonant with these relations. In other words, the structure of the relation between two groups in terms of relative status and power produces cognitions and feelings that are appropriate to the existing structure.

Clearly, history is replete with examples of hostile ideologies which have grown up between groups which differ in power and socio-economic status, particularly when the inferior position of one group is a direct consequence of the other's domination and exploitation of it. In that sense, then, we may simply appear to be re-stating the obvious when we say that power and status differences lead to hostile inter-group attitudes. However, when we examine how these attitudes arise we rapidly discover that 'the obvious' is more complex than it first appears. It is *not* necessarily the simple perception of gross status differences and power relations which is involved here. On that basis alone the average British citizen might

36

feel unmitigated hostility towards the Royal Family, which is far from the truth. The vital ingredient for hostility to appear would *seem* to be the perception of *competition* between groups. This factor was the focus of a series of seminal studies by Muzafer Sherif[343,344,345] in the early 1950s. These studies were something of a landmark in social psychology and deserve attention, not only for their intrinsic merit, but also for their relevance to recent developments in this area.

Sherif created a natural, 'real-life' laboratory for his experiments; with his associates he arranged a series of boys' summer camps in which experimenters would serve as camp leaders and so be able to contrive and control the activities of the camp; they could also observe the behaviour of the boys behind the 'blind' of an accepted role which would arouse no suspicions. For simplicity, these various experiments will be presented as one, except where indicated.

In the first phase of the experiment the boys were brought to the camp and for a period they simply got to know each other and familiarized themselves with their new surroundings. This was the communal stage, for all the activities were arranged on a single-group basis; meals were eaten together, the sleeping accommodation was undifferentiated, in fact everything that went on in the camp involved all the boys. The leaders/experimenters observed their behaviour closely during this period, noting the friendships that were formed and the social networks that developed. After a week this was replaced by the second phase in which the boys were assigned to two groups; this 'arbitrary' division ('for the purposes of simplifying the organization of the camp') was in fact carefully controlled to ensure that close friends were separated. From this point on the boys lived their lives entirely within the confines of their respective groups and there was no mixing or joint activities with the other group. They dined and slept in separate huts and went about their daily pursuits in isolation. The experimenters noticed that this phase brought about rapid changes in the nature of the individual groups. Each developed its own characteristic structure, hierarchy and customs, its own rudimentary culture. There was a growing awareness of the group as an entity, and a consciousness of themselves as members of it.

In the third phase of the experiment, Sherif once again brought the groups into relation with one another, but still operating as separate groups and in a specifically competitive context. He simply wished to look at the effects of *competition* on behaviour between and within the groups, and institutionalized this competition by building it into the structure of daily life in the camp. A points system was introduced whereby one group could achieve ultimate victory over the other and win prizes for all its members. Points could be accrued in a number of ways: through better performance in completing camp chores, victory in sports contests and other kinds of tournaments. This third phase signalled an immediate deterioration in the relations between the two groups; inter-group hostilities grew up, negative stereotypes towards the other group emerged, and own-group solidarity intensified. While this outcome was in some ways predictable, Sherif was nevertheless disturbed by the ease with which this antipathy had been fomented; both ethical and theoretical considerations prompted him to add a fourth stage to one of the experiments to see whether peace could be attained as easily as war, so that the boys would not leave the camp in the grip of this artificially-induced hostility.

He arranged matters so that situations would arise which compelled the groups to act co-operatively if they were to achieve certain goals which would benefit them all. These 'super-ordinate' goals were, for example, the retrieval of a food truck which had broken down and where the pooled resources of the two groups were required to pull it in, and the purchase of a film programme for their entertainment which neither group could afford to hire alone. Happily, these co-operative activities did succeed in reducing inter-group tension and hostility and in many ways the boys returned to the friendly atmosphere of the first phase.

The theoretical insights that Sherif provided — that intergroup competition leads to hostility and negative attitudes, while co-operation encouraged by the erection of super-ordinate goals produces positive attitudes — were less than earth-shattering, viewed after the event. However, had he argued in advance that the competitive stage based on a few sports contests and washing-up competitions would *not* result in hostility between boys who had got to know each other for a week, we would have been equally unsurprised; hindsight often determines what is 'obvious'.

What Sherif achieved was, as Tajfel[369] points out:

> . . . to create groups with a history which he has been able to control in order to look at the psychological effects of the developing inter-group relations. The fact that, under these simplified and controlled conditions, he has been able to re-create many phenomena which are usually associated with

long-term complex social and historical developments greatly adds to the significance of his work.

As significant as the detail of his theory is:

the kind of theory it is, or the approach to the problem it represents. The subjects who took part in Sherif's studies were 'normal' healthy American boys with no special personality or emotional problems which would distinguish them from the population at large. They behaved as they did as a *consequence* of a certain kind of inter-group relations which were imposed upon them, rather than creating a certain kind of inter-group relations as a result of their emotional or motivational problems. Group membership and inter-group conflict created their own uniformities of predictable social behaviour.

Beyond these innovations, the very meticulousness of Sherif's design and observational techniques has allowed other researchers to examine his work and to develop further interpretations that he himself did not attempt. Billig[32] is one who, while according Sherif's work the respect it deserves, goes on to give supplementary explanations of the phenomena, which may be quite as important as Sherif's original formulation. Billig looks in detail at Sherif's second experiment[345], and in particular at the second phase in which the boys have been separated into groups but have not yet been brought into institutionalized competition. The 'Blues' and the 'Reds', as they are called, are each in the process of developing a group culture and identity and they re-name themselves the 'Bull Dogs' and the 'Red Devils' respectively. But here Billig[32] notices some crucial developments which Sherif appears to have missed or ignored: 'The groups were not merely building themselves as strong, cohesive social units, but were doing this *in contra-distinction to* their perceived out-group.' (italics added). For example, boys who fraternized with members of the other group were referred to as 'traitors'; unfavourable comparisons were made between the groups; and the Red Devils refused to use any blue paint in the decoration of their hut, as this was the colour associated with the Bull Dogs. Each is a small consideration, but taken together with other examples they add up to a picture of emergent hostility between the groups well in advance of the stage of institutionalized competition. The implication is clearly that the development of in-group identity and

39

solidarity is inextricably bound up with consciousness of the out-group and competitive feelings towards them.

There was more evidence for this in the last of Sherif's experiments[344]. Here the boys came separately to the camp in two groups and remained unaware of each other's presence for some time. As soon as the existence of the other group was discovered it assumed a high profile in their lives, and there was an immediate clamour for contests, sporting competitions and the like. The role of the leaders/experimenters was interesting in this connection: they felt compelled to damp down these upsurges of rivalry in order that they emerge at the 'proper' time, that is, in the competitive stage. The question that all this prompts, and which Sherif overlooked, is whether the very fact of groupness *vis-à-vis* another group is in itself sufficient to promote inter-group rivalry and hostility?

The 'minimal group' studies

In recent years, Tajfel and his associates have carried out a series of experiments designed to answer this question by looking at the very minimum conditions necessary for numbers of individuals to perceive themselves as a group and behave discriminatorily against other groups. In the original study[372], a number of schoolchildren were divided into two groups after viewing reproductions of paintings by Klee and Kandinsky shown to them on a slide projector. While they were told that the division was on the basis of their preference for one or other painter, they were actually assigned to the groups randomly. In any case, this criterion had been selected as an unimportant and superficial basis for dividing up a group of children who already knew each other since they had been drawn from the same school. The children were then individually given a series of tasks which required them to simultaneously assign monetary rewards to *other* members of their own group (the in-group) and to members of the out-group. It emerged that there was consistent discrimination in favour of their own group and against the out-group, even though there was no obvious 'reason' for enmity. The children chose to do this quite independently as they had no opportunity to talk and decide upon a strategy that would benefit them all. Nor did each child stand to gain individually from discrimination as the rewards were to be paid to other people. Strikingly, the children often chose to discriminate in preference to 'maximum joint profit' strategies: in other words, some choices would result in a higher reward going to both groups, but these were eschewed in favour of the choices that provided the greatest differential between the groups, even though the absolute value of the reward to the in-group was smaller.

If we look at real-life situations where groups discriminate against one another, as in the case of racial discrimination, then these findings are thrown into relief. There are a number of factors which account for the discrimination: (i) there are obvious physical and cultural differences between racial groups which may be used as a reason for discriminating; (ii) there can be real or perceived competition for scarce resources, so that individuals may stand to gain by discriminating; (iii) there is frequently a history of hostility between the groups which may pre-dispose them to this kind of behaviour; and (iv) the participants in the discrimination are often not known to each other, so there is no real social relationship to mitigate the discrimination.

Turning back to the minimal group experiments, each of these factors is reversed: (i) there were no important differences between the groups to engender or rationalize hostility; (ii) there was no 'objective' competition between the groups because each *could* benefit more from a co-operative, maximum joint-profit strategy; (iii) there was no history of hostility between the boys; and (iv) there was a social relationship between many of them which cut across group lines. So if discrimination occurs in these minimal conditions, it is hardly surprising that it does so in real life when we add in all the more realistic reasons. But why does it happen, apparently, 'for no reason' in the experiments? Initially, Tajfel put forward this explanation:[367]

It is, however, possible that certain societies create or contribute to what might be called a 'generic' out-group attitude: in other words, that norms, values and expectations present in their modes of socialization and education foster or reinforce a tendency to behave differentially towards out-groups and in-groups even when such behaviour has little 'utilitarian' value to the individual or to his group, and even when a particular categorization has very little meaning in terms of the emotional investment that it represents and in terms of differences between groups on which it is based.

Subsequently Tajfel came to abandon this explanation, seeing it as little more than a re-statement of the experimental results. He and Turner[399] have been working towards a more genuinely explanatory theory which also admits the wealth of further empirical work that has flowed from the original experiments. Tajfel[370] has reviewed and collated this work, together with the theory of inter-group relations[375] which has grown from it. The theory is really a translation of Festinger's[115] theory of social comparison processes into the social psychological realm. Festinger proposed that individuals have a drive to compare themselves with others, that is, to evaluate their own characteristics and abilities against other people's, and to do so in ways that will preserve their own self-esteem. In other words, the do not wish to suffer by comparison, and this will tend to affect their choice of target, so that they select for the purpose people of similar or slightly inferior abilities. Also, it is sometimes necessary for individuals to 'see' others as inferior (even when they are not objectively so) to make sure this comparison comes out in their favour. Tajfel argues that the same kind of thing happens at the social level: that there is a need for every social group to create and maintain a positively-valued social identity, and that this is achieved in comparison to an out-group or groups.

The behaviour of the subjects in the minimal group experiments could then be interpreted like this: faced with a situation where they have been categorized into arbitrary groups, the boys attempt to impose a 'real-life' construction on this artificial situation. They behave as though the groups were meaningfully distinct and as though in-group norms were operating, even though they were not actually in contact with their fellow group members. Perhaps *because* the relationship between the groups was ambiguous there was a greater need to make social comparisons and established a valued in-group identity/devalued out-group identity, than in real life, where these values are more defined by objective factors. In any event, discriminatory behaviour against the out-group is one available means of expressing hostility and competition, advantaging one group over the other, giving it a basis for superior feelings.

Beginning this whole chain of events is the business of social *categorization*. In the minimal group experiments social categories were created by the experimenters in ways which illustrated the very minimum conditions necessary for social differentiation to take place. The categorization of people and human groups is not essentially different from the categorization of other objects and events in the individual's world and we can understand this better if we look at the basic 'laws' governing these processes.

Categorization, assimilation and contrast
In a classic experiment of Tajfel and Wilkes[376], subjects were

presented with a series of eight lines which varied in length by a uniform amount, and they were required to make judgments about the length of these lines. For one group of subjects the four shorter lines were labelled 'A' and the four longer lines 'B'. Compared with other groups who viewed lines which were not labelled at all, or were randomly labelled 'A' or 'B', the first group of subjects consistently exaggerated the difference between lines 4 and 5, that is the longest line in the shorter group and the shortest line in the longer group. In other words, by virtue of having the 'groups' of lines labelled, the subjects saw them as belonging to different categories and having more pronounced differences between them than in reality they had.

To a lesser extent they also 'reduced' the differences between lengths of lines within both category A and category B. These are known, respectively, as *contrast* and *assimilation* effects. They refer to the fact that when we have assigned stimuli to separate categories, we tend to accentuate the differences between those categories and the similarities within them. Similar processes operate in our perception of people who may be assigned to particular social categories on the basis of, say, skin colour: Secord, Bevan and Katz[339] showed their subjects photographs of people whose racial origin was somewhat ambiguous, and found that having categorized an individual as black or white, the subjects then went on to attribute to that individual a variety of other characteristics stereotypically belonging to that group. As Tajfel[368] points out, 'It can be shown that the more important a particular classification of people into groups is to an individual, the more likely he is to introduce sharp distinctiveness into his judgments of the characteristics of people who belong to the different groups.' Indeed, Secord *et al.* found that their anti-black subjects, to whom race was obviously an important criterion, were far more prone than others to exaggerate the differences between the 'black' and the 'white' photographs, and to exaggerate the extent to which the blacks had stereotyped negroid features.

Of course the very notion of categorization itself implies both some similarity between category members and some difference from non-members; that is what the process is all about. In establishing the category of (a) monetarists, (b) Rastafarians, or (c) 'born again' peanut farmers, we immediately create a further category into which the rest of the world falls, outside these categories. In the 1960s the 'student revolutionary' Jerry Rubin employed the same categorical device when he asserted that 'If you're not part of the solution, you're part of the problem.' But here we are concerned with the situation where discrete social categories (like 'black' and 'white') are imposed upon people whose characteristics largely overlap; then, assimilation and contrast effects over-accentuate differences between groups and common features within them, and thereby distort reality. Perhaps we should be less concerned with the violence that is done to objective reality in this way than the violence that is done to minority groups whose spurious 'differences' are used to justify their maltreatment.

Stereotyping

Central to this perception of human groups and their differences is the process of stereotyping. Although the term has passed into everyday language so that we 'know' what it means, psychologists themselves have differed in their use of the concept. Brigham[43] has reviewed the whole tradition of stereotype research since Katz and Braly's[207] classic study in the 30s. Katz and Braly presented one hundred Princeton students with a list of 84 character traits and asked them to list the ones they considered to be typical of ten ethnic groups: Negroes, Germans, Jews, Italians, Irish, Americans, Japanese, Chinese and Turks. When they then indicated the five traits they thought most typical of each group there was a very high degree of agreement in the way the traits were assigned. For example, 84 per cent of the subjects described Negroes as 'superstitious' and 75 per cent maintained they were 'lazy'; 79 per cent saw Jews as 'shrewd' and 78 per cent saw Germans as 'scientifically-minded'. What does this consensus represent? For Katz and Braly it represented 'fallacious thinking': 'Stereotyped pictures of racial and national groups can arise only so long as individuals accept consciously or unconsciously the group fallacy attitude toward place of birth and skin colour.' The fact that the questions *required* the students to produce stereotyped descriptions is perhaps less important than the ease with which they could be elicited and the degree of consensus in their exaggerated generalizations.

Many later conceptions of stereotypes have centred around the idea that they are essentially incorrect generalizations, either in direction — claiming attributes for certain groups that they do not in fact exhibit, or in magnitude — suggesting that a trait characterizes all members of a group when it does not. This second aspect of over-generalization is recognized by most theorists, but whereas Katz and Braly thought that a 'stereotype is a fixed impression which conforms *very little* to the facts' (italics added), many other theorists 'equate stereotypes with generalizations, which, although over-generalizations, may still describe situations which are extant, although to a lesser extent than that expressed in the stereotype' (Brigham[43]). There is disagreement, then, on the *degree* of exaggeration involved. While Katz and Braly seem to suggest that the stereotype need bear very little relation to the facts, the others stress the over-generalization of valid facts. The 'kernel of truth' hypothesis is relevant here, which suggests that stereotypes could not arise or be sustained over a long period if there were not an essential core of truth to them. What is in debate here is the size of that kernel. Of course, the debate cannot actually be resolved because it is simply not possible to determine whether all, or most, or few members of an ethnic group possess a particular characteristic; we are not necessarily dealing with easily measureable characteristics such as height, but perhaps with behaviour patterns or intangible personality characteristics which we cannot hope to assess across a whole population. We can only say that our knowledge of individual differences totally precludes the possibility that literally all members of an ethnic group will exhibit the same personality traits, and thus the most over-generalized stereotypes cannot be valid for all group-members. Because of this difficulty some theorists have set aside the issue of the absolute validity of the stereotype, but as Brigham points out, 'In this view, any generalization is a stereotype.'

Another common perspective has been to look at stereotypes as involving a flawed or illogical thought-process. This stems from the idea that stereotypes are usually acquired second-hand, from hearsay, rather than direct experience of the group concerned, and they are therefore accepted on the basis of very partial evidence. This is not the ideal, rational way of arriving at our beliefs, and so it is implicitly criticized, though it should also be said that this is precisely the way we acquire a lot of our information, and stereotypes are not exceptional in this respect.

Finally, many writers have stressed the *rigidity* of stereotypes, suggesting that they are inflexible and impermeable to new information; group members who do not seem to exhibit the expected stereotyped characteristics are seen as exceptions to the rule and the rule remains unchanged. In fact there is little empirical evidence on this, though it accords well with psychologists' stereotypes about stereotypes. Individuals' stereotypes may well be resistant to change because they fulfil a function: they help people to simplify the social world by categorizing other people into groups with 'known' characteristics: people are more comfortable if they think they can anticipate the behaviour of 'an Irish labourer', 'a Jewish shopkeeper' or a 'West Indian youth' and are ready to react appropriately to them.

Returning to the basic laws of perception, people may protect their stereotypes in the face of contradictory evidence by selectively perceiving that which confirms their belief and filtering out that which threatens them. Nevertheless, the accumulation of contradictory evidence over a long period may necessitate some adjustment to the stereotype. Certainly at the social level, widely-held stereotypes about particular groups do change over time. Schwartz[335] has shown how Americans are considerably less likely to endorse the old paternalistic stereotypes about, for example, black intelligence, since the significant social gains made by black people in the 1960s. One might guess that stereotypes about the Japanese altered a great deal between Pearl Harbour and the more recent camera and hi-fi invasion; perhaps they will also change back again if Japanese pre-eminence in micro-chip technology further undermines American industry.

What is common to virtually all discussions of stereotypes is the implication that they are *undesirable* and to be deprecated, 'either because they do not correspond to the facts about the ethnic group, or because they were arrived at through some unacceptable process' (Brigham[43]). The difficulty in validating or invalidating stereotypes has led Brown[49] to ask 'Is it possible that the social psychologist has used the word *stereotype* to stigmatize beliefs of which he disapproves but which he does not know to be false.' Nevertheless, both Brown[50] and Campbell[57] point to negative aspects of stereotyping which are indeed harmful, as Brigham points out in the following passage:

> Stereotypes are often not well-founded in direct experience; they sometimes serve to rationalize selfish behaviour; they are often not sensitive to contrary evidence; and they ascribe to racial inheritance that which may be cultural acquisition . . . the 'phenomenological absolutism' of the in-group member's imagery of the out-grouper [is naive because it] assumes without question that the out-group is as one perceives it, or as the in-group informs one about it. . . . The stereotyper believes that it is undesirable characteristics of the out-group that cause hostility, rather than recognizing that it is pre-existing hostility that has caused all possible between-group

differences to be interpreted in terms of the despicable characteristics inherent in the out-group.[43]

Stereotypes, attitudes and behaviour

Notice that much of this criticism of the stereotyper — pointing to
ethnocentrism and hostility — assumes that he/she is indeed prejudiced. However, it is not necessarily so. Clearly, where stereotyped characteristics are highly negative it would be difficult to
separate the two, but there are also overly favourable stereotypes of
particular groups (not least one's own) and ambivalent ones where
positive and negative stereotypes are attributed to the same group
(e.g. Jewish 'shrewdness' and 'exclusiveness'). For our purposes we
have concentrated on stereotyping in the context of prejudice, but it
is important to see it as a general mode of cognitive functioning
common to all, to once again avoid the error of regarding prejudice
and its associated styles of thinking as restricted to an atypical
minority.

As we have implied here, these cognitive aspects of prejudice are
not entirely separable from other aspects of our attitudes. In a
simple way we can regard attitudes as having three components.
Firstly, there is the *cognitive* component, which consists of the
beliefs and information that the person has absorbed in relation to a
particular attitude object, say a minority group. This information
may not necessarily be entirely correct, it may have been selectively
perceived or interpreted, but it is the 'factual' content of the
attitude. Conventionally the cognitive component of many white
people's attitudes towards black people has included the stereotyped
beliefs that they are less intelligent than white people, more
'primitive', amoral, athletic, musical, etc. Secondly, the *affective*
component of an attitude is the evaluative or 'feeling' component, in
that it is the actual feeling of liking or disliking for the attitude
object, the emotional colouration to the system; it is what we most
readily think of when we talk about attitudes in everyday language,
and it is essentially this dimension of favourability-unfavourability
that attitude measures try to tap. In the case of prejudiced racial
attitudes, the affective component includes feelings of hostility, even
hatred, towards a racial group; it may also include a fear component, and American researchers have noticed that this has
increased since whites have perceived blacks to be making social
advances which might threaten the existing social order[12]. Thirdly,
and finally, is the *behavioural* component; this is the disposition to
act or behave towards the attitude object in certain ways. It does

not refer to people's actual behaviour, but to their readiness to behave in certain ways; again, the behavioural component of a prejudiced racial attitude might include a disposition to socially reject black people, insult them, discriminate against them, or worse.

It is important to emphasize the difference between a readiness to behave in some way, and the behaviour itself, because there is by no means an automatic translation of our attitudes and dispositions into the behaviour that would appear to be predicted from them. Many factors intervene between what we feel, believe and are ready to do, and how we actually conduct ourselves in practice. Wicker[420] lists the following factors which also have to be included in the equation:

1 personal factors
    (i)   other attitudes
    (ii) competing motives
    (iii) verbal, intellectual, social abilities
    (iv) activity levels

2 situational factors
    (i)   actual or considered presence of other people
    (ii) normative prescriptions of proper behaviour
    (iii) alternative behaviour available
    (iv) specificity of attitude objects
    (v) unforeseen extraneous events
    (vi) expected and/or actual consequences of various acts.

In this context it seems unlikely that any attitudes will find direct expression in behaviour at all. Clearly this is not the case, but these factors do help to account for the generally rather poor correlations that have been found between people's measured attitudes and observed behaviour. In LaPiere's classic study[241] this was amply illustrated when he journeyed through the United States with a Chinese couple at a time when there was a good deal of anti-Chinese feeling. He listed every hotel and restaurant they visited and recorded the quality of their treatment in each; only once were they refused service. However, when he wrote to each of these establishments after completing the vacation, to enquire whether they were prepared to accept reservations from Chinese people, of the 128 (out of 250) that replied, over 90 per cent said they would not accept Chinese people, despite having done so 'in the flesh'. The study was methodologically flawed, but nevertheless demonstrates clearly the dangers in assuming that how people say they will behave will accurately predict how they do so.

A more contemporary illustration emerged from two separate studies of racial prejudice and discrimination in Britain in the mid-1960s. The first was a straightforward survey of British attitudes towards black 'immigrants', consisting of a 'prejudice-tolerance scale' on which people could be located according to their answers to four key questions (which 'provided an opportunity to express unconditional hostility towards coloured people') and to ten others scattered through the questionnaire, 'where an unfavourable attitude towards coloured people could be expressed'[320]. Overall, they found that only 10 per cent of their respondents were 'prejudiced' (when three or four hostile replies to the key questions was the criterion of prejudice), 17 per cent were 'prejudice-inclined' (having given two hostile replies), 38 per cent were 'tolerant-inclined' (one hostile reply) and 35 per cent were tolerant (having given none). There was a lot of controversy over these findings, not least because of the over-charitable criteria of prejudice-tolerance employed. However, in the same year a rigorous study of racial discrimination[295] presented a different picture. To investigate discrimination in housing, for example, the researchers sent equally-qualified white English, white Hungarian and black West Indian applicants to try for the same advertised accommodation. Similar tests were set up for employment vacancies and for public services from shops and hotels to mortgage facilities and hire purchase companies. In each case, applicants equipped with virtually identical life-histories but with different ethnic backgrounds all applied for the same commodity. These tests were then supplemented by interviews with the white and black people concerned in each instance.

In the area of housing, the West Indian encountered discrimination in the letting of accommodation on 75 per cent of the occasions he tried for it: 'Such discrimination was in most cases overt in the sense that the West Indian was just told that the accommodation had gone when it had not.' The figure did not include the occasions when the white applicant was told 'Come round quickly, I've got a West Indian coming at 7 pm, so get here by 6.30.' When the landlords were interviewed later, they all confirmed that they had in fact discriminated. In addition the West Indian experienced discrimination at nearly 75 per cent of the accommodation bureaux and estate agents tested: 'There was no less discrimination against the West Indian when he was applying for accommodation in a professional, educated role . . . than when he was applying as a bus conductor; if anything there was more.' On

64 per cent of the occasions he applied to purchase a house he experienced discrimination; in council house allocation, while 'no discrimination' was invariably official policy, it was found that a variety of processes operated to prevent black people getting council houses as easily as white people.

Very much the same situation was found in employment; three-quarters of the time the West Indian applicant was refused jobs that were offered to an equally-qualified white applicant later. Similarly, substantial discrimination was found in public services, particularly in motor insurance, where black applicants had difficulty in getting insurance cover and were often charged considerably higher premiums.

Clearly, this does not automatically mean that the many white people who discriminated in this way were prejudiced. It is possible for a person to be coerced into discriminating by social pressures, or by the employment policy of the employer — though it is also true that these 'reasons' for discrimination are often convenient excuses. Nevertheless, it is as wrong to assume prejudiced attitudes from discriminatory behaviour as the reverse. What is at issue here is the very different picture of British racial attitudes and behaviour that is painted by each of the two studies. Of course, the same people were not involved in both the studies, so it is not a true test of the attitudes-behaviour relationship, but one cannot help but be struck by the contradiction between an apparently 'tolerant' climate of attitudes and extremely discriminatory 'norms' of behaviour.

As an indicator of the real racial climate we would tend to place more reliance on the situation tests of actual behaviour; it is clear that responses to doorstep interviews are much more vulnerable to influences like the need to present oneself in a socially acceptable light. If expressed attitudes, then, are such poor predictors of behaviour, why do we concern ourselves with attitudes at all? We do so because an attitude is, first of all, a relatively stable, enduring orientation towards some aspect of the world. As such, it has a value in describing the individual which is much greater than any specific piece of behaviour we can observe, and which may be dictated more by the exigencies of a particular situation. It is a complex structure of beliefs, feelings and dispositions to behave in certain ways and, as we have seen, this structure may reflect aspects of personality, on one hand, and the influence of wider social reference groups on the other. An attitude is thus an essential bridge between the most 'individual' aspects of the person's psychological functioning and the most 'social' aspects; taken together, people's attitudes relate them to their social world; their attitudes help to define their social world and their place within it.

★

In these first chapters we have sketched in a historical backdrop to the study of prejudice, and introduced a social psychological perspective on the issue. The remainder of this book is devoted to *developmental* aspects of prejudice: the processes by which children come to develop racial attitudes *as a normal consequence of their socialization within a society where prejudiced racial attitudes are widely held,* rather than as a consequence of individual personality dispositions.

There is a further emphasis, too, which brings the wheel full circle in the study of prejudice, namely the experience of black people in such societies. As psychology turned its attention away from black people as the 'reasons' for prejudice and concerned itself with the causes of prejudice in white people, so there was a neglect of black people's experience as the targets of prejudice. The radical changes of the 60s and 70s have once more brought these issues into focus and we shall try to do justice to the burgeoning literature on this issue. Once again, the principal emphasis will be a developmental one; naturally a black psychology must start with the child for, as in a white person, none of the black person's attitudes, nor personality, nor way of being in the world appear suddenly in adulthood. *Pace* Wordsworth (and *pace* feminism), the black child is, of course, father to the black man, and the pressures which inhere in 'being black' are a reality which may structure childhood and adolescence more powerfully than any other influence.

3
The socialization of attitudes and identity

Attitudes are made, not born. Social attitudes do not unfold from germ plasm or inhere in particular genetic configurations; they are not innate, nor do they enter human tissue for transmission to future generations (for which we should be eternally grateful). They arise, are communicated and are sustained in human social life.

In recent times there has been a vogue for quasi-scientific writing which has tried to establish the essentially animal-like nature of human beings. Konrad Lorenz, Robert Ardrey and Desmond Morris, among others, have enjoyed enormous popularity through assuring vast numbers of people of their *instinctive,* and therefore inevitable bestiality. This has been dubbed the 'litany of innate depravity' and it rests on analogies drawn between aggressive behaviour in humans and instinctive aggression in various lower animals. These views have an easy appeal and have gained a wide currency among the general public. This has happened because people need to understand their aggressive feelings and behaviour and to justify them; and:

> if no other rational explanation appeals, or even when it does, instinct is likely to trump every other card in the pack because it appears to be so fundamental, so recondite, so all-embracing and so simple.[11]

Now while these notions have been principally applied to aggressive *behaviour,* there is a danger that they may be seen to embrace aggressive (or prejudiced) attitudes also. If the former is mischievous, the latter is alarming for people are virulent enough in their prejudices against one another without 'scientific' justification.

As Berger and Luckmann[30] have written, *'homo sapiens* is *homo socius'.* And in the last analysis, whatever analogies and equations between humans and animals may be employed, supported by science, anecdote or dogma, we are left with the monolithic fact of people as thinking, communicating organisms which separate them from all others. We may indeed retain some vestiges of instincts dating from a primitive past but we are not uncontrollably driven by them. Our capacity for thought enables us to rationally evaluate our impulses and anticipate their consequences, measuring them against past experience and future contingencies. Our language capacity provides the medium for this, and the means by which our thoughts are communicated to others, and theirs to us. Social attitudes are communicational phenomena above all else. As such, they simply belong to a different realm of discourse than that which is concerned with the vicissitudes of animal life.

Socialization

We are primarily interested in the child's social attitudes. If these are not pre-ordained then we have to consider the various sources of information and emotion in a relatively restricted social world. This world is bounded by the home, the street, the school and the mass media, yet within these limits the child will learn most of what he or she needs to know about the world. This knowledge is the child's cultural inheritance; its transmission is called the 'socialization process'. All the ways of doing things practised in the immediate group or the wider culture are conveyed to children, intentionally and by accident, with or without their realization. And the process begins at birth; the notion that children begin to absorb the culture with their mother's milk is certainly no exaggeration.

We are not concerned here with weaning and toilet training and the inculcation of table manners, but with a more abstract part of the culture. Nevertheless, while racial attitudes and identity could hardly seem further removed from these domestic imperatives, we may say categorically that they have their beginnings in the same milieu at the same time. For in the socialization process, children learn not only 'what to do' but also 'how things are' as 'we' see them. Learning the business of living in a culture is not only a question of learning skills but also learning *meanings*. Children begin to absorb and, to some extent, to construct for themselves a *description* of the world as it is, and not only the physical world of objects but all the events which impinge on their consciousness, from the passage of time to the love of their parents. In other words, they begin to order these disparate objects and events, and to make sense of them so that they may cope with them adequately. Otherwise they would be bombarded with a maelstrom of experiences which they could neither understand nor respond to appropriately.

The foundations of this ordering are laid by the parents, for their own construction of the world, of reality, is contained more or less explicitly in the way they explain things to their children. Older siblings, friends and later, teachers will largely complement the parents' 'structuring' of the child's experience. These principal figures who, more than anyone else, retail reality to the child have been called the 'significant others'[366]. Of these significant others, the parents are the most significant, and they are almost the sole performers of the role in the first few years of life:

> Because of his lack of ready access to nonsocial sources of information, the child is peculiarly vulnerable to those social sources appearing and reappearing in the immediate environment. Parents and older siblings find themselves in positions of great power, the power that comes with having answers (right or wrong) to resolve the child's uncertainties. In the early years of socialization this power is almost monopolistic. Alternative answers or explanations are absent and the child's earliest contacts with the broader universe are filtered through all the biases and distortions in his parents' conception of reality.[203]

In the beginning, then, the parents *define* the child's world: they explain that world, and themselves define its limits. That other realms exist beyond them need not concern the child:

> he does not internalize the world of his significant others as one of many possible worlds. He internalizes it as *the* world, the only existing and only conceivable world, the world *tout court*.[30]

What is this reality, this construction of the world which is absorbed by the child? It is the aggregate of *experience,* the experience of perceiving people, objects and events, discriminating between them, understanding them, evaluating them and reacting to them. And this aggregate of experience coheres in a symbolic representation of the world *coloured by attitudes values and beliefs about the world.*

It would be quite wrong to portray this as a kind of indoctrination, to depict the child as a passive *tabula rasa* on which parents write indelibly, at will. A very great deal of parental teaching is unconscious and occurs through example or implicitly. And the child is a very active participant, at first eager for information from the available sources, and later seeking out independent sources, which may retail quite different versions of reality. The child is striving to attain an understanding of the world and this is a positive constructional task, not merely an inert absorption of parental ideas. Nevertheless, as we have indicated, parents have a unique control over the information that is available to the child, and that is the raw material from which meaning is constructed. It is not surprising, then, to discover that children do become aware of their parents' attitudes and values from quite an early age, and frequently seem to swallow them wholesale, reproducing them as their own. How does this happen in terms of concrete, everyday behaviour? Three overlapping processes are primarily responsible: direct tuition, indirect tuition and role-learning.

Direct tuition
Clearly, direct teaching of explicit attitudes is the simplest and most obvious vehicle, though not necessarily the most influential. 'Your father and I think that . . . is wrong' is its simplest form. It can be applied to individual acts (read 'hitting other children' in the previous sentence), through more generalized patterns of behaviour (read 'playing with black children'), all the way up to social attitudes (read 'monetarism'). For many years the parents are almost the sole arbiters of what is 'right' and 'wrong' while their children are unaware that these are less matters of fact than opinion. The parents' exclusive satisfaction of the child's biological material and emotional needs ensures that they acquire a very high value. This is both a primary value, through the provision of tangible rewards, and a secondary value shown in the child's desire to please and receive approval as a reward. At the very least the parents' sheer power over the child underwrites their influence.

It seems intuitively likely that parents provide a great deal of direct instruction about values and attitudes. Most people can recall occasions from their own childhood when their parents declared their own beliefs about a particular issue, and encouraged them to feel likewise. It may have been a political, social or moral question — 'the trade unions', 'immigration' or 'capital punishment' but in any event the parents' statement of views is persuasive because it is authoritative in the young child's eyes. Although recollections of this kind are notoriously unreliable, there is a good deal of research evidence which bears them out.

One of the more revealing studies of this kind of influence was conducted in the 1930s in a rural community in Tennessee[179]. Horowitz and Horowitz were interested in the extent to which the social relations in a community were reproduced in the next generation by parents' active intervention in their children's friendships. They found that:

> The [child's] attitude towards Negroes seems to have its origin with the child's parents. Apparently parents give *direct instruction* in these attitudes and *cannot recall having done so.* [italics added]

Some short quotations from interviews with the parents and children illustrate this:

Mother: He never played with any Negro children. I have to chase them out of the back yard, they keep coming around, but I never had to tell C not to play with the niggers. . . .

Child: Mama tells me not to play with the black children, keep away from them.

Child: One time I slipped off and played with some coloured people, back of our house when she told me not to, and I got a whipping. . . .

Clearly these examples involve tuition in attitudes which are central to the social life of a particular community; we would expect there to be a good deal of direct instruction about attitudes and behaviour which have such a high profile. But far less immediate and crucial social attitudes are also the subject of direct tuition, as a study by Johnson[200] showed. He looked at the development of children's attitudes towards other nations, their parents:

> . . . claim to speak to their children quite a lot about foreign countries in general, about contemporary and past wars, and about specific nations . . . the parents' preferences for nations appear similar to those of their children.[200]

This by no means proves that they teach attitudes to the children directly or intentionally, for their discussions might be purely factual. However, it seems likely that their attitudes and evaluations of countries are made known to the child in the process. In fact it is precisely these elements of the discussion which seem to be most readily absorbed by the child, as we shall see later.

Related to the direct prescriptions and proscriptions that parents make are others which are more subtle, for particular attitudes are

56

implicit within them, not explicitly stated. Parents' attitudes towards different social classes, for example, emerge from a variety of ways in which they guide their children's experience: the comics they are allowed to read, the clothes and hairstyles they may affect, and the ways in which they are encouraged to spend their money and their time. Here we are talking about the encouragement of particular *styles* of behaviour, of whole social atmospheres created by parents rather than individual acts. They are rather less tangible than direct instruction but probably even more effective in communicating how 'we' think about things, how 'we' do things, and ultimately, who 'we' are.

Indirect tuition

This category includes the processes by which children reproduce aspects of adult behaviour, in this case their attitudes, without conscious or intentional teaching on the part of the parents. We shall concentrate on two of these processes, identification and modelling.

IDENTIFICATION

> Children of two years and older have a tendency to act in a number of ways like their parents. They adopt parental mannerisms, play parental roles, and in the later pre-school years *seem to incorporate in their value-systems many of the values, restrictions and ideals of the parents.*[336] [italics added]

In the absence of reward or punishment, or indeed any kind of guidance, the child's behaviour becomes a microcosm of the parents':

> It is as though the child had learned a principle 'to be like my father and mother'. He then incorporates many of their psychological properties into his own repertoire of properties . . . [this] leads to the hypothesis of identification which short cuts the direct training process.[336]

The term 'identification' has been used in a variety of different senses, so that a good deal of confusion surrounds the concept[332]. Different views of the aetiology of identification account for some of this confusion. The range of behaviour to which the term has been applied has been very wide, so that Mussen[284] has proposed that we restrict the scope of what we refer to as 'identification behaviour':

> Identification, then, may be described as an hypothesized process, accounting for the child's imitation of a model's complex, integrated patterns of behaviour, rather than discrete reactions or simple responses — emitted spontaneously without specific training or direct reward for emulation.

Freudian theorists have attributed a great deal of significance to identification. In fact it was Freud himself who originated the concept, first to account for the pathology of melancholia[126], and later[128, 129] to describe the development of the super-ego, ego-ideal and sex-typing. He suggested that the boy's identification with his father developed out of the resolution of the Oedipus complex, initiating the process of super-ego development. This he termed 'defensive' identification, in contrast to the anaclitic identification of the girl with her mother, based on attachment, love and fear of loss of her love. (Most of the different types of identification described by other Freudian theorists corresponds with one or other of these: 'defensive' identification (Freud, and Mowrer[278]) 'aggressive' identification (Bronfenbrenner[46]) and Anna Freud's[125] 'identification with the aggressor' relate to a similar process; they arise from envy of the model's control over 'resources', whether these be the love of the mother, or, as Whiting[419] suggests, also 'food, privilege, information, freedom, love and praise'.)

Without necessarily accepting Freud's sexual 'division of labour' we can nevertheless recognize the two kinds of identification he described. In the first, the child identifies with the model to allay fear of aggression and to enjoy the rewards that seem to accrue to that position:

> The child believes that if he is similar to the model . . . he would command the desired goals that the model can command. For a child, perception of similarity between himself and the model is rewarding and strengthens the identification response.[284]

Freud[127] rightly stressed that the model which the child imitates is not only the immediate image which the parents present, but also the 'ideal standard reflecting the parent's aspirations rather than his actual behaviour'. The other variety of identification which Freud called 'primary' or 'anaclitic' (and Mowrer[277] termed 'developmental identification') is rooted in positive feelings of love for the model, the parent, who provides love, nurturance, comfort, etc., and it is these primary rewards which ensure that the model acquires a secondary reward value for the child. The prerequisite of this identification is the dependency of the child on the mother[337]. Sears[336] describes how:

> Among the acquired forms of self-reward [are] the whole class of imitated maternal behaviour, such as gestures, postures, task performances, and expressions of feeling; and, ultimately, as the child's cognitive capacities develop, and *he begins to perceive and absorb belief-systems, values and ideological positions, he imitates these aspects of his available models also.* [italics added]

Few parents would need to be persuaded of the veracity of the identification process. Their children frequently hold up a mirror to their own behaviour, through their wholesale imitation of adult ways, including irrelevant details and accompanying mannerisms, which can seem like caricature, but simply underline the importance to the child of doing things *exactly* 'like my mum does'.

Clearly, identification is an important vehicle through which parents unwittingly transmit not only particular ways of behaviour, but their whole world view. Who cannot remember playground disputes in which the participants tried to win the day by appealing to the ultimate authority: 'My father says . . .'? We speak volumes to our children about our own attitudes every time we comment on a news item, refer to 'the stockbroker belt' or 'the tower blocks' with just a hint of evaluation in our voices, or make one of their friends just that bit more welcome than another. The idea of identification helps us to understand why children are motivated to attend to these glimpses of adult feelings and take them as their own.

MODELLING

Whether these phenomena are explained in terms of psychoanalytic theory or learning theory,[18] or indeed any other theory, it is clear that the child purposefully models his or her behaviour on that of the parents to a considerable extent. Learning theory explanations have the advantage of also accounting for modelling behaviour where the model is not one of the parents, for example when an older brother or sister is the model.

Various writers, in particular Bandura and his associates have put forward 'modelling' theories of, for example, aggressive behaviour[20, 412]; the underlying principles of the theory are equally applicable to other sorts of behaviour also. They simply propose that:

> . . . observation of aggressive models, either in real life or in fantasy production, increases the probability that the observers will behave in an aggressive manner if the model is rewarded, or at least does not receive punishment for aggressive behaviour.[20]

Empirical tests of the hypothesis have been largely confirmatory [19, 20, 228, 412]. It does seem that adult aggressive models do tend to encourage subsequent aggression in young observers, probably both through providing a model which enables the child to learn various aggressive acts, and through 'disinhibition', the fact that the adult's performance of these acts signals that they are permissible for the child and removes any inhibitions.

There is every reason to believe that verbal behaviour is also accessible to imitation in the same way. Children are sensitive to the social connotations of some adult speech very early on, long before they fully understand the meaning; hence young children often swear to each other or to their parents knowing the effect their words will have, while knowing nothing of the anatomy, bodily functions or sexual acts that the words denote! In the same way, more complex speech involving factual statements, or attitudes and values, is often imitated far in advance of any comprehension of the concepts involved, but with their evaluative or affective sense faithfully reproduced.

Pushkin[305] reports a vivid example of this; he administered a tea party test to a six-year-old white boy in which the child was required to invite a number of dolls (representing real people) home for a tea party. When asked why he had always rejected the black dolls, the boy replied, 'If I have to sit next to one of those I'll have a nervous breakdown.' There can be few more graphic examples of (one hopes) unintentional parental influence.

There have been very few systematic studies of the precise ways in which parents directly or indirectly teach children racial attitudes, those that exist are reviewed in some detail in Chapter 5. For the moment, the results of one study (which looked at children's attitudes in relation to their mothers' attitudes and behaviour) serve to summarize the general findings in this area:

The results unequivocally support the conclusion that the ethnic attitudes of children are related to the ethnic attitudes of their mothers . . . the transmission of ethnic prejudice is certainly not surprising since children easily adopt prejudiced attitudes if these are displayed by parents who typically have high reinforcement value.[277]

Role-learning

Role-learning, the third aspect of socialization we shall deal with, overlaps with both direct and indirect tuition. It is an important part of the socialization process, integrating the child into different facets of the social matrix, through the acquisition of behaviour appropriate to each.

From birth, individuals find themselves inexorably entangled in a web of relationships with others. The first roles to be played are 'infant' and 'child'; the supporting cast are the parents, brothers and sisters, and various 'extras' with little part in the action. All these people, however, have a clear idea of 'what' the child is — that is, the role of the child — and demand appropriate behaviour in accordance with that role. As Laing[231] has written: 'One is in the first instance the person that other people say one is . . . we discover who we already are.'

A role carries rather precise prescriptions for the occupant's behaviour. These prescriptions reflect the social reality of which the role is an integral part, and so similar roles will carry quite different prescriptions in different social classes, cultures or periods of history. Thus, for example, the role of 'the child' has altered dramatically over the course of this century in Western societies, from one in which the occupant was 'seen and not heard', to the vociferous and vigorous participant in family life that child-centredness has promoted.

In learning roles the individual must learn to 'behave, feel and see the world in a manner similar to other persons occupying the same position'.[338] So it also involves attaining a particular view of the world and subscribing to certain norms and values. The perspective is strengthened when the child comes to make emotional responses to conformity or deviation from these norms and values.

In the early years most role-learning takes place in relation to the parents; role-behaviour is essentially reciprocal behaviour, and the parents are the 'others' who recur most frequently in the child's world. Here again the parents directly influence the behaviour, shaping it to conform to *their* conception of correct role behaviour,

61

and implanting within it an appropriate conception of the world. And once again, it is not a calculated process of indoctrination, in fact it may be largely unconscious. But as children learn these roles and enact them, they become aware of the ways in which the roles relate them to other people and *their* roles. This growing awareness of dovetailing, or reciprocity, eventually enables them to look back at themselves from the other's position, which we refer to as 'taking the role of the other'. But from quite early on, children become aware of themselves *as* performers of their roles, the process continues into adulthood in exactly the same way, and in each new role:

> Both self and others can be apprehended as performers of objective, generally known actions, which are recurrent and repeatable by any actor of the appropriate type . . . it is not difficult to see that, as these objectifications accumulate ('nephew-thrasher', 'sister-supporter', 'initiate warrior', 'rain-dance virtuoso' and so forth) an entire section of self-consciousness is structured in terms of these objectifications.[30]

Clearly, the parents' attitudes and values enter into the process of teaching the child these early roles; how they conceive of a role in turn determines how the child behaves in that role and, ultimately, how he or she understands the reality that surrounds it.

Identity and social reality

Role-learning illustrates the two aspects of the socialization process that concern us most: children's acquisition of an understanding of the world about them, and their acquisition of an identity. For as they attain a perspective on the social world viewed from a particular role within it, so do they attain a notion of themselves *as* enacting that role. It becomes a part of their identity. Thus the person's view of the world and view of themselves are indissolubly linked, through the roles they play. They are opposite sides of the same coin, the currency being social roles.

Identity is a concept which has been much used and abused in psychological theory. The term 'identity' has been a repository for a variety of imprecise ideas about what people are and how they see themselves. It has been all things to all theorists, and it is not our intention to redefine it here in yet another way. It seems more useful to integrate the concept into a wider schema which does not exclude its previous usage, but operates at a different level of explanation. Peter Berger and Thomas Luckmann[30] have developed such a schema, aspects of which have already been introduced within this chapter.

Their thesis proceeds from the central idea that reality is socially constructed; the 'knowledge that guides conduct in everyday life' is taken for granted as reality. It originates in the thoughts and actions of individuals and is communicated socially. This 'knowledge' is not the body of ideas we refer to as intellectual knowledge; rather it is the ordinary commonsense knowledge of our environment, way of living and so on. However, we do not always view the world in exactly the same way. How we do so depends on who we are, where we are, what we are doing, why, when and how. In any one day, a man sees the world from the very different perspectives of early riser, father, Times-reader, commuter, bank employee, saloon bar raconteur, bedtime storyteller, and perhaps even great lover. In other words we pass through *different* realities as a matter of course, and we can recall them to consciousness at will.

It would be totally disorientating if all these realities involved *completely* different views of the world. In fact there is a strong common thread which runs through them all, the paramount reality, which orders our behaviour in a consistent way despite these variations. This is the reality of everyday life; it is largely shared with other people and it appears to exist independently of us all:

The reality of everyday life is taken for granted *as* reality. It does not require additional verification over and beyond its simple presence. It is simply *there,* as self-evident and compelling facticity. I *know* that it is real.[30]

It is this everyday reality which smoothes the transition between the different realities that our lives involve, so that we hardly notice the passage from one to another. But each way of being in the world has its own perspective on the world, its own universe of meaning. This applies not only to the major roles of 'parent' and 'child' but also to the fleeting 'walk-on' roles already mentioned. And we get momentary glimpses of yet other perspectives as, for example, when we show unusual courage or fail unexpectedly or pass before some fortuitous social mirror.

Each of these different spheres of experience involves different ways of construing the world and hence different ways of construing ourselves. Each requires different qualities and behaviours from us; each emphasizes some of our attributes, and ignores or actually suppresses others, and we construe ourselves accordingly. Different realities require different identities. At the rally I am a Fascist but return home to become a loving husband and father.

The recognition that, theoretically, people possess as many identities as they have attributes, distinguishes this approach from the many previous conceptions of identity as a somewhat stationary, unitary entity. However, it is no more true to say that 'identity' is the sum total of attrributes that individuals possess, of demographic categories to which they belong, and of roles they play. But these are the raw materials of identity. At a given time, identity is an abstraction from this mass of characteristics each individual possesses — a sample of them on which a particular reality focuses. Any situation in which he or she finds him or herself has its own reality. This acts like a filter; it filters out the less relevant attributes (our Fascist's passion for cats for example) and amplifies the salient ones (his anti-Semitism). These are the elements of identity the person sees him or herself as having in this social reality and which are acted out. And the 'filter' is simply the 'knowledge' of that reality and the attributes appropriate to it.

What we customarily understand by 'identity' becomes, in this system, simply the identity construed by the individual in the every-day reality — that is, the identity construed from the small number of attributes which recur again and again in the different realities encountered. These form the central core of identity; they provide an ongoing sense of self which gives a foundation of consistency throughout the day's activities.

None of this implies that each inhabitant of a particular social reality has exactly the same identity. Any one individual will arrive at a notion of identity partly as a result of the pressure a particular reality exerts — in the ghetto, for example, 'race' will be a crucial aspect of identity for many people, figuring importantly and frequently in their experience, and often with highly emotional overtones. Yet for some long-standing residents, who do not happen to mix frequently with white people, the importance of race may have receded, so that other attributes such as 'being the friendly neighbourhood mailman' are more central to their notions of them-selves. Other differences in the identities which individuals deem important arise from the different attributes they possess and develop, their different experiences, and of course differences in personality which produce different emphases on each of these. Nevertheless, to the extent to which people occupy similar realities in any given social situation, so will there be some consensus as to

64

the importance of particular attributes, and some correspondence of identities. Our Fascist's friends have not gathered to discuss his passion for Siamese cats, and the reality of the rally and its aftermath will focus less on his affection for animals than his disaffection with people; similar concerns unite all those present, who will thus construe their identities similarly.

Childhood identity

For children this system is very much simpler. Their social experience is far more restricted, as is their cognitive development, so that they do not alternate between different perspectives on their own and other people's behaviour with the dexterity of adults. That is, they inhabit rather fewer social realities — the home, the street, the school and the recreation ground — with correspondingly few identities. Yet essentially the same process operates: social reality is made evident to them in an unsophisticated form mediated by the 'significant others' in their world. The significant others monitor the child's behaviour according to the rules of that reality and convey to him or her the qualities which are called for. Through these appraisals children absorb an idea of their standing in terms of these qualities, that is, a rudimentary sense of identity. The young boy is aware that his mother believes the sun to shine out of his very mouth, his teacher perpetually reprimands him for talking in class, while in the gang he has to compete for supremacy like everyone else. In each of these situations he perceives himself to be a slightly different person, but with some qualities common to each.

The central qualities which recur in many different realities, and so contribute most to the child's enduring sense of identity, will be different from one social milieu to another. Some, however, are likely to be crucial in most contexts. The child's sex, for example, determines behaviour, dress and treatment in every situation in which children find themselves. It not only figures frequently, but also the context — that is, surrounded by emphatic taboos — impresses it firmly in their minds: consider the reaction from both teachers and friends if a boy goes into the girls' cloakroom at school, or wants to play with dolls in the gang. Age, too, is a very important attribute. It sets limits on permissible behaviour and it locates the child in the hierarchies of the family and the school; we would thus expect it to be an important aspect of the child's identity.

Age and sex are relatively simple categories that the child fully understands. However there are categories which are conceptually complex and not fully understood by the child, which nevertheless

65

crucially contribute to identity. Certainly religion is just such a category for Ulster children. Young children continue to demonstrate this aspect of their identity in the streets, even without profound knowledge of the historical, ecclesiastic, or dogmatic issues between Protestantism and Catholicism. It is sufficient that from the earliest age the children associate the religious category-names with their adult evaluative connotations, and from that basis evolve an intense identification with their own group, and rejection of the other group. More will be said about this process shortly.

Where the relations between groups are the subject of strong feelings, or where they are regulated by widely-held values and norms, or where they are institutionalized in compulsory segregation, we would expect the relevant attribute (like 'race' or 'religion') to enter most strongly into people's identities. Further, the more explicitly the category figures in the social reality, the more pronounced this is likely to be. In racially segregated areas, then, race may be more crucial to the inhabitants than in unsegregated areas, even though the opportunities for inter-racial contact are reduced. Thus the *de jure* segregation of the American South may have enhanced the salience of the race category in comparison with the *de facto* segregation of the North. Morland[273] provided some evidence which points in this direction; he found that Southern white children had a significantly greater ability to make racial distinctions than did Northern whites or blacks. Moreover, Horowitz and Horowitz[179] showed that this pronounced intrusion of the 'race' category into the social reality can enhance the importance of the racial aspects of the child's identity over and above all others — even fundamental ones like age and sex. They compared the importance of sex, age, race and socio-economic status identifications in their young Southern subjects; using three separate tests they found consistent clear evidence that with children in these communities race is the most fundamental distinction: 'The general order of importance of these attributes appears to be race first, then sex, age and socio-economic status.'

We have shown, then, how social attitudes and identity are closely linked; both emanate from the reality that surrounds the child. A multiracial society creates realities which demand a heightened awareness of particular attitudes and identities. Here children come to view their world through race-tinted spectacles, whether they are black or white.

★

We can summarize the argument so far in the following way: in the course of socialization, society teaches children not only ways of doing things but also ways of seeing — that is, its *values*. Parents are central to this process; they are the interpreters and instructors. They encapsulate and inculcate society's message, by accident and design. Children come to hold many of these values as their own; among them are values concerning other groups in the society — social classes, religious denominations and racial groups are the most obvious of these. Not all parents share the majority's attitudes and values so that their children may develop dissenting views. But that young children will absorb many of their parents' views is automatic and inevitable. And to the extent to which a view of the world prevails among a majority of adults, so will that perspective influence the next generation. As far as those children's attitudes and values are concerned, this is the beginning rather than the end of the story. All kinds of influences intervene before adulthood to affect these processes, among them the education process. But whatever dissenting voices the child encounters, we should be clear about the strength of social pressures urging conformity to the majority view, exerted in the socialization process.

Our central concern, racial attitudes, is not a special case but one part of this larger view. In the remainder of this chapter and in the following chapters we single out this aspect of the socialization process and its consequences. In the previous chapter we considered whether society teaches us particular ways of seeing groups which are 'different' from ourselves and saw how easily hostility was fomented between groups, no matter how superficial the differences between them. We now turn to look at the development of national attitudes in children, where there are more cues to differentiate the parties than in the 'minimal group' experiments, but no obvious physical differences, nor immediate context of competition, as in the case of racial groups.

The development of national attitudes

The early studies of national attitude development in children tended to focus on their cognitive abilities; their capacity to handle the rather complex concepts of nations, countries and so on. The emphasis lay on their evolving ability to understand the logical relations between these concepts and between the entities they denoted. Piaget was the main exponent of this approach, and in his earliest study[298] he investigated the child's attainment of part/whole relationships and the concept of inclusion, as applied to the relations between a town, a district and a country. For example, he examined the child's progress from the stage where it might be denied that one could be, for example, simultaneously Parisian and French, to an eventual grasp of the correct relationship.

In a later study Piaget and Weil[299] described the development of the child's notion of nationality as a dual process of cognitive and affective development: 'The cognitive and affective elements may be said to be parallel or isomorphous.' In other words, at the same time as children learn to handle concepts of nations and absorb factual knowledge about them, they develop *affective* dispositions also. Learning about other countries is also learning how to feel about them.

As Jahoda has written:[187]

. . . a child's intellectual grasp of his environment begins in his immediate vicinity and only gradually extends outwards. One can think of this as a series of concentric circles with the child at the centre.

This process of understanding the spatial relations between towns and countries, and the conceptual relations of the self to class and nationality groups is paralleled by affective development. In the young child, evaluations of, or attitudes towards other countries (according to Piaget and Weil) are initially egocentric or personal, to be replaced subsequently by acceptance of the family's values about other nations, finally giving way to attitudes based on wider societal values.

Implicit in those approaches which emphasize the factual and cognitive aspects of attitude development is a 'rational' model of attitude development. People like to think of their attitudes as evaluations, based on a rational appraisal of the facts, the end-product of some deliberation. To describe national attitude development as an almost simultaneous absorption of facts about countries and production of feeling about them does not rule this out. In theory it allows the feelings to be a response to the facts.

However, more recent research has exploded this idea. It is now clear that the relationship between two cognitive and affective elements of national attitudes is not a simple isomorphism, nor are the 'feelings' necessarily a rational response to the 'facts'. This emerged from a study by Tajfel and Jahoda[373] in which they investigated the development of concepts and evaluations of foreign nations among six- to seven-year-old children. In particular they looked at the relation between the children's preferences for various countries and their factual knowledge about them — in this case, the size of the countries concerned. This was achieved by successive individual comparisons of the children's preferences for four countries (America, France, Germany and Russia), each with the others, and similar comparisons of these countries with regard to distance from the child's own country, and determination of the relative size of the child's own country and the other four countries:

> One aspect of the results can be described as follows: at the ages of six and seven children in Britain agree rather more about which countries they like and dislike than about practically anything else about those countries . . . (they) agree rather more that they prefer America and France to Germany and Russia than that *both* America and Russia are larger in size than *both* France and Germany. There is no theoretical difference between the learning of these two kinds of 'facts'; *and, if anything the knowledge of facts about preferences crystallizes rather earlier than the corresponding knowledge of facts about size.* [italics added]

Before this study, the possibility that the affective elements could emerge *before* the items of knowledge on which they were supposed to be based, (according to folk-psychology and common sense), had not been widely accepted. The child's development of national attitudes was now clearly seen as a process of social learning; this consisted of learning various 'facts', some of which might be items of information about the countries themselves, but more importantly a variety of social 'facts', such as 'Britons don't like Germans'.

These findings blur the distinction between the cognitive and affective elements of national attitudes. The precise relationship between these two elements was the subject of a study by Johnson *et al.*[201] with children of seven to eleven years. They found that children knew most about the countries they liked and disliked strongly and least about the ones they felt neutral about. The knowledge they demonstrated, though, was not necessarily the basis for their preferences, for it contained information about geographical position, population and so on. One interpretation of this is that 'there may simply be more information "in the air" referring to the nations the child is expected to like or dislike strongly . . . the relationship . . . may tell us more about the "propaganda environment' in which the child lives than about intra-individual processes

69

involved in the formation of attitudes'[201]. Together with evidence from an earlier study[199], they conclude that 'some evidence exists for believing that knowledge is not an essential pre-requisite for the development of emotional reactions to other nations. As Horowitz[180] puts it, "Within the individual the sequence is frequently the development of a prejudice first and the perfection of the techniques of differentiation later." The results of the present study are certainly congruent with that view.'[201] So these studies call into question the notion that children's knowledge and conceptual development need to be very far advanced before they are able to reproduce, if not understand, national attitudes. This is important for our discussion for it emphasizes the child's sensitivity to the emotional and evaluative nuances of adult attitudes at an early age.

At the same time as children develop attitudes towards other nations, they absorb an evaluation of their own nation; these are reciprocal aspects of the same process. Simply:

> As a function of age, children develop an increasingly stable system of preferences for various foreign countries and a more consistent identification with their own country.[259]

And, as with attitudes towards other countries, 'children do come to "prefer" their own country to others well before they are able to form, understand and use appropriately the relevant concepts of countries or nations'[375].

This emerges from a comprehensive study of children's national attitudes which was conducted in England, Scotland, Holland, Austria, Belgium and Italy[375]. One test in the study required children to assign photographs of young men to boxes labelled 'I like him very much', 'I like him a little', 'I dislike him very much'. In the first of two sessions separated by two weeks the children were asked to sort the same photographs into boxes labelled (for example) 'English' and 'not-English' in the case of the English subjects, 'Scottish' and 'not-Scottish' for the Scottish subjects, and so on. The children had been told that some of the photographs were of people of their own nationality.

In most of the locations children tended to assign the photographs they liked better to their own national group. That is:

> . . . through an association of national verbal labels with preference sorting of photographs one can elicit from young children a clear index of preference for their own national

group . . . children clearly prefer those photographs they classify as own nation to those they classify as not own nation. [Although this relationship weakens with age] . . . it would be naive to assume that this decrease is due to a decrease in nationalism.[374]

It seems likely that the younger children base both the preference judgment and the nationality judgment on the same criterion: simple liking. The child's choice could then be interpreted as unconsciously saying 'I like him *because* he looks English' or 'Because I like him, he must be English.' Either way there is a clear association between liking and one's own national group. However, it may be that the older children approach the two tasks using different criteria — for example, basing nationality assignment on some physical stereotype of the national group rather than just on the basis of liking, thereby reducing the correlation between the judgments.

The exceptions to this rule were the Scottish children. They did not show this pattern of national preference, that is they did not always prefer the photographs they identified as 'Scottish'. One possible explanation of this is that the category 'not Scottish' was interpreted by the children to mean 'English', and their preference for the photographs they assigned to this category reflects the relatively less favourable evaluation of 'Scottish' compared to 'English' that has existed in Britain. At first this seems to be a rather far-fetched explanation for the devaluation of Scotland and things Scottish is relatively mild and more a matter of history than a contemporary issue. However it was borne out in another part of the study[374] which employed the same tests with English, Scottish and Israeli children. The English children discriminated in favour of their own group, and this decreased slightly with age, as before. The Scottish children did not discriminate in favour of 'Scottish' when choosing between 'Scottish' and 'not Scottish'. When further Scottish children were tested and given the choice between 'Scottish' and 'English', the children discriminated in favour of the English. In other words they demonstrated a preference for another nation, and an implicit devaluation of their own nation. Though this is a very significant phenomenon for our discussion, there must be some doubt as to whether these findings would now be replicated as they pre-date the advent of Scottish Nationalism as a political force.

Equally interesting results emerged from the sample of Israeli children; two groups were tested, some of Oriental origin and some of European origin. They were shown twenty pictures half of which depicted young 'European' Jews and half young 'Oriental' Jews. In choosing between 'Israeli' and 'not Israeli':

> The national preference results which were obtained in other countries are — not surprisingly — strongly replicated. . . . the correlation based on the overall degree of liking of the photographs and their assignment to the category 'Israeli' is very high (among the highest of any of the national group).[374]

Further, *both* groups of children preferred the 'European' photographs; and the difference between the frequency of assignment of these photographs to the 'Israeli' category and frequency of assignment of the 'Oriental' photographs to this category was highly significant.

There are several interesting issues here. Firstly, the high level of preference for their own nation clearly reflects the heightened national consciousness of Israelis, as a result of their historical experience and contemporary tensions in the Middle East. Secondly, there is evidence among the 'Oriental' children of some devaluation of their own group and preference for the 'other' group in the society, that is, Jews of European origin. This is thought to be a reflection of the more dominant role played by European Jews in the Israeli state, further evidenced by the children's assignment of the European photographs to the 'Israeli' category. The Oriental children, then, combine side-by-side a pronounced preference for their own national group above all others, and a devaluation of their own 'ethnic' group within the society, through their preference for the more dominant group.

The burden of all these studies is that the development of attitudes towards the child's own country and other countries is primarily a result of social influence. The child is dealing with abstract entities — nations — with which there is no direct contact (and whose members are not obviously distinguishable from one another by virtue of physical or other characteristics). The sources of both factual and evaluative information are therefore social sources — parents, siblings, peers, teachers, together with some non-human equivalents like comics, books and television. Within this system children acquire a preference for their own country and an enduring identification with it. At the same time they develop a pattern of preference for other countries in advance of some of the simplest items of factual knowledge about them. These preferences and dislikes derive from contemporary and historical national alignments; they mirror the portrayals of their own and other countries current in their social world. And this operates even in situations where no overt inter-group tension or strife is evident, and where the group is not substantially disparaged. Children are apparently sensitive to the most subtle nuances of social influence and incorporate them in their nascent attitudes.

The development of racial attitudes
In this light, the emergence of rudimentary racial feelings in very young children is easily understood. While, as we have seen, the development of *national* attitudes is not assisted by any cues other than adult attitudes, the development of racial attitudes is virtually the opposite extreme. For over and above adult teaching, the process is assisted by direct experience of contact between the races, obvious physical differences like skin colour which distinguish them, and often strict rules governing conduct between them.

Contact ensures that these issues enter directly into the child's experience in a concrete way. Wholesale physical differences, and hence high visibility, make discrimination between the groups and labelling them extremely easy. Rules of behaviour establish patterns of responding to other racial groups which are consistent with adult attitudes towards those groups, whether or not children have yet developed those attitudes for themselves. But we must not lose sight of the fact that while these cues help to foster and reinforce children's attitudes, they only complement the central role of adult influence.

Here we must anticipate Chapter 5, in which a detailed picture of the course of racial attitude development is presented; for the moment we need only an outline of this. In a multiracial society white majority-group children show evidence of being aware of simple racial differences from a very early age, sometimes as young as three years old. In the following years they begin to show feelings about these groups; these are simple evaluations which invariably take the form of preferring and identifying with the in-group, and showing some dislike or rejection of other racial groups. These evaluations are picked up from significant others and various media of communication, as we shall describe in the following chapter. Soon after, around the age of five, rudimentary versions of adult attitudes may be mouthed, and the first understanding of the social roles of whites and blacks appears. Versions of adult stereotypes are reproduced, and the process of absorption of the society's colour values crystallizes into fully fledged racial attitudes.

For black children brought up within the same society, things are rather different. They are surrounded by the same values and attitudes, and these are made real to them in a number of ways: they pervade all the social life and the institutions of the society and the children cannot help but absorb them. They speak directly to black people, for within those attitudes is a picture of their group and, by implication, of themselves. The more derogatory is this portrayal, the more unacceptable is the 'identity' it imposes. Even without the more lurid racial stereotypes which tend to accompany tense inter-racial situations, the inferior social status of the minority, underwritten by their colour, ensures them a devalued identity.

In the context of national groups implicitly devaluing themselves, as we have seen, it is not surprising to find that some children from racial minorities have apparently sought to avoid the imposition of a derogatory identity, by 'preferring' or identifying with whites. This response to the inferiorizing pressures of racism pre-dates the growth of black consciousness and has been largely superceded by it, but it is a psychological phenomenon which is of enormous importance: it illuminates the individual's range of responses to oppression, whether as a member of a racial, national, religious, sexual or political minority, and it is given due weight in Chapter 6.

4
Culture and prejudice

If we consider the complex of factors that lies behind the emergence of racism in any one society, we can identify three main categories: the *cultural* determinants, the *social structural* determinants and the *individual* or *personality* determinants. Each has been utilized by various schools of thought to 'explain' prejudice; any one on its own is inadequate to the task, but taken togther they can account for the genesis of racism in a society, its proliferation through the culture, and its transmission to future generations. It is this last aspect which has been given the greatest emphasis so far. The reason for this continuing emphasis is as follows: once racism has emerged within a culture, has become widespread and established, then the cultural factors (of the three groups we have mentioned) become singularly important agents in its continuance. When racism has taken root in the majority culture, has pervaded its institutions, language, its social intercourse and its cultural productions, has entered the very fabric of the culture, then the simple process by which a culture is transmitted from generation to generation — the socialization process — becomes the most important 'determinant' of prejudice. For then it reaches all sections of the population, including those who are neither objectively nor subjectively threatened by black people, nor stand to gain anything by discrimination against them — in other words, those who have neither 'social structural' nor 'personality' reasons for prejudice. This is why such emphasis was laid in the last chapter on the socialization of attitudes in children.

When, in addition, the culture retains a residue from past race relationships — any legacy of assumptions and attitudes about black people from the days of slavery, or from the periods of imperialism and colonialism — then we see that contemporary racism builds upon some submerged but enduring cultural foundations. These too assist the transmission of prejudice to children as we shall see. The first part of this chapter deals with all these cultural factors — both the traditional foundations and the contemporary content of prejudiced racial attitudes. 'Social structural' and 'personality' factors are not overlooked, but are considered in the next chapter as 'intervening variables', factors which add to or subtract from the basic process of attitude transmission. They materially affect the incidence of prejudice within various groups of adults and therefore equally affect *their* children's attitudes in turn. For the moment, we turn to a brief survey of cultural influences on children's attitudes.

Racism in children's literature

Until the advent of film and television, books were among the most influential carriers of culture. While this influence has diminished, they remain a telling mirror of current social values, including racial values, and these may in turn influence the reader's attitudes. Literature enjoys a privileged position in our culture. 'The book' as a source of information and knowledge has a mystique and an authenticity which is unrivalled by other cultural media. It is one of the means of communication that underpins our entire education system. This crucial role is most evident in the priority we accord to 'learning to read', the necessary condition for participation in every other aspect of education. Inability or retardation in this sphere handicaps the child to an extent which is comparable to mental or physical handicap. Both the process of reading and reading materials themselves acquire a halo of value that simply does not attach to film or television or ordinary conversation in the same way. The emphasis we place on reading is not lost on the child: many tangible rewards are offered for success, above all the manifest approval of parents and teachers.

While older children and adults can be more objective and critical of the *content* of books, there is little basis for the young child on which to discriminate between 'good' and 'bad'. The first glimpse of a new reality which reading offers is likely to be potent and influential, making the child more vulnerable to the message of the book, invested as it is with all the highly positive connotations we have described. For this reason we have to look rather closely at the reading material we provide for children and divine the message it conveys. Whether fact or fiction, information is seldom conveyed in a social vacuum; it often implies, or is conveyed in an atmosphere which implies, certain social values.

When we look at the portrayal of racial minorities in children's literature, it is clear that it has traditionally been characterized by omission and derogation in equal measure. In other words, until quite recently children's literature has virtually ignored the existence of black people and, where they have been acknowledged, their treatment has been at best patronizing, at worst racist, and nearly always stereotyped. Walters[411] has pointed out that minority children suffer as a consequence of their group's omission from schoolbooks:

> The acceptance of white skin as associated with all that is important enough to be in books, pictures and 'school-learning' tends to be an unconscious rejection of the child's own colour.

Dorothy Kuya[229], writing in similar vein, talks of the humiliation of the child whose group is ignored in this way. Not only are such children deprived of the recognition of their group by the book and by their peers, but also of figures with whom they can identify. This state of affairs is also detrimental to white children; for an unrealistic picture of the social world is presented which does not acknowledge the existence of a multiracial society, or a multiracial world for that matter.

The ways in which racial minorities have been *devalued* in children's books are more complex and sometimes quite subtle. This derogation operates principally through (i) the disproportionate selection of 'dark' figures for 'bad' roles, and (ii) the attribution of bad characteristics to people *because* they are members of a particular racial or national group; overlapping with these is the use of stereotypes. Stereotypes may be artificially good, bad or neutral, but they are all bad in the sense that they are over-generalizations and, as we have seen, exaggerate the differences between groups and the uniformities within them. While this makes for ease in categorizing people, it ignores the characteristics and experiences which are common to all people and which could be portrayed as a bond between them, and the huge variations in personality and life-style within any one group. There is a 'kernel of truth' in some of these stereotypes, or there was once. But they are usually generations out of date, or refer to minorities within the races or nationalities concerned, or practices which are a profoundly unimportant part of people's lives. It would be easy indeed to emerge from a childhood spent with some of these books believing that Africans seldom come out of the jungle, Chinese men wear pigtails, and French men (who affect droopy moustaches and dress only in striped jerseys and black berets) dine exclusively on frogs and snails.

Mary Waddington[410] described how many books introduce foreign people through:

> . . . a romantic and entertaining fantasy of ancient heroes or quaint but abandoned customs. So many books, pictures and films show the unusual quaint aspects of life in other countries, and children are left with the idea that *all* Dutch children wear clogs, and *all* Eskimos live in igloos despite Rotterdam being one of the most modern cities in the world, and Eskimos probably using more helicopters than we do in Britain.

British books, inevitably, view the rest of the world from a British perspective; the quaintness of these images underlines their *'differentness'*. These people deviate from an unspoken norm: the customs, habits and values which constitute the British way of life. Deviation from the 'normal' often connotes inferiority as Kozol[226] explains:

> It was not that we were told anything was wrong with looking odd or peculiar but simply that we were made to feel, beyond possibilities of redemption, that this 'oddness', this 'differentness', this 'peculiarity' is something from which we can feel ourselves indescribably lucky to have been spared. It is the inexorable quality of differentness which seems so evil here. A bitter little perjury is perpetrated upon children even before they are old enough to understand exactly why it is that things that are made to seem so different, strange and peculiar, are precisely the things which it is easiest to despise.

We will look briefly at a few examples culled from a selection of books which are widely read by children. Although Charles Kingsley's *Water Babies* is a well-loved and apparently harmless children's story, it is a good example of how we accept children's classics uncritically and pass on some malignant stereotypes in the process. Listen to Kingsley's description[219] of Dennis, an imaginary but typical Irishman:

> You must not trust Dennis, because he is in the habit of giving pleasant answers; but instead of being angry with him, you must remember that he is a poor Paddy and knows no better; so you must just burst out laughing; and then he will burst out laughing too, and slave for you, and trot about after you, and

show you good sport if he can — for he is an affectionate fellow and as fond of sports as you are — and if he can't, tell you fibs instead, a hundred an hour; and wonder all the while why poor old Ireland does not prosper like England and Scotland, and some other places, where folks have taken up a ridiculous fancy that honesty is the best policy.

If that passage at least has a gloss of patronizing warmth, consider another one, where Kingsley describes how 'young ladies walk about with lockets of Charles the First's hair (or of somebody else's when the Jew's genuine stock is used up)'. Similarly, even ·C.D. Lewis's apparently benign adventure stories contain an incident where some boys pawn some toys and describe their meagre payment from the shopkeeper as having been 'Jewed'.[238]

Stereotypes of French people, whale-eating Eskimos, swarthy and operatic Italians, and dour penny-pinching Scots abound. Further afield, aliens come in for more exotic treatment; in fact there seems to be a correlation between the distance from England of a particular nation, and its potential for bizarre, comic or savage treatment by the author. Arthur Ransome shipwrecks some of his characters off the coast of China.[311] One of their Chinese captors claims to:

Talkee English velly good. You mean Melican Missee? Melican boy? . . . Chang is velly gleedy man. Chang wants to get lich quick . . . He will make Lord Mayor San Flancisco lite a letter to Amelica.

Naturally all the Chinamen have pigtails and long twisted moustaches, while the women have strapped feet. With the exception of Missee Lee, who was educated in England, the women are all shown to be stupid and petty. While the men work, 'Their yellow bodies were naked to the waist . . . "like yellow frogs", whispered Roger.'

This brings us on to the treatment of racial as opposed to national groups. First of all let us look at the treatment of 'black' and 'white' as colours which are rich in connotative meaning. They are repeatedly used as descriptive devices to convey atmosphere, mood, threat, human characteristics, morality and to enlist the support of the reader for good over bad. Often characters are 'coloured' in this way to distinguish the goodies from the baddies, Right and Wrong or, most unfortunately, Us and Them. As Kozol[226] remarks:

Once upon a time there was a woman who had two daughters. One of them was beautiful but the other was ugly. . . . When you read this . . . you know, even before you look, which daughter is going to have yellow hair, and which one will have dark hair.

Like, for example, Marusia, heroine of one fairy-tale of Williams-Ellis's: 'She was a beauty that girl; Marusia the Fair they called her. Her skin was as white as milk . . . And what's more, Marusia was as kind and good natured as she was pretty.'[426] But Charles Kingsley once again provides the best example of polarity of black and white. *The Water Babies*[219] is a moral tale of Ellie, 'a clean, white, good little darling' of a wealthy family, and Tom, a little chimney sweep. When he enters her room by mistake:

> . . . The room was all dressed in white; white window-curtains, white bed-curtains, white furniture and white walls, with just a few lines of pink here and there. . . . Under the snow-white coverlet, upon the snow-white pillow lay the most beautiful little girl that Tom had ever seen. Her cheeks were almost as white as the pillow and her hair was like threads of gold spread all about the bed. . . . [Tom] stood staring at her as if she had been an angel out of heaven. . . . Looking around, he suddenly saw standing close to him a little ugly, black, ragged figure with bleared eyes and grinning white teeth. He turned on it angrily. What did such a black ape want in that sweet young lady's room? It was himself reflected in the great mirror.

This symbolic black/white, bad/good theme recurs monotonously throughout the book. Were that not enough, the final associative link is made with black *races* when Tom talks to a family of 'heathens'. They are very stupid and call on a pow-wow man to attend to their son, who 'rattled, brandished his thunderbox, yelled, shouted, raved, roared, stamped and danced corryborry like any black fellow'.

It is too easy to write off these moral tales as archaic and unimportant. The evaluative connotations of black and white are hammered home relentlessly throughout children's literature and it is unfortunate that there will be many children, black and white whose only experience of black figures in books will be characters like these. Somewhere between the symbolic representation of 'black' and 'white' people and the *actual* portrayal of different races comes the nearly-human 'Golliwog'. His adventures were originally written in 1900[401]; they were inexplicably resurrected in 1967. Golliwog himself is a ludicrous caricature but the traditional association with black people makes him a more serious influence than he appears. In one of his adventures, the authors manage to cram all the stereotypes of black people into one scenario. Golliwog, the laughing, crying, rubber-lipped, nigger minstrel figure, finds himself in Africa, where he is surrounded by — wait for it — savage cannibals:

A fearful tribe of cannibals
All armed with weapons grim,
Brandish their spears
And spite of tears
Prepare to finish him.

It is said of their king (and, needless to say, the scalp is not Golliwog's):

This scalp so fair
He longs to wear —
Such trophies he holds dear.

Many other stories furnish examples of African savagery, cannibalism, primitive rites, exotic headgear and clothes, or lack of them; where stereotypes are not so derogatory, they invariably stress the simple-minded backwardness and uncultured life-styles of Africans. This shades into the image of the slave-like Uncle Tom figure, happy and lazy, loafing and finger-clicking, abounding with natural rhythm — the patronizing stereotype of the American 'Negro'. And of course where black Americans do enter into children's literature this is precisely the treatment they receive. Two examples stand out: *Nicodemus and his New Shoes*[177] and the *Little Black Sambo* books.[22] Both depict in words and pictures black people (and perhaps most damagingly, black children) as laughable doll-like figures, who speak in music-hall Negro dialects: Nicodemus opines, 'Lawdy lan', if you don't hole dat chile by de han', she is boun' to git into trouble.' And the children sing a characteristic song: 'I got shoes, you got shoes, All o' God's Chillun got shoes.'

H. Lofting's 'Doctor Doolittle' books are among the worst offenders (and among the most popular of children's books). The author[246] feels free to pass on 'adult' racial insults like 'darkies', 'work like niggers', 'coon'; and he puts the following words into the mouth of his character Prince Bumpo (and one can predict, correctly, from his name that he will be dark-skinned and large-lipped):

> White man, I am an unhappy prince. Years ago I went in search of the Sleeping Beauty, who I had read of in a book. . . . I at last found her . . . she awoke, but when she saw my face she cried out 'Oh, he's black!' And she ran away and wouldn't marry me. . . . If you would turn me white, so that I may go back to the Sleeping Beauty, I will give you half my kingdom and anything else besides.

The Prince would like blue eyes too; for a time his face is turned 'white as snow, and his eyes, which had been mud-coloured, were a manly grey'. Just to hammer the message home, one of his actions is met with the remark, 'Serve him right, if he does turn black again! I hope it's dark black.'

It is no exaggeration to call this material racist, albeit in an apparently innocent form. Its message — shame over blackness, a desire to be white — is unmistakeable, and it would be an insensitive child who was not aware of this; objective evidence of a telling awareness of these sentiments in both black and white children will be presented in later chapters. Nevertheless it is sometimes argued that the older books cited here are no longer read by children and are therefore not influential. To take three examples cited so far, Kingsley's *Water Babies* was recently reprinted in a glossy paperbound edition, Dr. Doolittle's various adventures sell upwards of 25,000 copies a year, while Little Black Sambo is now in its umpteenth printing and was recently re-issued complete with wall-poster to adorn the reader's walls. No-one, however, would contest the popularity of Enid Blyton's 'Noddy' books and yet, as Dixon[94,95] points out, her use of black figures (in the 'harmless' form of golliwogs) is unfortunate to say the least. These benign nursery creatures nevertheless perpetrate a variety of vile deeds upon our hero, including what must be the earliest recorded black 'mugging' in children's literature. Blyton also displays her unerring racial sensitivity in *The Three Golliwogs* by naming the central characters 'Golly', 'Woggie' and 'Nigger'.

Stories which, unlike these, involve real people rather than fantastic figures deserve careful scrutiny as they come closest to 'reality', and therefore may be taken by the child to be realistic. The

82

indefatigable Biggles is only the most famous, or infamous, example of a whole genre. Adventures stories for boys, instilling the values of manhood and courage, require dangerous situations with which to confront their heroes. By the same token their adversaries must be instantly recognizable as brutal and wicken men simply by virtue of their appearance. What better recipe for racial steretyping? Thus the white men in Foster's *Dragon Island*[120] encounter a tribe of 'the ugliest savages ever created'. On hearing war-drums,

> They [the British] imagined the scenes in the village; the natives, their naked bodies glistening in the firelight; the old men seated by the tom-tom, thumping incessantly; spitting flares, lighting up a ring of cruel faces.

When they are not savages they are merely simple, with child-like pleasures, and easily bought by the more intelligent white man:

> I have promised them a stick of tobacco each if they have a meal ready by the time we get there,' explained the hunter with a grin. 'If I know anything about the Malays we shall find a feast.'

But Biggles, from his sheer volume of adventure and unrivalled popularity, should have pride of place in any ethnocentric rogues' gallery. His creator, Captain W.E. Johns, locates him in an atmosphere which is not years out of date but generations. As Barnes[26] has written:

> Captain Johns' socio-political attitudes are those one would associate with a not unduly intelligent Empire-builder of the late Victorian 'white man's burden' period.

This is not only evident in isolated incidents but in the whole world view that emerges from the books — one which is palpably biased and distorted. The reader receives the following impression:

> that nearly all the world's surface was jungle and desert, inhabited by bestial savages: that civilization was only to be found in a place called 'Home' or 'England' whence men came by private aeroplane to solve the problems of the dark places of the world; that these problems consisted always of evil men plotting the world's destruction . . . that these evil men could

be easily recognized — big, black Negroes, harsh Prussian officers, fat suave Eurasians.

However, there is a sub-category of non-white people who are invested with some humanity; their qualities, however, are usually defined *in relation to* the white man — loyalty to him, trust given to him — and these qualities are credited to the white man's race and culture. For these characters have invariably benefited from the civilizing effect of a British mission school, or have spent time in England. Their virtue often has another significant correlate: they are usually lighter-skinned. For example, Kadar Bey in *Biggles Flies South*:

> was . . . a native, but obviously one of the better class, and his skin was not that much darker than that of a sun-burned white man. . . . His clothes were of good quality and might have been made in London; indeed, but for his distinguishing tarboosh, he might have passed for a European.

But even these elevated beings never threaten the white man's superiority.

It has been argued that this kind of analysis reads too much racialism into merely old-fashioned books where there was no harmful or deliberate intention by the author, and whose influence on the child will be minimal. Perhaps the best rebuttal of this point of view comes from Captain Johns[197] himself:

> I teach . . . under a camouflage. Juveniles are keen to learn, but the educational aspect must not be too obvious or they become suspicious of its intention. I teach a boy to be a man. . . . I teach sportsmanship according to the British idea. . . . I teach the spirit of team-work, loyalty to the Crown, Empire and to rightful authority. . . . The adult author has little hope of changing the outlook, politics, or way of life of his reader, whose ideas are fixed. The brain of a boy is flexible, still able to absorb. It can be twisted in any direction . . . upon the actions of his heroes will [a boy's] own character be formed. Upon us, who cater for him at the most impressionable age of his life, rests a responsibility which has been perceived by at least one political party. Biggles, therefore, may have some bearing on the future of the country.

Finally it is worth looking at kinds of reading experience which are common to all children. The books by which children *learn* to read are obviously the first books with which they have an 'unadulterated' personal relationship. For the first time a child can read a book alone and absorb its contents first-hand. This novelty value makes those contents very important. They are memorable to the extent that many adults can recall the characters of their first reading books. But, most significantly, these readers give access to another world, one of the first alternatives to the here-and-now daily lives that children encounter. And as the books originate from teachers and parents the child must often equate that world with the 'real' world of adults which he/she is about to share. Add to this the mystique surrounding the induction process — learning to read — and the sanctions and rewards offered for enthusiastic participation, and it soon becomes clear to the child that there is something very important about this whole process.

Adults may look at children's readers from a purely structural point of view — the acquisition of vocabulary, grammar, sentence construction and so on — but the child does not. The young reader cannot help but attend to the contents because in the interests of learning they are repeated with such remorseless regularity. For example:

I like sweets. You like sweets. You and I like sweets. You want toys. I want toys. You and I want toys. . . . Here are shops. We like shops. We like sweet shops and toy shops.[281]

Some time ago there was some long-overdue analysis of this world of school readers. Childs[66] looked at the Ladybird reading schemes:

Peter and Jane are privileged people. They live with their family in a comfortable house with a pleasant garden, and they have a friendly dog for company. Father drives a large car. Mother is a good housewife; she bakes cakes, assiduously waves people goodbye, and purchases execrable hats. They live in a middle-class idyll. As children they are improbable; but in the chintzy world of painted sunlight which they inhabit, they are no doubt firm friends of Dick and Dora (Happy Venture Series), Roy and Carol (Let's Learn to Read), Ruth and John (Beacon Readers), and everyone's first literary acquaintances, Janet and John.

Even for the middle-class reader there is a marked air of unreality about these books; frozen in the early fifties, a world free of traffic and television, in which children are always obedient, happy, and free to pursue a life of pure hedonism (abetted by adults, unworried by shiftwork and inflation — and not a working mother in sight — whose function seems to be to satisfy their children's every whim). Money is unquestioningly available for treats and trips, but above all, for buying things. Our Ladybird hero and heroine are such voracious little consumers that 'keeping up with the Janes' must be an expensive business for their readers. In the course of the first ten short books they acquire dolls, a rabbit, ball, racing car, fish, boats, a kite, tent, colour camera, balloons, skipping rope, scrapbooks, gun, and endless sweets. Peter himself should be given the last word on the subject as he is seen arranging his toys in a huge new cupboard: 'We have a lot of toys. Sometimes I forget about some of them.'

Clearly, this semi-detached and sports-jacket world is irrelevant to working-class white children, let alone black children. Stewart[360] looked at the ways the most popular children's reading schemes handled minority groups and found that native American Indians came off worst, stories stressing 'savagery, cruelty, cowardice and ugliness', and that while blacks were seldom mentioned explicitly, there were any number of stories in which 'the villain or enemy is brown or black with other undesirable characteristics as well'. In the case of Chinese, Japanese, Maoris and Arabs, 'the exotic differences between these people and white people is stressed . . . often the foreigner takes on rather a grotesque form and they are seen to be in a subordinate relationship with white people'. (There have been multiracial readers on the market for some time (for example, *Sparks*) and other series with occasional naturalistic non-white figures; even Ladybirds now have a sprinkling of (lightly) tinted faces, but the exemplary books in which such figures do *not* seem like a 'token' inclusion remain in the minority.)

Racial bias in children's books is not restricted to fiction and reading-schemes. It can also be identified in conventional school literature and curricula, whether in the teaching of history, geography or a variety of other subject areas. For the most part, history continues to be taught from a Eurocentric perspective, and while an emphasis on domestic history is inevitable, it is unfortunate that international history teaching should be so dominated by 'our' point of view. Thus are children conditioned to the notion of Europeans 'discovering Africa and bringing civilization to its jungle-dwelling inhabitants, whose culture is portrayed as a 'blank and brutal barbarism'.[84] The idea that we continue to teach such outdated stereotypes might be laughable were it not for the fact that precisely this kind of account of the 'Age of Discovery' can be elicited from children at will. Only exceptionally is there any awareness of the existence of civilization before the arrival of Europeans; of the means by which 'the natives' were controlled (rather more emphasis being given, in these accounts, to the Bible than the gun); of the motivation for exploration and colonization (other than a swash-buckling ambition to discover new territories and plant the flag); or, most important of all, of the contribution made by the exploitation of these countries' natural and human resources to our mercantile and industrial pre-eminence. To give one example, the Industrial Revolution is rightly celebrated in our history lessons for giving Britain an unassailable lead in industrial development that was to last for more than a century; less often are children taught that the capital which financed it was principally provided by the profits from the slave and sugar trades.

History and geography combine in our elementary teaching about 'people from other lands' in the sense that the 'human geography' involved is usually years out of date. For many years there has been a taste for introducing children to the diversity of human groups, nations, cultures, and geographical circumstances through books which offer brief portraits of 'typical' individuals from a number of more or less exotic places. Inevitably this amounts to an exercise in caricature, a brief excursion 'around the world in eighty stereo-types'. The absurd simplification involved does violence to reality and encourages stereotyped beliefs through enshrining them in 'factual' materials, giving them a bogus legitimacy. Thus we institu-tionalize bias and distortion where genuine knowledge should pre-vail. One example will be sufficient to illustrate this kind of approach. In common with many books the reader is invited to visit some foreign children and sample their way of life first hand. In this extract we are to benefit from the Southern hospitality of Ruth and Harry who live on a cotton farm in Alabama:

> Let us pretend that we are taking a walk through the cotton fields on their father's farm. . . . Now that the bolls have begun to open the pickers are starting their work. The pickers are mostly Negroes. Harry calls them 'darkies'. He says that every Autumn his father hires darkies to pick his cotton. Some of the farmers have big machines for picking cotton. Harry's father is one of many who do not use picking machines. He

says no machine can do this work as well as the darkies do it by hand.

The darkies move slowly to and fro through the fields, picking the cotton from the bolls with their nimble fingers. . . . The darkies are as happy picking cotton as the peasants picking grapes in the vineyards of sunny Italy. Those nearest us are singing an old song that they learned from their fathers and grandfathers when they were children. Listen carefully and you can hear the words:
'Oh de cotton fields are white
And de pickers are but few
If your fingers isn't nimble
Sure you nebber will get through.'

Now Harry's father is coming down the road in a big wagon drawn by a pair of plump brown mules. The darkies touch their caps as he drives up. . . . 'Good mornin' Marse Henry', they say, and there is a smile on every face. It is easy to see that Mr. Jackson is a kind master, and that the darkies all like him. 'Marse Henry' is their way of saying 'Master Henry'. . . .'[9]

The passage almost defies comment, but it is necessary to point out that its harmfulness is in no way vitiated by the age of the publication. The stereotypes it employs were no less patronizing when it was first published in 1958 and although there have been strenuous efforts to remove this kind of material from the classroom, this particular instance was identified in current use in an inner London primary school, 70 per cent of whose pupils are black.

Moving to textbooks for somewhat older children, as early as 1962 Hatch[164] pointed out some rabid stereotyping of races and nationalities that passed for fact in history and geography readers. Glendinning[141] later analysed history textbooks and apparently found little change over the intervening nine years, the same mixture of jingoism, ethnocentric versions of events or historical developments, or at best 'patronage' of 'under-developed' peoples predominating. Cameron[56] suggests that much of the reason for this has been buck-passing between teachers and publishers, neither taking the initiative to secure changes in archaic textbooks, which are therefore simply reprinted in their original form. She cites the example of *Our Neighbours and Their Work for Us* whose title gives some clue to its imperial perspective. First published in 1935, it was reprinted regularly over a thirty year period, apparently without

88

substantial revision if the following passage on the West Indies is anything to go by:

> The heat of the sun makes the work of growing sugar too hard for white people. Even the natives on the plantation work in very light loose clothes.

Or *Work in Other Lands,* first published in 1935, tells us that in Ceylon:

> Each of the plantations where tea is grown and picked and packed is looked after by a white man. . . . He sees that all the people who work on his plantation work well and honestly.

As Cameron comments, 'presumably he has to keep his eyes peeled'; as this extract is drawn from the revised 1956 edition it is interesting to speculate on the nature of the material which was discarded in that revision.

If our textbooks' treatment of African and Asian countries has been colonial or neo-colonial in tone, then we might hope that a new generation of writers and teachers might now acknowledge the social and economic progress of Third World nations rather than continue the stress on underdevelopment. There are tensions and conflicts of interest here; on the one hand there is a need to redress the very negative picture of Third World peoples that has always been purveyed; on the other hand, a kind of positive propaganda for the achievements of these nations could be equally far from the truth. The latter has not presented itself as a serious danger, if only because there continues to be a rather negative picture of the Third World presented in our geography teaching, although for different reasons than previously. Owen[290] points out that Third World studies have added a new dimension and a social relevance to geography teaching, by dealing with topics like poverty, the urban explosion, over-population etc., but that these very topics reinforce an image of underdevelopment. This image is actively fostered by the development agencies as a fund-raising device, and they provide a great deal of educational material about these countries for use in the classroom. Our very notions of development and underdevelopment are Eurocentric. For example:

> We teach India within the framework of the Rostow Economic Model. It recognizes five stages of economic growth and the

further a country is along the continuum, the more developed it is. So India is at stage 3 (for the most part) while we are naturally at stage 5! . . . Yet to teach this way is misleading. . . .

> India is at stage 3 because it has hardly no machines People live in huts and make tools to use. They have no machines so they make pots and baskets to sell.
>
> (boy aged 14)

> America is at stage 5 because the local villages have lots of shops and they are also in the space race. America is deep into electronics, their trade is world-wide, their exports are high and their main aim is to always be ahead in the western world. America is stage 5 because they're on top.
>
> (boy aged 14)

It is easy to see how, in the mind of the child concerned, this continuum of economic development is equated with a scale of virtue; development and civilization are made synonymous with science and technology. And it is reasonable to suppose that these evaluations will attach to the peoples concerned not just the abstract notions of their countries. In this way we continue to teach a subtle sense of superiority to white children and, concomitantly, preserve the notion of non-white inferiority.

Of course these issues remain controversial; it would be quite wrong to give the impression that all authorities agree on the necessity for revision of our perspectives in geography teaching. Or it may be that the principles are accepted while the practical implications are met with less enthusiasm; this was Dawn Gill's[137][138] recent experience in preparing an analysis (commissioned by the Schools Council) of geography syllabuses followed in secondary schools, including the Council's own 'Geography for the Young School Leaver' syllabus. Her report was critical of the syllabuses' assumptions concerning, and approaches to teaching about, the countries of origin of Britain's non-white population; it also raised questions about the teaching of urban geography, and migration. Though there may be room for disagreement about some of her analysis, the report concludes with a body of recommendations which should, at the very least, inform a thorough debate on geography teaching in a multiracial society. At the time of writing,

90

the Schools council seems unwilling to accept and publish the report in its present form.

★

Since the first edition of this book there have been several other reviews of racism in children's literature, notably those of Dixon[95], Zimet[431], Stinton[361] and Hicks[169,171]. As a result of the considerable expansion of interest in the topic, few people in education can now be unaware of its implications for their practice. To assist them there are published guidelines for assessing children's books for their suitability for the multiracial classroom[202]. In addition, there are a number of regular publications (*Children's Book Bulletin*[65], *Dragon's Teeth*[100], and the *Bulletin* of the Council on Interracial Books for children[52], from America) which continually review new publications. There are also compilations of recommended books and resources for different age groups by Taylor and Hurwitz[379], Stones[365], Elkin[109] and Hicks[170]; the most recent, comprehensive, and probably the best is by Klein[222]. The fact that there has been enough interest to sustain all this written activity testifies to the effectiveness of the *National Association for Multiracial Education* and other pressure groups who have scourged publishers for their racist sins of commission and cajoled them into making good their omissions. The success of this pressure is reflected in the fact that there are enough good books now published to make up respectable 'recommended' lists.

This does not, however, signal the end of the issue. Some books are still being published which should be handled with care (if handled at all) in a multiracial context — or even in an all-white classroom. As recently as 1976, *The Colour Factory* was published and while it is by no stretch of the imagination racist, it unfortunately continues the time-honoured assocation between black, dirt and unpleasantness: as the children in the story visit the room where black is made, Tom says, 'I should like to make black.' 'It's too dirty,' said Lyn. 'It's very dirty,' said the man. 'We have to take care that it does not spoil the other colours.'[85] The text is perfectly innocent in one sense, but not in another as we shall see shortly.

More important is the continuing use of some of the older generation of books which we have reviewed in these pages. As financial pressures in schools preclude the wholesale replacement of outdated books, there remains a need to monitor their use. They do have a utility, however, which their authors never conceived: to illustrate to older children how 'facts' change over time, and to show them graphically what racism is, and how it affects them through the books they read.

Comics

Children's comics are usually considered frivolous but essentially harmless reading matter. For the most part this is true, and the worst objections that educationalists could raise to them are that the adventures of Korky the Kat, Roy of the Rovers and Wonder Woman are not very elevating for the child. However, many comics have a more serious aspect. George Orwell realized this, and in an article on 'Boys' Weeklies'[289] he argued that they relayed an out-dated view of society. He felt that this was a conservative force because it encouraged a reactionary ideology in the minds of future citizens which could only help to shore up their society against change. His belief in the powerful influence of comics over children's minds was purely intuitive, for there was no hard evidence to support his case at the time. Nevertheless the sheer circulation figures make his view plausible; children in Britain, for example, buy over ten million comics a week and some of the more popular titles outsell all the major adult weekly magazines put together.

Broadly speaking, the comics for younger children are the most harmless. But as the comics reach out towards an older audience they devote an increasing amount of space to war stories. We believe war to be undesirable, and yet we make it the staple fare of young boys' fantasies. Fictional war is presented to the child in comics as a scenario in which the nobler qualities of men emerge: courage, endurance, patriotism, self sacrifice, comradeship and moral strength. To be on the right side is to be on the side of Right. And this is the crux, for wars are the highest (or lowest) expression of Us against Them, and these are *our* qualities not *theirs*. In comics' portrayal of war, a complex socio-political phenomenon is reduced to crude and simplistic violent episodes between groups and individuals of different nationalities, mouthing staccato sentiments, presented in strip-illustrations which can easily be absorbed by the just-literate reader. Loyalties must be left in no doubt, so that the enemy is invested with exactly the opposite characteristics to our side, not only making the distinction unmistakeably clear, but also justifying their slaughter.

In Johnson's[199] fascinating study of British war comics he found:

The enemy is described, either by the comic itself or by British characters, as 'deadly and fanatical; lousy stinking rats; brainless scum; swine; devils; filthy dogs; slippery as snakes; or slit-eyed killers'.

As Orwell maintained, the world view and the alliances the reader is called upon to support are years out of date, in this case dating back to the Second World War. Others, particularly American comics, include more contemporary enmities against 'Commies' in general and the Russians and Chinese in particular. (Some which are set in the Second World War have a timeless quality about them; no doubt the Australian soldier who 'didn't fancy the idea of his country being overrun by yellow men' would still support a 'White Australia' policy today.)

Johnson analysed comics for older boys and war comics, looking at both the number and nature of references to different national groups. Countries involved in the Second World War were mentioned very much more frequently than other nations; however the way in which the Allies were mentioned was very different to the treatment of the Enemy nations. Taking as an index the use of derogatory nicknames, the Allies' nicknames ('Limey', 'Yank', 'Aussie') (which are fairly mild anyway) were used in less than 6 per cent of the references to these countries, while the much harsher 'Nazi', 'Gerry', 'Kraut', 'Boche', 'Hun', 'Jap' and 'Nip' comprised over 38 per cent of all references to Germany and Japan.

Johnson was naturally interested in the possible effects of this material on children's day-to-day attitudes towards the countries involved. With a group of Oxford primary school children, he obtained their ranked preferences for various countries, which produced the following order of preference: England, Australia and America, France, Italy, India, Germany, Russia and China, and Japan. He then partitioned the children into those who regularly read Boys' and War comics and those who did not, and looked at the nationality preferences of each group. While the rank order of preference for the *entire* sample is as above:

. . . the enemy nations, Germany, Japan, and Italy, are liked less by the children who read War or Boys' comics [than by non-readers] while the Allies, America, Australia and France, are liked more. Russia, India and China which do not appear in the comics as involved in the war, show the smallest differences in preference between the two groups of children. There seems also to be a stronger identification with the children's own nation, England, in the case of the Boys' and War comic readers.

Clearly, the effects on children of reading war material as it is presented in comics is far from trivial, and it may also be long-lasting.

It is interesting that the Japanese were the most disliked group. This may be due to reports of their atrocities, though it is arguable whether these were any worse than German war crimes, or than Dresden or Hiroshima for that matter. An alternative explanation is that there are two reasons for antipathy towards the Japanese; they are both an enemy and an alien racial group. Both the author and the illustrator can play on the extra 'meaning' which attaches to such groups: it is easier to portray them as enemies because they even look different from us. And all the traditional overtones of mystery, danger, inscrutability, barbarism and animality which surround our feelings about foreign races make it easier to invest Orientals (or blacks) with the bestial quality the Enemy must have.

This introduces the question of how comics treat *racial* as opposed to *national* groups, irrespective of whether they are involved in wars or not. Jennie Laishley[233] looked at this issue by analysing some sixteen comics over a six month period; 162 issues were examined, including comics for very young children, boys' comics, teenage girls' magazines and a general knowledge magazine. When most comics contain at least five stories, it is significant that only twenty stories from the entire sample featured any non-white figures at all. Of these:

> . . . eight treated these characters in a wholly unfavourable fashion, that is, they were represented as, evil, treacherous, violent or stupid. Three stories included characters who, although not treated in a strongly unfavourable manner, were nonetheless represented as rather limited stereotypes. Two stories included a single non-white in the background of the story, who had little or no personality, and two further stories included characters who had a personality of their own but whose status was subordinate to the white hero or heroine of the tale.

While the war comics have lost nothing in popularity, a new generation of science fiction comics commands an increasing share of the market. It is interesting that the writers' projections for the

94

next millenium are beyond even the extreme Right's wildest dreams: an exclusively white world, save for the extra-terrestrial beings who have taken over the villain's role. '2000 AD' includes no black characters as such, although one of its heroes is Black Hawk ('once a roman centurion . . . now a gladiator in a savage alien arena!') whose ancestry is unclear, though probably not entirely Caucasian. Of contemporary fantasy comics, Wonder Woman and Superman occasionally include background blacks; however, in a recent adventure of Green Lantern/Green Arrow (a Lincoln green clad duo, who are a strange union of Batman and Robin Hood), the single black portrayal is of a violent looter.

The mass media
During the past thirty years television has grown from a luxury enjoyed by a privileged minority to a vital ingredient of virtually every household. In many homes it is almost the only source of entertainment and information and it provides these services for many hours every day. It is arguably the single most important purveyor and mirror of contemporary culture.

The novelty and attractiveness of rapidly changing visual images ensure the medium's interest-value for all but the very youngest children. This accessibility is increased by the television companies' (and advertisers') acknowledged cynicism in broadcasting material which is often tailored to the lowest common denominator of their audience's intellectual capacity; proportionally very little televised material is of a level that would be incomprehensible to the average eight to ten-year-old. It is not surprising that television has come to play an increasingly central role in children's lives. It can have an easier and more dynamic appeal than reading, or many other active pursuits. Its influence is reinforced by harassed parents who use the device as an electronic child-minder and as a reward for good behaviour. For all these reasons we should attend rather closely to the messages it conveys for they are surely influential in shaping the child's view of the world.

It is only within the last ten years that the networks have taken at all seriously the demands for greater and better representation of minorities in programming. Before this time the medium was almost exclusively white, the tiny proportion of programmes which included black characters portraying them as happy-go-lucky, unreliable 'coons', maids and manservants, entertainers or athletes. This message was clearly not lost on one American child who referred to a black infant as a 'baby maid'. In Britain, in the era before black immigration, the television treatment of black people was principally in the context of 'foreigners', with all the ethnocentric overtones the term implies. An early study, *Television and the Child*,[173] pointed out that 'Negroes' were most often seen 'in dance bands and variety shows'; even after Britain had acquired a substantial domestic black population, for many years the single most regular exposure of 'black' people on the television screen was *The Black and White Minstrel Show*, an enduring monument to the programmers' racial insensitivity.

American television responded slowly to the changing racial climate of the 1960s. In the mid-sixties a token move towards 'integrated' TV began when a few black actors were called upon to play comparatively major roles, as assistants to white detective heroes like 'Ironside'. In 1968–9 the television industry announced that important changes in programming to include black people were to be undertaken. The net result of this was an increase in the incidence of blacks in commercials; in dramas, 37 per cent of the total had at least one black character compared to the previous figure of 32 per cent. As far as the kinds of roles blacks now took, it was found that there was virtually no increase in major roles, a significant increase in minor roles (from 29 per cent to 46 per cent) and a decrease in the use of blacks as background figures[98].

Of course the sheer quantity of exposure is only one consideration; the kind of portrayal is equally important and while this has markedly improved in recent years there remain key areas of characterization which are questionable. This was particularly true of the first attempts to deal with race and race-related issues, in the context of comedy. In Britain, a number of programmes attempted to grasp the nettle by acknowledging white prejudices against blacks through the use of a central character like Alf Garnett in *Till Death Do Us Part* (Archie Bunker in the American cover version, *All in the Family*), a lovable bigot whose outrageous racism could be satirized and defused through simply allowing the character to have his head and say the unspeakable. The notion that prejudices thus aired could be laughed away is an appealing one, though not particularly convincing; there is certainly no evidence that the programmes had this effect, and if anything there was a general increase in racist humour among the population at large and in the repertoires of stand-up comedians. A similar programme, *Love Thy Neighbour*, whose central motif was the relationship between neighbouring black and white couples, derived most of its humour from the frequent exchanges of more or less good-natured racial insults between the menfolk. By voicing these sentiments in a humorous context they were given a kind of acceptability they would never otherwise have enjoyed; another consequence was to give people a whole new vocabulary of racial epithets and many teachers noted the immediate use of these expressions by school children in the playground within days of each episode being screened. Having witnessed this usage in classrooms at the time, let alone in the freer atmosphere of the playground and beyond, one is not inclined to underestimate the influence of such programmes.

Broadly speaking this era has passed to be replaced by some fairly dire attempts at black situation comedy (*The Fosters, Mixed Blessings*) with only *Empire Road* to leaven the diet of cheap stereotypes served up in *It Ain't Half Hot Mum* and *Mind Your Language*. In serious drama there is a distinct trend to represent ordinary black people more realistically and to handle racial issues with greater sensitivity. On both sides of the Atlantic there has been a noticeable increase in minority newscasters and commentators though we are a long way from the stage where their presence is entirely unremarkable.

More worrying is the presentation of black people in 'factual' contexts: in news items, journalistic programmes and documentary features. There is an endemic bias here (which also applies to sound broadcasting, and the Press) which is related to the need to boost or hold audiences, or sell copies. Because these media, first and foremost have an entertainment function, dramatic human-interest items are at a premium and, as every newsperson knows, *bad* news is good copy. Husband[183] describes this:

[It is a] journalistic fact that bad news — e.g. murder, rape, disasters, deviance, etc. — makes 'good' news. Even a superficial perusal of the press, or other news media, will provide ready evidence of the frequency with which negativeness is reflected in news copy. If we look at the possible consequences of negativeness as a news value in relation to race relations we begin to see that it is likely to be harmful. At its simplest it means that stories of racial conflict are likely to predominate over stories of harmonious race relations. Similarly the negative behaviour of minority groups becomes a more frequent item of news content than do their positive achievements. Stories of criminal acts . . . become more accessible than stories of socially meritorious behaviour. . . . The fact that negativeness also applies to reporting of the host population does not detract from the seriousness of this bias. For the generally negative image of the ethnic minorities created by such coverage is likely to be consistent with stereotypes already held about minority groups. Pressures towards selective perception are therefore likely to amplify the negative image presented in the news media.

There have of course been guidelines and journalistic codes of conduct drawn up to try to correct these biases. While they have managed to extirpate some of the more explicit racism from the media, they can have little effect on the overall context within which black people are portrayed, which does not necessarily *appear* to be a racist one. And yet it effectively adds to the negativeness Husband referred to by surrounding black people with the aura of 'a problem'. It began with 'immigration' as a problem (despite the net outflow of population) and has continued through every conceivable social problem of the inner city which pre-dated black immigration (but which, since immigration, can be conveniently laid at their door) to more recent racial disturbances, even where these were provoked by white extremists. Naturally inner city crime, or riots where blacks have been seen to figure prominently, are further grist to this mill. That black people are a problem is even entrenched in the language of the 'balanced' studio discussion of race relations: 'prejudice' is acknowledged as the negative pole of the debate, but the most positive term that can be used to describe the opposite is 'tolerance', which is not even neutral but concedes there is something noxious to be tolerated.

As Troyna[398] writes, based on his survey of press and radio coverage of race in the 1970s:

> . . . the findings showed that different media produce a version of the 'reality' of race relations in Britain which is characterized by an emphasis on negativity. In other words, black people tended to get into the news for negative reasons. In 1976, for example, the headlines were dominated by the inflow of ethnically Asian refugees from Malawi, the accommodation of two of these homeless families in a four star hotel, and the action taken by young Asians in Southall as a reaction to the racial murder of Gurdip Singh Chaggar. In 1977, 'race relations' tended to make the news as part of the saturation coverage of anti-NF demonstrations in Lewisham and Ladywood and because of the racial assaults on young

Bengalis in Southall and Brick Lane, and the following year saw the re-emergence of 'immigration' as a pre-eminent theme in the media — particularly with emphasis on debates about further restrictions on entry into Britain.

During the mid–late 70s the emphasis of the media in the area of 'race relations' changed substantially from an habitual concern in the 1960s with the number of black people entering Britain, to the problems alleged to be associated with their presence in the country. On the other hand, our analysis clearly showed that there has been little *qualitative* difference in this coverage — the 'external threat' has simply been transmuted into 'the outsider within' as the media continue to project a limited and ethnocentric picture of the world. As part of the media's representation of reality, cultural differences are disparaged and the black population seen as a problem to, and essentially different from, the mainstream of the society.

Two recent events suggest that press coverage of race-related themes has not got off to a particularly auspicious start in the 1980s. The Press Council[303] has lately rebuked the *Sun* newspaper for its sensational and inflammatory reportage of a black protest march in London ('Blacks go on rampage . . .'). More notable, perhaps, in the context of the blanket press coverage of the 1981 inner city riots, which were largely identified with blacks, is the case of the 'white riots' in Everton[276], a five-day period of street fighting requiring the attention of scores of riot policemen, which was almost uniformly ignored by the press. Clearly, discrimination and bias can take many subtle forms.

Race, colour and culture

In Chapter 1 an issue was raised that gives some insight into the relationship between culture and prejudice against black people. It was shown that in our culture, and in many others, the colours 'black' and 'white' have traditionally had very strong *evaluative* overtones, and we have just seen that these overtones still persist in contemporary children's literature. In our language, literature and art, white is conventionally used to depict all things good and pure and black to denote badness and evil. It is arguable whether these usages may affect the way we think about objects which bear these colours — and perhaps even 'black' and 'white' people too. However, although we can find any number of illustrations of this 'colour-code' at work in everyday speech (black mail, black mark, black sheep, etc.) in books and in pictures, this is a far cry from explaining people's prejudiced attitudes or behaviour towards racial groups. However, Williams and his associates in the USA believe there may be some kind of link between the two, and this has been the subject of a whole series of studies.

Their first study looked at the different connotations of a series of colour names — black, white, yellow, red, etc. — and particularly at the different *values* associated with each. Using a technique called the 'Semantic Differential' it was possible to discover the *evaluative* connotations of each colour name. Perhaps not surprisingly, white and black differed most in this respect, connoting 'good' and 'bad' respectively[421]. In a later study[425] these American results were replicated in Germany, Denmark, Hong Kong and India, so this is not a phenomenon which is restricted to the white Western World.

The next step was to find out whether people's values about colours, like 'black', spilled over into their feelings about *people* of different colours, like 'black people', and from there into names of racial groups, like 'Negro'. For the white subjects it was found that colour-linked groups of concepts (like 'black, black person, Negro') had greater similarity of connotative meaning (that is, were evaluated in a more similar way) than did groups of concepts which were not colour-linked. So in other words:

> racial concepts have connotative meanings similar to the colour-names with which they are linked by custom.[422]

Of course, to find that they have similar connotations does not prove any cause-effect relationship between them: one could cause the other, or vice versa, or they could both be caused by something else entirely.

The issue is whether *colour* values in any way determine racial values. The experiments described show that the two sets of values are congruent; they point in the same direction, as it were. People who rate the colour black negatively also rate the concepts 'black person' and 'Negro' negatively; but that does not prove that they do so *because* they rate black negatively. That would imply that colour values came first and values about black people came later by association. Indeed, another of Williams' studies[158] showed how this process might work. It was shown that the connotative meanings of colour names can be *conditioned* to terms with which they are associated. When subjects learned to associate certain stimuli with particular colours, they later rated those stimuli in the same way as they rated the corresponding colours. In other words, the stimuli they had been made to associate with the colour black was rated negatively even though at face value it had nothing to do with blackness. Is it not possible then, Williams asks, that having learned the values our culture attaches to the colours black and white, we then learn to associate the same values with black and white people, giving us negative and positive evaluations of them? The argument is the more plausible for the demonstration that these values can so easily be conditioned to irrelevant concepts, let alone concepts which even have words in common (e.g. black, black people).

Clearly the issue of what gives rise to what can only be settled if we trace these processes as far back as possible until we find how, and in what order, these values originally develop in individuals. This entails studying children at the age when they are beginning to use language and to learn the conventional meanings of words like black and white. Renninger and Williams[312] conducted a study of pre-school children in which they tried to find a direct answer to this chicken-and-egg problem. In the words of the authors:

> The principal purpose of this investigation was to study the degree of awareness of the connotative meaning of white as good and black as bad among Caucasian pre-school children. A secondary purpose . . . was to attempt to determine whether awareness of colour connotations develops prior to, concurrent with or subsequent to the children's awareness of racial differences between Caucasian and Negro persons.

Two sets of materials were used with the children, one to assess their colour awareness and one to determine their racial awareness. In the former the children were required to finish off stories that the experimenter began for them using cards with black and white figure drawings. Their score was the number of times (out of eight opportunities) that they completed the stories by using black to indicate a negative evaluation and white a positive one. Six, seven or eight answers of this kind were respectively labelled 'low', 'medium' and 'high' awareness. This seems rather a strict criterion, but even so, 7 per cent of the three-year-olds, 20 per cent of the four-year-olds and 43 per cent of the five-year-olds fell in the high awareness category. Perhaps a more meaningful picture is given by combining these categories, in contrast to those children who made five or fewer responses of the prescribed type, thus showing little awareness.

Then, 29 per cent of the three-year-olds, 73 per cent of the four-year-olds and 81 per cent of the five-year-olds showed a considerable degree of awareness.

The second test involved a kind of jigsaw puzzle with black and white figures that the child fitted together; the interviewer asked a number of questions about them, exploring (i) whether the child preferred the dark-skinned child or the light-skinned child as a playmate, (ii) whether he/she could apply a racial name to the dark-skinned child, (iii) whether he/she could connect the labels 'negro', 'coloured' and 'white' with the appropriate figures when the labels were supplied by the interviewer, and (iv) whether the child segregated the families in the puzzle arrangement. On (ii), (iii) and (iv) there was a clear tendency for racial awareness to increase significantly with age between three and five years. More surprising were the answers to section (i): over 80 per cent of *all* age-groups preferred to play with the light-skinned child depicted in the puzzle. So there is evidence of both racial awareness and, significantly, racial *preference* from three years old onwards.

This study does not give us conclusive evidence as to which develops first: colour values or racial values. Both are present to some extent even in the youngest children. The authors simply conclude:

> The results of this study indicated that Caucasian children are learning the evaluative meanings of black as bad, and white as good, during their pre-school years, the period in which awareness of race is also developing.

This suggests a concurrent development of colour and racial values, and it is certainly true that the data do not support the idea of colour values *preceding* racial values. But we should consider an alternative interpretation for, if anything, the indications from these data are that the process operates the other way around. Recall that while 29 per cent of the three-year-olds showed an awareness of colour connotations, over 80 per cent of them were aware of racial differences and based their playmate preferences upon them. In other words, racial values seem to be already quite strongly established in three-year-olds while pure colour values are only slowly being learned. So we have to allow the possibility that adult racial norms and values instil into the child a very early awareness of racial differences and values, *before* colour values, and that logically the former may influence the latter rather than the other way around.

However this is pure speculation and we can offer no further evidence on the matter.

Despite this evidence, Williams and Morland[122] have put forward a theory of racial attitude development which gives a more crucial role to the influence of colour values than other writers have acknowledged. And they suggest these values have an earlier origin than we have so far considered. Race bias, they say, develops as a result of three separate but mutually-reinforcing influences:

1 Experiences in infancy common to all members of the species, which interact with certain biological dispositions to produce a fundamental white-positive, black-negative association.
2 Subsequent exposure to 'the cultural practice of employing the colour white (or light) and the colour black (or darkness) to symbolize badness. Such symbolism abounds in the mass media, in children's literature, in Judeo-Christian religion and, through idiomatic speech, in the very fabric of human communication.'
3 The interaction of these factors with specific cultural teachings about race *per se*.

The second and third influences are already familiar to us. It is the first factor which is both novel and controversial. Williams and Morland say:

that virtually every child has experiences early in life which lead to development of a preference for light over darkness. This is based primarily on the child's visual orientation to his environment and the disorientation he experiences in the dark, and may be further strengthened by the fact that his major need-satisfactions occur during the daylight hours. *In addition to a learned preference, one may speculate that the young human may have an innate aversion to darkness, perhaps based on an evolutionary history in which avoidance of the dark was an adaptive characteristic.* [italics added]

Not only could this be the basis of the individual child's orientation, it would also explain the wider phenomenon of cultural colour meanings:

Colour symbols are not seen as arbitrary conventions but as cultural elaborations of shared human feelings. Further there is little danger of the symbols losing their meanings because . . .

103

[they] . . . are continually being re-established in successive generations of young children. . . . We believe that the main impact of cultural symbolism is to confirm the child's own feelings concerning light and darkness and to consolidate this learning in conceptual form. Prior to the cultural messages the child *feels* that white is good; following the cultural messages, the child *knows* that white is good.

On to this evaluative foundation is built a superstructure of information and attitudes which is specifically *racial*; but within this racial learning Williams and Morland continue to stress the importance of *colour* and explicitly counsel against the use of colour names to distinguish between racial groups precisely because of the association with this evaluative system.

The authors concede that their ideas about innate biological dispositions and pan-cultural experiences are speculative, and they wish to avoid the implication that: 'The light-dark preference of the young child is the sole — or even the principal — determinant of his race and colour biases.' Inevitably, though, the novelty of these suggestions and the need to argue the case for their acceptance assures them a central role in their theory. The ideas present many difficulties, and to some extent these are acknowledged by the authors. As regards the 'biologically-based' component of the child's aversion to darkness, they concede that: 'Although the demonstration of other innate fears in children . . . makes such speculation plausible, we know of no empirical findings which require such a theory.' Their suggestion that the dark comes to be associated with fear and disorientation and the day with better visual orientation and need-satisfaction is more persuasive; these are indeed universal cultural experiences, and the learning process involved may account for why children do not show fear of the dark from birth — a fact which detracts a great deal from the 'innate' part of their theory.

However, it is important to realize that equally plausible speculations can be made concerning this nearly impenetrable realm of early experience. Perhaps the most compelling of these would be that the child's earliest experiences take place in the total *darkness* of the womb, in perhaps the most favourable environment for warmth, security and immediate need-satisfaction that the individual will ever enjoy; later thrust into the 'booming, buzzing confusion' of the outside world, the infant only ever approaches this previous state when tucked up, warm relaxed and sleeping in the darkness of the bedroom. This alternative and credible account of pre-natal and infant experience would suggest the opposite to Williams and Morland's theory: that *these* cultural universal experiences will lead to children developing a *positive* association with darkness not a negative one. It would then remain to account for later developments like fear of the dark in terms of learning from parents, from simple stories and fairy-tales; and for the development of colour and race values as a result of specific cultural messages about colour and race, not early experiences.

The point of this is not to supplant Williams' and Morland's theory, but to demonstrate how this kind of speculative 'biologism' can be adduced in support of diametrically-opposed arguments. Neither can be proven by methods presently available to us; in fact the elusiveness of any 'proof' is precisely what allows us the latitude to speculate. But harmless as this may seem, there is also something in the very nature of untestable biologism which counsels caution, particularly in this controversial area. 'Innate biological dispositions' as explanations of human behaviour, like 'instincts', tend to prevail over other kinds of explanations, as we argued at the beginning of Chapter 3. They carry the connotations of 'basic', 'root' causes and so appear to be the most fundamental, the *real* explanation. This elevates their importance over other factors (like subsequent *learning* experiences, which may in reality be far more important) and their biological basis makes their influence appear to be both inevitable and intractable. Having witnessed the socio-political repercussions of Jensen's theories concerning race, heredity and IQ (see Chapter 7), it seems unwise to argue for *any* 'innate' component to racism without compelling proof. However such a theory is hedged with reservations and qualifications in a scientific context, its simplification and translation into a public arena carry the danger that it may be interpreted as a buttress and justification for racism, which is certainly not the authors' intention.

We should regard this area of theory and research concerning colour values *not* as a viable alternative account of the genesis of prejudice, but rather as describing some contributory factors: colour values provide an evaluative framework, chiefly operating through language and pictorial imagery, which reinforces race prejudice and gives it greater credence. In addition it assists the learning of *race* prejudice, to which we turn in Chapter 5, by simplifying for young children the division of the world into categories of opposites, whether they be colours or evaluations.

5
Children's racial attitudes

Until now we have simply referred to 'the course of children's racial attitude development' in a general way; we now need to specify and differentiate that process more closely. Mary Ellen Goodman,[146] one of the first American workers in this field, proposed a simple three-stage schema to describe the process: *racial awareness, racial orientation* or 'incipient attitude, and true *racial attitudes*. They are not discrete phases and they overlap to some extent, but they always occur in the same order: each is necessary for the next to appear. The first phase is the simple awareness of racial differences, the ability to discriminate persons of one racial group from another; the second is the emergence of rudimentary feelings about different racial groups, and the final stage is reached when these have been elaborated with more complex information and stereotyped notions into fully-fledged attitudes. While this describes the broad outline of the process it lacks detail. More recently Katz[212] has adopted a more cognitive approach and suggests a series of eight overlapping but separable stages by which the child comes to construct a version of the social world which is coloured by racial attitudes, as follows:

1 early observation of racial cues (skin colour, hair, facial features, etc.) starting well before the age of three, leading to:
2 formation of rudimentary concepts about black people, labels for which may be provided by adults, and often accompanied by some evaluative information;
3 conceptual differentiation: the stage in which the learning of the racial concepts is reinforced, through encountering positive and negative instances of the concept, the child testing his/her grasp of the defining characteristics of the concept against adult feedback. For example, the child will learn that skin colour is not the only determinant of 'race' because this person is called 'black' as a result of her hair type and facial features, even though her skin is light-coloured;
4 recognition of the irrevocability of cues: the child's mastery of

the notion that certain person-cues, like size and age, are subject to change, while others like sex and race are immutable;

5 consolidation of group concepts: by this stage the child can identify and label positive and negative instances and understand the permanence of group membership; consolidation, then, is the further development of stages three and four and completes the functional inter-relationship of the perceptual and cognitive aspects together with the evaluative content; this process typically begins somewhat before five years of age and continues for some time;

6 perceptual elaboration then takes place, proceeding from 'us' and 'them' categorizations of groups, and involving greater differentiation between groups, while intra-group differentiation is less pronounced, particularly in the case of the out-group;

7 cognitive elaboration: 'the process by which concept attitudes become racial attitudes':[212] this simply refers to the elaboration of 'incipient' attitudes into 'true' attitudes through school experiences, contact with children of other races, and contact with the attitudes of teachers and peers;

8 attitude crystallization, in which the child's attitudes fall increasingly into line with those in the immediate environment, thus becoming supported, stable and rather resistant to change.

To an extent, Katz's schema is hypothetical in the sense that it is not yet supported in every detail by empirical evidence (however, see, for example Katz[210,211,213,214]). Just as Goodman's schema is short on cognitive detail, Katz's system rather underplays the affective aspects; we would do well to bear both in mind when considering the mainstream of research findings in this area.

The methods used in this kind of research are mostly variants of the same basic technique. Because it is impossible to use verbally sophisticated measures with young children, the questionnaires and attitude scales that are used for studies of adult attitudes are obviously impractical. Instead, an interview is conducted with the child in which the researcher presents a variety of dolls and/or pictures representing the various racial groups in the child's environment. These are made the basis of a series of questions that are put to the child, the idea being that the children react to these figures as if they were real people and in this way demonstrate their feelings towards the groups that the figures represent. This methodology has been employed in some forty years research work in the USA and although it has become more refined in recent years, it has not escaped criticism, as we shall see later.

One of the most remarkable discoveries in this area is just how early in a child's life he or she begins to develop racial awareness. The ability to recognize and label racial differences and also to identify oneself in racial terms seems to be established between three and five years old, according to a number of studies.[178,308,359] The lower limit of this phase may be very early indeed for some children; Ammons[8], for example, found that 20 per cent of his *two*-year-old subjects and 50 per cent of the *three*-year-olds were able to discriminate skin colour and facial differences between black and white dolls. Kenneth Morland, a distinguished researcher in this field, has conducted a number of studies with children of this age range. In an early study[271], he found that this ability to recognize racial differences improved rapidly over the period from three to six years, the improvement being most marked in the fourth year. And in a later study[273], he found patterns of self-identification in three-year-old children which did not differ significantly from those of older children, suggesting that they were already well-established at this age.

Morland's method of testing for racial-recognition ability was typical of many in this area. He simply showed a series of multi-racial pictures to the children, and asked 'Do you see a white person in this picture?' and 'Do you see a coloured person in this picture?' If the child answered either in the affirmative, he/she was asked to point to the figure concerned. The terms 'white' and 'coloured' were agreed to be the most common racial designations in the area where the study was run. So this racial awareness not only involves the ability to distinguish between different skin colours, etc. but also to recognize and use the labels which are applied to each racial group.

The measure of *self*-identification in racial terms involved showing children pictures of white and black children of their own age and sex, pointing to each in turn and asking 'Do you look like this child?', 'Do you look like *this* child?', 'Which child do you look more like?'. Not surprisingly, as white children's racial awareness increased, so did the ability to identify themselves correctly: 71 per cent of three- to six-year-olds chose the correct figure, a picture which remained static over the age range.

The first positive and negative feelings about racial groups — Goodman's racial orientation stage — can also appear as early as three, though it is more usual at four to five years. Many studies[307] [359,404,405] have shown these first evaluative dispositions in the three to six years age group. Ammons[8] found that these rudimentary attitudes became more widespread with age; while only 10 per cent of three-year-old children showed negative feelings towards black figures, by the age of four this had grown to 40 per cent. In testing racial orientation the child might be presented with a series of pictures of black and white children, and simply asked which he or she would prefer as a friend, playmate, and so on. When Morland[275] put questions of this type to young white American children, he found that some 82 per cent of them showed a clear preference for their own race over the black figures.

Of course, preference for one's own race over another does not automatically imply rejection and hostility towards the other group, simply a greater favourability towards one's own group. Morland[272] conducted some tests to see whether black children would be accepted in a situation where there was not an either/or choice to be made between black and white figures. He found that relatively few of the children made an outright rejection of black figures, citing their race as the reason. A larger proportion were not prepared to accept black playmates 'for other reasons', some of which may have been excuses; and 20 per cent would not accept black playmates at all, indicating a far greater degree of hostility. It should be stressed that these kinds of findings have been replicated in any number of other studies.

The phases of racial awareness and racial orientation, then, are the foundations of racial attitude development. If there is a quarrel with the Goodman schema it is that it tends to separate these phases, when the evidence we have considered suggests a simultaneous learning of 'facts' and 'feelings' about groups. It is difficult to imagine that parents, black or white, in multiracial areas like Handsworth of Toxteth for example, could say anything at all of a factual nature about race to their children without also communicating something of their attitudes, so it is far more likely that the cognitive and affective aspects are absorbed together. As Kenneth Clark[69] has written:

> The child's first awareness of racial differences is . . . associated with some rudimentary evaluation of these differences . . . the child cannot learn what racial group he belongs to without being involved in a larger pattern of emotions, conflicts and desires which are part of his growing knowledge of what society thinks about his race.

Therefore although we find empirically that racial orientation is evident somewhat later than racial awareness, there is evidently a good deal of overlap between the two, and it may simply be that it takes longer for racial orientation to be overtly expressed.

The essential significance of this period has been well expressed by Harding *et al.* as follows:

> In what sense, then, can we speak of an ethnic attitude, inchoate or otherwise in the very young child? The fact is that his ethnic awareness is by no means affectively neutral. He reveals clear preferences for some groups while others are rejected. Thus a fundamental ingredient of an inter-group attitude is present: an evaluative orientation that is expressed in in-group versus out-group terms.[159]

This 'attitude' is expressed very simply: in preference for one's own group and strong identification with it, and in rejecting or hostile feelings towards the out-group. The sentiments the child will utter are equally simple; for example, children's spontaneous remarks about black figures during tests of racial orientation are often of the following kind: 'He's a stinky little boy, take him away!', 'I don't like him, he's a blackie!', 'He's no good.' 'He kills people.' Or, as described in Chapter 3, the child may 'model' sophisticated adult attitudes and retail them without fully understanding the concepts involved, but with the feeling behind them faithfully reproduced. The complexity of these utterances is not important. What is crucial is that the child has absorbed a simple polarized evaluation of the groups involved, so that one is positive, good and liked, the other negative, bad and disliked. Into this evaluative frame of reference can be fitted all the more complex information the child will subsequently encounter. But selective processes may operate to absorb only information that is congruent, so that the establishment of this first, basic evaluative foundation is extremely influential in determining the course of later attitude development.

It is precisely when this process starts to happen, that is, the absorption of more complex information about racial groups, stereotypes about their characteristics, and notions of social status, that we say the child is entering Goodman's third phase, of true racial attitudes. This generally begins between seven and nine years. In Trager and Yarrow's[395] research with children of this age they found that:

> concepts and feelings about race frequently include adult dis-

tinctions of status, ability, character, occupations, and economic circumstances. . . . Among the older children stereotyping and expressions of hostility are more frequent and attitudes more crystallized than among the young children.

An indication of this was the children's allocation of poor housing and menial employment to black people (and superior environments to whites) in doll and picture tests. Once again, this could be simply a recognition of real life status differences between the groups rather than prejudice. But it has been shown that:

> There is a tendency for hostile feelings towards Negroes and a perception of Negroes in inferior roles to appear together; however, many children who show a dislike for Negroes show no awareness of the status factors studied.[307]

Among the reactions to the black dolls in this study were the following: 'He is coming out of jail.', 'They are gangsters.', 'He would be digging dirt.', 'He doesn't have no work.', 'All ladies who are coloured are maids.', 'He's a coloured and he carries knives.' — clearly an intricate mixture of social status references and outright hostile feelings.

As we have seen it is not difficult to identify the sources of information which provide the child with the raw material of stereotypes. What is less easy to tease out is the origin of hostile *feelings*, the actual emotional, evaluative thrust behind rejecting attitudes. To say that they are modelled from the parents is not quite adequate; it implies a passive process, which can explain how children learn what they should feel about things, but not how they actually come to feel them themselves. At one level, the learning process is a simple marriage of two pairs of concepts: good-bad, and black-white (as applied to people). The very simplicity of this scheme of things cuts directly through all the conventional objections to the idea that children can have racial attitudes (on the grounds that the issues are too complex for them to handle.) The good-bad concept is one of the simplest (and one of the first) pairs of polar opposites that the child meets. Yes-no, positive-negative, smiling-frowning are all expressions of the same contrasting evaluations and are present in parent-communication — in both directions — from the very beginning. One of the first things which parents try to teach their children is the concept of '*no*', in relation to fires, cookers, stairs, electric plugs or valued objects of their own. Even earlier they may show disapproval of something the child does. All of this is a long time before the child has produced any speech so it is done at an almost non-verbal level through facial expression and tone of voice. Thus children become very discriminatory concerning their parents' affective tone and from early on they can discern from these things alone what is approved of and what evokes disfavour. It is with this well-developed ability to grasp what is positive and negative, what is liked and disliked, just from subtle nuances of parental tone and gesture that the child attends to parents' and others' information and comments about black people and white people. And we have seen that some awareness of racial differences (which provides the other concept pair — black people/white people) can be attained as early as three-years-old, so that the marriage of concepts can be achieved at this time. From then on, everything that follows will tend to reinforce this disposition. Greater exposure to black-white imagery in language and literature will help to cement the evaluative connotations of the colours, and exposure to specifically racial information will elaborate and strengthen the orientation towards black people. It is impossible to precisely identify the stage in which the child will introject 'adult' attitudes to the extent that they will be felt as the child's own. It is probably not any one point, but a cumulative process which may be to do with the opportunity to voice these sentiments in social situations. In other words, the more the child is called upon to declare his/her beliefs in public or feels impelled to do so, the more he or she is identified with them and feels them to be his/her own. What may begin as simply mouthing beliefs that have been gathered at the breakfast table, may end as one's own attitudes, particularly if the emotions are engaged by being called upon to defend this view or if one's social acceptance is contingent upon them. Peer groups frequently provide the arena for this kind of display of family-views and loyalties, and insofar as racial views figure there they are likely to be deemed important.

Of course, not all the elaboration of attitudes and reinforcement that we have described is straightforward, for not all of the information and experience the child encounters will be congruent with these rudimentary attitudes, or could be made so. As the complexity of the child's world grows, so do the problems in maintaining a simple view of things.

Older children
Beyond the age of seven or eight years there is a continuation of the trends we have described, that is, a gradual intensification of preju-

dice[267] [279]. However, there is a less marked increase than in the preceding years, and in some respects it levels off in early adolescence. During this time, too, the organization of the child's attitudes undergoes some change, in the direction of greater *differentiation, integration* and *consistency*. As outlined in Chapter 2, we may conceive of attitudes as having three components: the affective or emotional component, the cognitive or 'intellectual' component, and the behavioural or action tendency component; our feelings, beliefs and behavioural dispositions, in this case towards other racial groups. The process of differentiation may occur within each of these components. For example, the affective component may become differentiated to allow that a child likes one particular black child, while disliking black people as a group. Or the cognitive component might become differentiated to admit both the good and the bad attributes of the group or individual. Blake and Dennis[35] found just this process operating in their adolescent subjects. Or the behavioural component may be differentiated as children comply with the demands of the integrated classroom while effectively segregating themselves in the playground.

In other words, the components become less 'global' and more fitted for rationally handling the more complex information about groups that the child is now encountering. While the admission of discrepant 'positive' information may 'tow' a negative attitude in a more positive direction, this does not automatically happen as the item can be perceived as exceptional, atypical of the group and its stereotype. As we have seen, this creation of an 'exceptional' subcategory may appear to be more rational than a blanket stereotype, but it has the effect of innoculating the stereotype against contrary information. It must be recorded that only a few studies have given concrete evidence of this differentiation, but most writers have assumed the process to be at work in the transition from simple 'childish' to adult attitudes.

At the same time, the three components undergo integration, so that there is greater consistency between them. Thus the child who has always disliked black children as a group but has previously accepted them as playmates may begin to alter this. The behavioural component may fall into line with the affective component as he or she withdraws from inter-racial contacts and spends more time with his/her own racial group. Horowitz[178] found increasing correlations between the three components of attitudes, with age, in his five to fourteen-year-old white subjects.

Radke, Sutherland and Rosenberg's[306] study of seven- to

thirteen-year-old children well illustrates the form that racial attitudes take during this period. When confronted with pictures of black and white children and asked to assign a variety of favourable and unfavourable dispositions to them, the white children 'show clearly their acceptance of the attitudes of their culture toward the Negro . . . in each grade (i.e. at each age level) the white children assign many more undesirable than desirable characteristics to Negro photographs.' However, among older children there was a greater tendency to attribute a few good characteristics to the black figures. Overall though, there was not a single case in which a good characteristic was more frequently attributed to a Negro figure than to a white one, and the proportion of children making pro-white, anti-Negro assignments averaged across all the picture presentations was 80 per cent.

The investigators also measured the children's preferred choice of 'friends' from the same photographs. Around 90 per cent of the white children chose friends from within their own racial group. However, from measures of the children's real-life friendship choices inside the class, within the school, and from the community at large, an interesting picture emerges. A majority (76 per cent) of the younger white children chose black friends from within their class; this declined sharply among the older children to 53 per cent. It should be stressed that the school concerned had a white population of only 15 per cent; therefore the choice of white friends in any one class is severely limited. When this constraint was removed and the children were free to choose friends from other classes within the school, the proportion of younger children choosing exclusively white friends jumped to 92 per cent and to 100 per cent for the older ones. And 100 per cent of both age groups chose white friends when they were allowed to choose from the wider community. In other words there is consistency between rejection of black figures in the picture tests and the children's real-life friendship choices, which increases with age.

Of course, a better indication of the actual course of racial attitude development across the adolescent years would be obtained if we could observe the process in the same children, rather than compare different children, at different age-levels. One of the very earliest studies, by Zeligs[429], adopted this kind of longitudinal approach with children who were twelve years old at the beginning of her study, and who she re-interviewed at ages fifteen and eighteen. Over this six year period she noticed relatively little change in the children's attitudes towards various ethnic and national groups: most of the races towards which favourable and unfavourable attitudes were expressed on the first occasion were again mentioned in the same way six years later, as were the reasons children gave to explain their attitudes. Changes towards certain races made the attitudes of older children more like those of the adults whose attitudes were tested in contemporary studies at the time. A later study by Wilson[427] also confirmed an increasing stability and consistency (and decreasing variance) in racial attitudes over the thirteen to eighteen age range.

Of course not all children will follow this 'typical' pattern of racial attitude development. Other factors will intervene to modify the learning process, sometimes amplifying the cultural messages about race and accelerating the process, sometimes insulating the child from this learning, delaying and diverting it. Naturally individual children, too, will differ enormously in their personality and experience, and therefore differ in their receptivity to such messages. We refer here to the 'social structural' and 'individual' determinants of childhood 'prejudice'.

Social structural factors in children's racial attitudes

Very few studies have successfully isolated social structural factors in a controlled way. More often, comparisons have been made between different geographical and social areas, on the assumption that they differ with respect to the variable in which the researchers are interested, say, 'socio-economic status' or 'interracial contact'. As a result, few clear-cut findings emerge, usually because of the influence of other factors which have not been controlled for, and which may interact with the variable in question. Take the case of 'socio-economic status' as an influence on children's racial attitudes. Despite the rather consistent findings in studies of *adults* (e.g. Lipset[242]) that there is a correlation between higher socio-economic status and less prejudice towards blacks, it is only just possible to discern this relationship from equivalent studies of children. Some studies have found *no* differences in attitudes between different status groups[34], and Morland's studies[272, 274] showed both that low-status whites were more prepared to *accept* black children (chosen from pictures — 'Will you play with this child?') than higher-status whites, but that on preference measures, where the child had to choose between the races, more of the lower than the upper status group preferred the whites and rejected the blacks. The latter finding was confirmed in a different context by Landreth and Johnson[234]; and Chein and Hurwitz[64] identified more positive out-

115

group attitudes among their higher status Jewish subjects. Another confirmatory study illustrates the difficulties in interpreting these studies. Chyatte, Schaefer and Spiaggia[68] found that children of professional fathers (*sic*) showed significantly less 'prejudice verbalization' than did children of non-professional fathers. This points to the whole complex of differences which go hand-in-hand with socio-economic status differences, in this case 'education'. This factor alone could account for all the differences so far described which have been attributed to status differences. 'Intelligence' is a related factor which may have contributed to these results; for Singer[353] found higher intelligence to correlate with decreased prejudice.

When we consider the extent of *de facto* residential segregation in America, or in Britain for that matter, it is clear that differences in status among whites also ensure differences in the amount of contact with blacks. 'Inter-racial contact', then, is another accompanying factor which could account for the findings described above. Studies of contact are reviewed by Amir[7]; while they demonstrate that it is not so much the quantity as the quality of contact that is important, we should briefly note an early study by Horowitz[178] which produced some unexpected findings. He compared the racial attitudes of schoolchildren in New York, Georgia and Tennessee in both segregated and mixed schools. The children in New York from an all-white school showed neither more nor less prejudice than those from a mixed school, who would have more contact with black children. More surprisingly, 'the Southern groups tested showed no more prejudice than that shown by the children in New York City'. Further, 'comparison of the Southern samples showed no difference among them in spite of differences in mode of living represented by sampling urban and rural living'. Clearly, this is a case where many more factors are being varied in the course of the comparison between different areas than simply contact alone. Nevertheless, it is surprising that in spite of the variation of a number of factors between each situation, this uniform picture of hostile attitudes persists. Horowitz's conclusion reinforces the argument that it is the qualitative aspects of inter-racial situations that are important: 'Attitudes towards Negroes are now determined not by contact with Negroes, but by contact with the prevalent attitude towards Negroes.' The implication, of course, is that an overall climate of hostility exists towards black people, across the length and breadth of the United States, and it is absorbed by children uniformly, that is, irrespective of their direct experience of black people, and of the institutionalization of racism through segregation in particular areas.

Individual factors in children's racial attitudes

Of the individual differences that might be expected to affect attitudes, the sex of the child is potentially one of the most important. However, while the vast majority of studies have involved subjects of both sexes, very few have published any data on sex differences. The reason for this may be less neglect than a reflection of the same situation described in those studies which have reported data — very few consistent differences by sex in children's racial attitudes. While Koch[225] describes a slight trend for her white female subjects to choose own-race figures as friends more frequently than do white boys, and Goodman[146] refers to sex differences in racial awareness, Springer[356], Morland[271], and Chyatte *et al.*[68], found no such differences, and the latter are more common findings. As Vaughan[405] concludes, 'Significant attitudinal differences by sex, then, are yet to be demonstrated.'

The earlier emphasis on the role of parents in forming the child's attitudes directs us to the most obvious source of individual differences: the kind of parents the child has inherited. We know that children's racial attitudes[6, 148, 149, 179, 277, 309] and behaviour[254] often show close similarity to those of their parents. What is at issue here is whether there are other reasons, over and above the existence of prejudice or positive attitudes in the parents which help to determine the attitudes of their children. Are there other factors, like more general social attitudes and values, child-rearing beliefs and practices and so on, which affect the process?

The major research initiative in this area remains the classic Authoritarian Personality Study[3], reviewed in Chapter 2. Recall that the researchers tried to identify the kinds of family styles child rearing practices and parental beliefs in the backgrounds of those subjects who were highly prejudiced — on the assumption that it was this complex of experiences which had shaped their personalities in such a way as to make them more receptive than most to racial prejudice. Harding *et al.*[159] have described the findings this way:

> . . . highly prejudiced subjects, in contrast to those who were tolerant, showed a more rigid personality organization, greater conventionality in their values, more difficulty in accepting socially deviant impulses as part of the self (for example, fear weakness, aggression, and sex) a greater tendency to externalize these impulses by means of projection and more inclination to be status- and power-oriented in their personal relationships.

These personality attributes as well as others (for example idolizing one's parents, impersonal and punitive aggression, dichotomous thinking) represented the defining features of the authoritarian personality. These attributes in turn were found to be related to early childhood experiences in a family setting characterized by harsh and threatening parental discipline, conditional parental love, a hierarchichal family structure, and a concern for family status. The unconscious conflict involving fear of and dependency on parents, on one hand, and strong hatred and suspicion of them on the other, seemed to be contained by an authoritarian personality structure tuned to expressing this repressed hostility towards members of socially-sanctioned out-groups.

Of course, this does not resolve the issue of how far children's prejudices reflect the creation of this personality structure within them, and everything which flows from it, or how far they simply represent the direct transmission of attitudes in the socialization process, from prejudiced parents who *also* subscribe to these kinds of beliefs about child-rearing. The truth of the matter may well be a mutually-reinforcing combination of the two: parents who are *themselves* authoritarian (and therefore more likely to be racially prejudiced) tend to create prejudiced children, by both direct and indirect tuition concerning race, and by their child-rearing beliefs and practices — which create authoritarian structures in their children, which in turn make them more receptive to learning their parents' and other people's prejudices. While that cycle is hypothetical, the simple fact that home backgrounds of an 'authoritarian' type do tend to produce children who are disposed towards prejudice is reasonably well established[6,148,149].

★

Cross-cultural comparisons: New Zealand, South Africa, Britain
All the studies described so far have come from the US, but this pattern of racial attitude development is by no means an exclusively American phenomenon. We find that very similar patterns have emerged from studies of other settings where there are substantial non-white populations who are the subject of prejudice and discrimination.

Although the New Zealand racial situation is not as severe as in America, Ritchie[317] has shown how very derogatory stereotypes about Maoris have had a wide currency among the white population. The 'good' stereotypes have been based on the 'noble savage' concept, while the bad ones depict the Maori as 'wilfully poor . . . breeds irresponsibly, dirty . . . children moronic and undisciplined . . . virtually unemployable and grossly irresponsible if not plainly criminal'. Thompson's analyses of newspaper items[385] suggest a wide circulation of bad stereotypes, a high percentage of the themes implying unfavourable attributes such as 'lazy', irresponsible', 'ignorant' and 'superstitious'.

It is perhaps not surprising then that Graham Vaughan's[403,405,406,407] studies of white ('Pakeha') children's awareness of race differences and attitudes towards the Maori minority show an essentially similar picture to the American studies: awareness begins in early childhood and increases through the middle childhood years, and there is evidence of strong own-race preference and other-race rejection from as early as four years old, which peaks between six and eight, and tapers off somewhat towards adolescence. The attribution of unfavourable stereotypes to Maori figures follows a similar course, though with somewhat greater differentiation of stereotypes among the older children.

Of course it is very difficult to make cross-cultural comparisons because of the differences in the methods different investigators have used, differences in the samples of subjects tested, and variations in the cultural contexts. However, if we tried to predict a cultural milieu which embodied all the necessary conditions for the 'familiar' pattern of majority-minority attitudes to emerge, South Africa would very quickly spring to mind as an obvious candidate. Gregor and McPherson[153] circumvented some of the methodological problems involved by using an identical method to one of the best known American studies, by Clark and Clark[71], in their study of white and African children. Not surprisingly, the African children tested showed an unequivocal orientation towards the in-group and rejection of the out-group, 83 per cent liked the white doll best, 90 per cent said that it had a nicer colour, 93 per cent thought the brown doll was the bad one and 100 per cent correctly identified themselves with the white doll. These are even higher percentages than in the equivalent American studies. (The responses of the black children to these tests in both New Zealand and South Africa will be discussed in the next chapter.)

The race relations situation in Britain differs from those already discussed in the sense that it is a 'newly' multiracial society. Nevertheless, the history of British attitudes towards 'black' nations dating from the days of slavery, imperialism and colonialism, taken together with intense and pervasive prejudice and discrimination against recent black immigrants, suggests that a comparable race relations climate exists. Pushkin's[304] study of children in three London boroughs was the first to deal directly with British children's racial attitudes. He conducted his study in one area in which few immigrants lived, and two areas with a high immigrant population, one of which had been the scene of some racial incidents. His subjects were mostly white children between the ages of three and seven years, to whom he administered a number of doll and picture tests. Another dimension was added by his structured interviews with the children's mothers, which produced information about their ethnic attitudes, their child-rearing practices and those of their parents, and their social mobility aspirations. He found that the white children's preferences for their own group were present in the nursery-school age range, increased with age, and frequently increased in hostility to a noticeable extent in the sixth year. He found no relation between the children's attitudes and the child-rearing practices of their mothers. But a substantial proportion of the racially 'hostile' children had mothers who were also rated as very hostile. So the central role of parental influence was demonstrated here: so too was the role of wider social pressures, as the greatest hostility amongst both children and mothers was found in the area where there had been marked racial tension. As Pushkin concluded, his results point to:

(1) the reflection of strong ethnic attitudes of mothers in their young children, and (2) the importance of the kind of contact (between races), through attitudes prevalent in the area, in the formation of young children's attitudes to the ethnic outgroup.

In Laishley's[232] study of nursery school children in areas which were not racially tense, it appeared that the children had not yet internalized any negative evaluation of black people and were relatively unaware of skin colour differences. Laishley stresses the low age range involved in the study and suggests that children only a little older than these may well show different reactions. That this is sometimes the case is shown by Brown and Johnson's[48] study of three- to eleven-year-old white children. While their youngest children did not show consistent preferences for one racial group over another: 'Children between the ages of five and eight years show a marked increase in the attribution of negative statements to shaded figures and positive statements to white figures.' These findings were largely confirmed in Richardson and Green's[314] contemporaneous study where a majority of English children preferred white skin colour to dark in the pictures they were shown. The researchers added an original, if somewhat macabre, dimension to this kind of work by assessing whether this preference was still upheld when the white figure involved was visibly physically handicapped. Only the white boys in the study showed a significantly greater preference for the white handicapped figure over the dark figure; however, 'on average, boys and girls, coloured and white, preferred light to dark skin colour' when neither of the figures was handicapped.

Jahoda, Thomson and Bhatt's[188] study of Scottish school children employed a somewhat different methodology from other studies (requiring the child to construct preferred facial features by super-imposing a number of celluloid sheets upon one another, each of which contained one facial feature — nose, eyes, hair, skin colour, etc. — chosen from a range of different racial types in each case. Despite the difference in the task, they nevertheless found an essentially similar pattern of preferences as in other studies, in that their six-year-old subjects showed a balance of preferences towards their own group's facial features, a tendency which increased sharply and significantly by age ten. However, the substitution of an Indian experimenter changed the direction of these preferences, an issue we will return to in due course.

Milner's[262, 263, 264] studies were principally concerned with West Indian and Asian children's attitudes and identity, and these findings are reported in the following chapter; however, each study also involved a large number of native English children whose responses are relevant here. The studies were conducted with five- to eight-year-old children in two large English cities with substantial black populations. While the conventional doll and picture tests were employed, the materials used embodied some refinements over previous studies. In many cases the dolls used have been simple peg-like figures, or at the other extreme, the over-glamourized, commercially-produced toys which have been equally unrealistic. In this study the basic figures used were realistically proportioned scale models, with skin colour, eye colour, hair colour and type, and facial features appropriate to each of the groups they represented. The children were required to choose between an English doll and a West Indian or Asian doll (depending on which group predominated in the locality) in response to questions put by the interviewer, and a different pair of figures was presented for every question to minimize the association between them.

Once again these English majority-group children predominantly favoured the white figures and rejected the black and brown ones (despite the novelty of the latter and their intrinsic attractiveness, compared to those used in other studies). The vast majority of children selected own-group companions for various activities and only six per cent favoured other-group figures more on these questions. *All* the children attributed some negative stereotypes to the minority figures and positive ones to the white figures. None of them showed any hesitation in identifying themselves as white nor in maintaining that they would 'rather be' the white figure given the choice. Many of their spontaneous comments about the black figures, or the reasons they gave for rejecting them, evidenced considerable racial hostility. While this was often expressed in childish terms, it also frequently took an adult form, in which the parental origins of the sentiments were fairly clear. One six-year-old maintained that the black doll was the 'bad' one 'because he should have learned the language before he came over here', and other comments made suggested a degree of hostility that would not have disgraced the National Front or the Ku Klux Klan. While these were perhaps exceptionally hostile examples, the overriding impression was of a generally negative feeling towards blacks in line with current adult prejudices.

The studies of British children's attitudes reviewed to date were all conducted around the beginning of the 1970s. There have been a number of further studies over the following decade which have yielded a broadly consistent picture: despite some significant changes, the similarities with the earlier studies are greater than the differences. Norburn and Pushkin[287] did a follow-up study involving many of the children who had taken part in Pushkin's earlier study eight years previously. They found that in general, the proportion of children expressing 'extremely unfavourable' and 'very unfavourable' attitudes towards blacks had declined somewhat, but the 'moderately unfavourable' category had increased by 67 per cent. Part of this was due to a movement from the other end of the scale, such that none remained in the 'very favourable' or 'extremely favourable' categories; in other words, there was an increasing concentration of children towards the middle of the scale, but the large rise in the proportion of children in the 'moderately unfavourable' category meant that the total disfavour score (combining all three 'unfavourable' categories) had increased over the eight year period.

Milner's second study[265] replicated aspects of his earlier study conducted five years previously, with the same five- to eight-year-old age range, as part of a larger investigation of the educational implications of children's racial attitude development (see Chapter 8 and Appendix). Essentially the same high level of own-group preference and out-group rejection was apparent in the second study, and a similar level of positive and negative stereotyping of the groups. There was, however, a small (and *statistically* insignificant) proportion of children who 'preferred' and positively stereotyped black figures in the tests, whereas none of the previous sample had responded in this way. There are one or two other indications of marginal improvements in white children's attitudes. In a small scale study conducted by Doddrell[96] (supervised by the present author), a small but determined minority of white children were quite unwilling to make any choices between black and white figures, adamantly maintaining that there was no difference between them or that the obvious difference did not matter. This was the first time, to the author's knowledge, that children have reacted in this way, and although it is an idiosyncratic response which probably reflects the thoroughgoing positive multiracial philosophy of the school the children attended, it may be a significant development — and one which should inform the debate on multiracial education policy.

Davey and his associates have provided the most recent evidence on children's racial attitudes in Britain[81,82,83]. In a substantial study conducted in the late 1970s, their findings show a continuation of the trends recorded earlier in the decade. Race, it seems, was still a crucial basis for categorization amongst British primary school children: in one part of the study children were set two tasks designed to assess the relative importance of race, sex, age and status in their categorization of people. When the children simply had to sort photographs of people differing according to these criteria, 'in all ethnic groups, both sexes, regardless of geographical locale or demographic concentration, sorted the photographs by race, or pigmentation first. The sex and ages cues alternated . . . for third place, while dress was always the residual or ignored cue.' The other task involved pairing photographs of children playing on a roundabout in a park, according to who they thought would be playing together. Anyone familiar with the rigid playtime division between the sexes in primary school children will not be surprised that on this task, 'the sex cue moved into first place, followed by race, with dress coming a poor third.'

What of children's feelings of liking or disliking for other ethnic groups? On a test which required the child to express preferences for photographs of children from their own and other groups by comparing each picture with every other one, the white children put the well- and poorly-dressed white children in the top four positions (out of twelve), the only ethnic group to do so. On a further test where the child had to share sweets between children photographed playing in a park, the results:

> . . . yielded three broad groups of children, the 'ethnocentric', who consistently favoured their own group, the 'fair-minded', who attempted to distribute the sweets evenly between the groups, and the out-group preferers, who predominantly favoured other groups at the expense of their own. There were significantly more ethnocentric children among the whites than either the West Indian or the Asian groups.[83]

A Stereotypes test confirmed this general picture: the white children showed a greater readiness to assign the favourable attributes exclusively to their own group. The impression given by the study is one of strong in-group preference, but rather milder out-group rejection and hostility, when compared with Milner's findings nearly ten years earlier. With different samples of children and different tests, exact comparisons cannot be made but there are indications of a slight improvement in white children's racial attitudes over the period. For example, whereas 100 per cent of the white children in the earlier study said they would 'rather be' the white figure (given the choice of 'black' and 'white' figures), the equivalent figure was 86 per cent in Davey's study. Clearly, this change in the previously unthinkable prospect of preferring to be black or brown is a rather significant development, albeit involving only a small minority.

Attitudes versus behaviour
An important issue which we have not yet examined is the question of what children's racial attitudes, as measured in these kinds of study, actually tell us about their *behaviour* in everyday life. Do 'prejudiced' children necessarily behave in a hostile way towards blacks in practice? After all, we have only presented evidence of children's expressed attitudes, an interpretation of the material we have elicited from them in possibly artificial experimental situations. Researchers have often presented their data on attitudes as though it were predictive of behaviour, even though (as we recall from Chapter 2) the situation is not that simple. By far the greatest research effort has been devoted to the attitudes side of the

equation, partly for its intrinsiç value, and partly for sound 'economic' reasons. As Vernon[409] put it:

> Words are actions in miniature. Hence by the use of questions and answers we can obtain information about a vast number of actions in a short space of time, the actual observation and measurement of which would be impracticable.

Isaac Deutscher[91], among others, has pointed out the many fallacies involved in this kind of inferential jump from one sphere to another. He argues cogently that in many cases it is a 'dubious assumption that what people say is related directly to what they do'. This is simply because reality places many demands and constraints upon our behaviour which may not operate when we are simply expressing our attitudes. To take an extreme (and extremely unlikely) example, South African blacks *might* have very positive attitudes towards whites and wish to integrate and socialize with them; in reality, *apartheid* proscribes any such behaviour. Ascertaining their attitudes would not, in itself, tell us very much about their everyday behaviour and the legal limitations on it; similarly, if we were to deduce their attitudes from observing their behaviour we would be misled. In other words the *situation* in which behaviour takes place will determine whether that behaviour is a reflection of the individual's attitudes, or whether it is an accommodation to other influences such as social or legal pressure. So it is not possible to make a simple statement about how children will interact with other races based on the attitude studies described so far. To say that 'it depends on the situation' is not an equivocation but the best possible account of what happens in reality.

It is actually very difficult to study children's behaviour directly, and in particular to determine whether individual acts or friendship choices are influenced more by race than by other considerations, such as the personality and attractiveness of the children involved. It is also, of course, extremely time-consuming. One such study, by McCandless and Hoyt[254], found a degree of racial cleavage even among pre-school children in the US, but very few studies have been based upon this kind of naturalistic observation. The majority have used sociometric techniques which really measure neither 'pure' attitudes nor behaviour. The child is required to indicate the names of other children in the class/school/locality, in order of preference as 'best friends', 'someone you would like to sit next to in class', or some other criterion. A matrix can be constructed from the pooled choices of all the children in any locale, such that a complex picture of the children's friendships emerges, identifying those who choose each other, those who are most frequently chosen (the 'stars') and those 'isolates' whose choice of others is not reciprocated. If the children are identified by racial group in this 'sociogram', it is possible to see how far friendship choices are made across racial lines. Once again there are problems of analysis and interpretation here, because the simple fact that A chooses B in the task does not guarantee that he/she does so in the flesh, and in any case there is ambiguity about what that choice represents. Is B chosen because or in spite of his/her race, and is C rejected because or in spite of his/her personality?

Nevertheless, the sociometric studies of friendship choice and play behaviour in the US provide a fairly clear and consistent picture of race-related behaviour. In an early study of elementary school children, Criswell[76] found that 'in classes of coloured and white children containing minorities of four or more Whites [there was] an increase of racial cleavage with age. Separation into racial groups is usually absent until grade three. Cleavage reaches its highest point in grade five.' (Grades 3–5 cover approximately the nine to eleven age range). In a subsequent study[77], Criswell again found that the eleven-year-olds showed the greatest in-group preferences, and indeed Moreno's earlier study[270] had found little racial cleavage before this age. However, we must set against that McCandless and Hoyt's discovery of cleavage among pre-schoolers in actual behaviour. Koch showed that this process of mutual withdrawal into their own ethnic groups slowly increased over the whole period from eight to sixteen years[225], and this picture was broadly confirmed by the work of Loomis[248] and Lundberg and Dickson[249]. (Interestingly, more recent studies in the post-desegregation era by St John[362], and McConahay[255], show little if any improvement in inter-racial friendships.)

British sociometric studies of race cleavage parallel these findings. Rowley[326] looked at the friendship choices of 1747 English, Indian, West Indian and European children in both primary and secondary schools and found that at all ages children tended to choose children of their own ethnic group (90 per cent of the English, 75 per cent of the Indian and 60 per cent of the West Indian children choosing in this way); there was a slight, though not statistically significant tendency for in-group choices to increase with age. Kawwa's[216] and Saint's[331] studies show the same picture of predominantly in-group friendship choices. Once again the most recent evidence is from

126

Davey's studies; Davey and Mullin[82] presented three sociometric questions to a sample of nearly four thousand children in multiracial schools in London and Yorkshire. The children were asked which other children they would like to sit next to in class, play with in the playground, and invite home from school. They found that 'a significant degree of in-group preference characterized the friendship patterns of all three ethnic groups', confirming the low levels of inter-ethnic friendship found by Jelinek and Brittan[193] and by Troyna[397]. Furthermore, the operation of wider social pressures was evident in the fact that the children were even less willing to take home friends from a different ethnic group, or play with them in the playground than they were to sit next to them in class. Without detailed observation, there is no way of knowing how far these choices correspond to the children's actual choice of friends and companions in each of the three social situations (although there is no obvious reason why these should diverge). However, Davey and Mullin did compare the *preference* choices of the children who consistently chose own-race friends on the sociometric items, with those of the children who had more other-race friends according to the sociometric test. It emerged that the children who had no other-race friends were far more likely to express a preference for their own group on the preference test.

Imagination and reality

A great deal of the evidence we have so far presented derives from studies of children's racial attitudes, using doll and picture tests. We have postponed until now any discussion of the validity of these procedures. (This discussion is, of necessity, a technical one, and the general reader may prefer to omit this section.) In recent years there has been a certain amount of criticism of these methods, questioning how far they can be said to predict real life behaviour, that is, children's actual racial feelings and friendship choices. Of course there is a serious question as to whether we should expect them to do the latter, given what we know of the tenuous connection between attitudes and any one piece of behaviour in adults. Nevertheless, the issue is worth pursuing for it would considerably strengthen our confidence in the account of racial attitude development we have provided if we could indeed point out some consistent behavioural correlates.

It could be argued from an overview of the studies described in this chapter that children's racial attitudes and behaviour do follow parallel courses: that own-group preference on attitude measures from the pre-school years onwards *is* manifest in own-group friendship choices, albeit somewhat later, and that the two converge towards rather consistent own-group oriented attitudes and behaviour in adolescence. Two problems arise from this, namely that the developments are not strictly contemporaneous, so that we have to account for the delay in own-group preference being expressed in behaviour; and secondly that the studies concerned have seldom involved the same children. In other words we are comparing one group of children's attitudes with another group's behaviour. Hraba and Grant[182] say that where attitudinal and sociometric measures have been used with the same children, there has been 'a lack of relationship between doll-choice and friendship', although we have just seen that Davey and Mullin demonstrated a significant relationship[81]. In the Hraba and Grant study, the discrepancy may reflect a number of specific situational factors like the racial composition of the neighbourhood, which literally prevented some of the children from having the requisite number of friends of one race in proportion to their doll choices of the same group; but beyond these situational considerations, there are other factors which may contribute to the disparity. Of these, the principal factors (affecting all such comparisons) which may differentiate 'attitude' and 'behaviour' measures, are that (a) the *tasks* are very different, as are (b) the areas of psychological/behavioural functioning they are attempting to tap.

It is unfortunate that various critiques of methods in this area have tended to pose the alternatives in almost a competitive way, with at least the implication that, say, 'behaviour' measures are in some sense more 'real' than 'attitudinal' measures. Teplin[381] essentially argues this case; she distinguishes between 'projectively-based methods', 'which questions respondents as to their feelings about dolls, photographs, drawings or other inanimate attitude objects', and 'reality-based methods', 'which utilize questions pertaining to individuals of the child's acquaintance'. Noting that the former type of method predominates in the literature, and in the context of her argument that 'the findings derived from studies employing this methodology may have little to do with assessments made by more reality-oriented methodologies', she suggests that this 'calls into question the assumed equivalence of the predominantly-used method and real life experience'. This implicitly devalues these attitude studies (or indeed all attitude studies), and we might take issue with the notion that a person's attitudes are any less important a part of his/her 'real life experience' than observable behaviour.

128

The other side of the same coin is the inflated value of the socio-metric studies (whose shortcomings we have already discussed) and the equation of them with 'reality'. Surely they provide a better measure of *a* reality, the immediate reality of the classroom or play-ground, but whether the friendship choices made in that context tell us very much about how the child will relate to members of other racial groups beyond the school — or beyond childhood — is another matter. An argument that these wider and longer-term racial orientations are as much influenced by enduring attitudes as by situationally-specific friendship choices on sociometric tests, would be plausible and reasonable to sustain.

However, in a later contribution Teplin[382] elaborated this critique and presented data which compared the responses of children to tests of each type. Four tests were involved, as follows:

(1) a behavioural-intention method in which children were required to choose children for specific classroom activities, (2) a paper-and-pencil questionnaire whereby youngsters chose classmates for hypothetical activities, (3) a reality-photo-choice measure where children expressed preferences among a group of photographs of their classmates, and (4) an imagination-photo-choice measure for which children chose from a group of pictures that were completely unknown to them.

Thus, only the last measure approximated to the doll and picture technique, the other three being variants of the sociometric method. She found that 'methods 1, 2 and 3 were all highly correlated; the majority of correlation coefficients were above 0.85. In contrast, the statistical relationship between method 4 and all other methods was extremely low'.

The most interesting comparison is between methods 3 and 4: they are almost identical (so that the discrepancy in the results could not be attributed to a gross difference in the task or materials) save for the fact that the children in the photographs were known to the subjects in method 3 and unknown in method 4. This single salient difference is clearly crucial to the outcome of the tests. It highlights once again the extent to which situational factors, like racial compo-sition of the group, peer-group friendship networks and individual personality considerations (in both the chooser and the chosen) may prevail over crude racial categorizations in determining friendship choices in these tests. In contrast, the method 4 tests of underlying attitudes towards members of racial groups who are unknown to the children produces a picture of own-group preference. As Teplin suggests:

> . . . while the imagination-photo-choice method would seem to reflect a child's racial/ethnic stereotypes, reality-oriented situations are more amenable to the discovery of traits which may be in conflict with the child's stereotypical conceptions and/or expectations of that race/ethnicity . . . in short, the exhibited discrepance between imagination and behavioural intent may reflect the respondents' tendency to perceive their classmates to be 'exceptional' individuals, i.e. not possessing the stereotyped characteristics thought to be associated with their racial/ethnic group.

She also acknowledges that:

> the findings of these studies . . . should not be interpreted as demonstrable evidence of the inadequacy of any of the methodologies, nor indicative of a method-artifact or internal validity problem. Rather, the seemingly low convergent validity between the imagination-photo-choice measure and the reality-based methodologies seems to indicate that each measures a unique theoretical construct, so that all should be regarded as important to the understanding of inter-group relations in children.

Other criticisms of 'projectively-based methods' and their interpretation are more directly relevant to their use in studies with black children, and these are discussed in the following chapter. However, two other discordant voices should perhaps be mentioned here. Katz and Zalk[215] did not find the strong preference for white dolls found in other studies in their research with three- to five-year-old children. In investigating whether children base their choices on cues other than skin colour, they equipped their 'white' dolls with dark brown hair and eyes of the same shade as the 'black' dolls. Although they set out to 'clarify some of (the) ambiguities in children's doll preference behaviour', it seems that their modification of the stimulus figures in some ways increased these ambiguities. While it may be interesting to know which race-typed human features are the *most* influential in prompting racial categorizations and determining preferences, we are left with the fact that real people com-

130

bine most or all of them, and that reducing the distinctiveness of figures representing these groups does not tell us very much about how children will react to real people who are physically and socially more distinct than these modified figures.

Finally, Ballard and Keller[17] found rather low correlations between six different variants of 'projectively-based' tests of racial awareness. Their sample was rather small and there are some objections to repeated testing of the same children with different measures. Principally, though, their finding must contend with the huge literature which has accumulated over the last forty years of this kind of research, which, allowing for enormous variation in subjects, locales and methods, has yielded a remarkably consistent picture. To be sure, we should welcome any evidence of changes in the direction of less own-group oriented racial attitudes in children; but although there are indications of some changes here, we cannot yet assert that these have significantly altered the picture.

The argument that projectively-based methods constitute a rather blunt instrument applied to a rather sensitive and volatile phenomenon clearly has some force. However, as we shall see in the next chapter, it is nevertheless responsive to changes in the wider social milieu. Sociometric measures also have an important part to play in mapping exising friendship patterns in specific social contexts. But so long as we wish to have some indication of racial orientations that transcend the exigencies of particular situations, and that will be brought to bear in contacts with unknown people as well as familiar classmates, we will continue to need more general attitudinal measures of the doll and picture type.

6
Race and the black child

Until now we have focused solely upon the development of racial attitudes in white, majority-group children; we now move to consider the consequences for the black child of living at the 'sharp end' of racism. While acknowledging individual and social structural factors, we have given far greater emphasis to the simple consequences of the socialization process in transmitting adult racial attitudes to children, and the kinds of messages about race which are to be found throughout our culture and its productions. Of course, black children are socialized within the same broad cultural milieu and within the same racial climate. While the messages about race which black and white children receive are the same, the implications are radically different. Whereas white children are encouraged by these images to value and identify with their own ethnic group, and indeed to deem it superior, black children are confronted with an image of their group which is at worst derogatory and at best ambivalent. If, as we have argued, these are the raw materials from which the child's racial attitudes and identity are constructed, then it is almost inevitable that the black child will take in some of these negative messages. Two consequences suggest themselves: to the extent that the devaluation of the group is felt to have personal implications, some aspects of self-esteem will be affected; and/or this initiates a dynamic process, for the individual and the group, directed to reverse this valuation and to retrieve a positive self- and group-identity.

Within the last fifteen years we have seen the literature on black identity emphasize the first of these consequences, only to be rapidly supplanted by an emphasis on the second. Unfortunately they have sometimes been posed as competing explanations, gaining or maintaining ideological supremacy; we will argue that both perspectives are absolutely essential to an understanding of black identity processes — for they are chronologically and psychologically linked. For these reasons it is necessary that our account of racial attitude and identity development in black children also follows a chronological course.

As before, we begin in the USA where there emerged the first evidence that white racism intruded into black children's attitudes. In the classic experiments by Kenneth and Mamie Clark[72], and Horowitz[181], it appeared that a minority of black children were unwilling to specifically identify themselves *as* black. They asked the children to choose between black and white dolls in response to the question: 'Give me the doll that looks like you', and found that a third of the children chose the white doll. This was not a perceptual mistake, as nearly all the children had labelled the black and white dolls correctly on other questions. Mary Goodman[144] found the same phenomenon, and suggested this reason for it:

The relative inaccuracy of Negro identification reflects not simple ignorance of self, but unwillingness or psychological inability to identify with the brown doll because the child wants to look like the white doll.

Far from showing an inability to *discriminate* racial differences, if anything the evidence suggests that black children are more rather than less aware of racial differences and their significance than white children. Several studies, for example by Goodman[146], Porter[300], Hartley *et al.*[161, 162], have shown an earlier development of racial awareness in minority-group children than whites; and Landreth and Johnson[234] surmise that 'environmental influences directing attention towards skin colour may be effective earlier in Negro than White groups'. It seems more likely that the choice of a white doll on an identification question represents a *heightened* awareness of the negative connotations of the black figures: Morland notes that some children who identified themselves 'correctly', 'did so reluctantly and with emotional strain'[271].

The children's responses to other tests also suggested a highly positive orientation towards whites and a somewhat equivocal feeling for their own group. Goodman's[145] black subjects, aged 3½ to 5½, made more out-group preferences than did the whites (64 per cent cf. 7 per cent), showed less antagonism towards the out-group (9 per cent cf. 33 per cent), less friendly responses towards their own group (56 per cent cf. 93 per cent) and more antagonism towards the in-group (24 per cent cf. 0 per cent). Morland's studies [271, 272, 273, 275] showed very similar results and a majority of the black children he interviewed went as far as to say they would 'rather be' white than black.

The evaluative climate which surrounds black people seems to be subjectively real to these young children. So too are the subtle nuances concerning gradations of colour. Landreth and Johnson[234] used picture-and-inset matching tasks with both black and white children; whereas the white children perceived them as intended, that is, *as* matching tasks, many of the black children perceived them as *preference* tasks. Having done so, they tended to choose white in preference to black, white over brown, and brown over black.

The form and content of black children's attitudes in these studies (mostly conducted in the 1950s and 1960s) are predictably similar to white children's attitudes. For example, in one study[307], rejection took the form of ascribing inferior roles to black characters in story-telling tests. In another[359], black figures were chosen less often by black children for playmates, companions to go home with, and guests for a birthday party. In completing unfinished stories involving black characters, the black children more frequently placed own-race figures in negative positions, and said they were more likely to be the aggressor, the 'badman', or the loser in a contest, and less likely to give aid.

There is not a great deal of data on the development of these attitudes with age. The few relevant studies suggest a decrease in out-group orientation as the black child gets older. For example, the Clarks'[72] seven-year-old subjects chose the white doll as 'nice' and the black doll as 'looking bad' less often than did their younger subjects. Increasingly, reality obtrudes too strongly for children to mis-identify themselves to any great extent after the age of eight or nine and similarly, the realities of racial cleavage in friendship patterns lie behind the tendency for choices on tests of preferences for friends and companions to become less white-oriented with age.

All of the studies cited so far date from before the growth of black consciousness in the USA; they are based on a long tradition of research which presented quite a uniform picture of these attitudes over a twenty-five year period. For obvious reasons, all this was to change in the 1960s, a development we do justice to in due course; for now we need to set this picture in a wider context. For it was not solely a black American phenomenon; just as white American racism has its counterparts elsewhere, as we have seen, so too do the reactions of the devalued 'minority'*, who are its target, including those who are in the numerical majority (as in South Africa) but whose oppressed status is equivalent to that of disadvantaged minorities.

Out-group orientation is not an inevitable consequence of racism and minority-group status. Some studies of ethnic groups, perhaps less disparaged than the ones we have dealt with so far, show no such orientation, for example Springer's[355] work with Caucasians and Orientals in Hawaii. However, a great deal of work with Jewish children, (e.g. Chein and Hurwitz,[64] Fishman,[117], Harris and Watson[160], Meltzer[258] and Zeligs and Hendrickson[430]), while using a variety of different methods, generally confirm the foregoing picture of minority children's attitudes.

Many of the studies in the last chapter, conducted across a range of cultural settings, also involved black children. Vaughan's[403,405,406] New Zealand studies, it will be recalled, suggested that white majority ('Pakeha') children developed race awareness and attitudes along similar lines to white American children. Correspondingly, a significant minority of the Maori children identified with the out-group (on doll and picture tests) though this declined by age nine, as did other-race favouritism on preference measures. But until then the Maori children:

. . . tend to favour other race figures when assigning stereo-types that refer to desirable or undesirable attributes; tend to prefer other-race figures as playmates, and tend to prefer other-race dolls to 'take home'.[404]

It seems also that a much less explicit racism can penetrate into childhood to affect the child's attitudes and embryonic identity; this is borne out in situations where the minority is both less visible and less obviously disparaged than are black Americans or Maoris. Werner and Evans[417] used structured doll-play interviews with young Mexican-American children, who showed the familiar preference for white figures, and generally evaluated lighter skin as good and darker skin as bad. The socializing role of the school was brought out by the finding that these responses were much more prevalent among children with school experience. The children also showed a substantial amount of out-group identification. Interestingly, 25 per cent of the sample indicated that the white man-doll was larger than the darker one, even though they were actually equal in size. These remarks were quite gratuitous as no questions about size had been asked. Werner and Evans comment that this phenomenon is reminiscent of the classic Bruner and Goodman[51] experiment in which the working-class children over-estimated the size of coins of high value, as compared with middle-class children, because of their enhanced subjective value.

Once again we turn to South Africa to consider the opposite extreme to these situations, that is, where a highly visible black population is the subject of virulent racism. Gregor and McPherson's[153] replication of the Clarks'[72] study has already been mentioned in part; they found a pattern of identification and preference among white children which was more strongly pro-white and anti-black than any of the American studies. They also found that the African children 'give evidence of marked out-group orientation'. On the preference questions their responses were at a similar level to the white children's, and in the same direction: 76 per cent liked the white doll best, 79 per cent thought the brown doll 'looks bad', and on the crucial identification question, 34 per cent chose the white doll as looking more like them. This is a very substantial minority, though not as great as has been found in some studies. Perhaps there is a curvilinear relationship between racism and out-group identification. That is, the latter increases as hostility increases, but tails off again as the status gap and hostility are so great that out-group identification becomes totally unrealistic or involves danger.

One particularly important study embodied both a cross-cultural comparison and an attempt to test the notion that racial attitudes are a function of dominant-subordinate status relations between groups (for which 'race' is simply a rationalization, and a marker). Morland did this by gathering data in Hong Kong from Chinese children and comparing it with white and black American data collected by the same methods. The island of Hong Kong is one in which, Morland says, 'the most appropriate description of the social structure . . . [is that] . . . the Caucasians and Chinese might be said to hold parallel positions . . . a multiracial setting in which no race [is] clearly dominant.' There were no significant differences on tests of racial acceptance, but on tests of racial preference all three groups differed significantly. 82 per cent of the white Americans and 65 per cent of the Chinese preferred their own group compared to 28 per cent of the black Americans. Morland writes[275]:

. . . a plausible interpretation of the differences between the American Caucasian and the Hong Kong Chinese is that race differences carry more importance for status in a multiracial society that has dominant and subordinate races than they do in a society in which races have parallel positions.

There was a similar pattern on tests of racial identification: the

136

white Americans being the most in-group oriented, the black Americans the least, and the Chinese effectively falling between them (although half of the sample were 'not sure, or insisted that they looked no more like one than they did the other'). So the Chinese children preferred and identified with their own group less than white Americans and more than black Americans. Morland sees these data as a reflection of the fact that, in Hong Kong:

> . . . there is no dominant race to maintain its superior position, and no subordinate race to show unconscious preference for the identification with the dominant race.

Social status, then, lies near the core of racial attitudes and when political, economic and cultural subordination are underscored by skin colour differences, the divide between the high status majority and the low status minority is wide indeed.

Finally, we should consider some studies conducted in Britain where, as we have seen, the climate of prejudiced racial attitudes has encouraged a pattern of childhood attitude development among whites which is similar to the American model. Broadly speaking, the first studies in the early 1970s showed that black British children's attitudes also paralleled their American counterparts'. Milner's[262, 263] studies replicated many aspects of the classic American research work, with the children of West Indian and Asian settlers in Britain. Both groups of children showed a high level of out-group preference in choosing companions for various activities, over 70 per cent of each group making predominantly white choices on these questions. 68 per cent of the West Indian children and 65 per cent of the Asian children consistently attributed good characteristics and stereotypes to the white figures and bad ones to their own-group figures. However, clear differences emerged on the identity questions: in response to the standard identification question, 'Which one of these two dolls looks most like you?', 48 per cent of the West Indians and 24 per cent of the Asians maintained that the white figure looked more like them. When asked, 'If you could be one of these dolls, which one would you rather be?', 82 per cent of the West Indians and 65 per cent of the Asians indicated the white doll rather than their own-group figure. In addition, 35 per cent and 20 per cent respectively misidentified one or more family members when asked, 'Which one of these two dolls looks most like your mother/brother/sister?'

Two things stands out from these findings: the levels of out-group orientation displayed by these children are comparable with the American results (and the highest recorded in any British study), but there are nevertheless significant differences between the groups involved. One explanation for the latter difference might be that the Asian settlers as a group are the subject of less prejudice and devaluation than the West Indians. However, there is no evidence that this is the case, in fact the evidence suggests that the white community is in *one* sense undiscriminating in directing similar levels of prejudice at 'coloured' people, irrespective of their country of origin or colour or culture.

Two other factors may help to account for the differences in the children's reactions to prejudice. Firstly the Jamaican children's parents were socialized within a society which bore an indelible British trade-mark (in every sense of the term) dating from slavery, colonialism and neo-colonialism. This engendered a strong 'white bias' in the culture, such that lighter skin became a passport to higher status positions; indeed, a person might be referred to as white simply as a result of their economic success. There were many other indications of the highly positive evaluation which attached to whiteness, like the references to 'improving' one's colour by marrying a lighter-skinned person, and the desirability of whiteness was reflected in a variety of cultural media, including educational materials which originated in the Mother Country, Great Britain. Unfortunately, when the West Indian immigrants came to Britain and tested the Mother Country's familial feelings, it transpired that she was prone to child-abuse: their hopes for integration were soon bruised and battered by racism. The Asians, on the other hand, desired no such thing, and maintained a much more detached and independent relationship with the host community, preferring to live within their own communities, providing their own goods and services not least because of their wish to protect and foster their own cultures. Despite the traumas of immigration the Asian child was securely located within a family which embodied a long cultural tradition, and its own language, diet, dress and religion. These were all things which were valued highly, and gave the child a positive sense of who he or she was — an identity — and one which was quite independent of anything that the prejudices of white society said about their group. It was not, then, that prejudice against Asians was necessarily any less intense, but rather that it had to contend with a greater social and cultural insulation, and greater positive resources of identity, and thus may not have penetrated so far. It is salutary to note that, despite this resistance, a quarter of the Asian children misidentified and a very substantial majority maintained they would rather be white, rather convincing evidence of the derogatory pressures which prejudice exerts.

This is, of course, simply an interpretation of the findings; it is perhaps time to move away from this litany of research studies to consider their meaning, and that is also a matter of interpretation. It must be made clear from the outset that the meaning of misidentification and out-group orientation has always been a controversial issue, and never more so than in the last few years. To some theorists it has seemed nothing more than an experimental artifact, to others nothing less than a perfect microcosm of black identity-conflict. Above all, these different interpretations of the same phenomenon have emanated from different periods of recent history, and our understanding of them should recognize this, and not be divorced from the wider social considerations which have undoubtedly influenced them. We shall therefore approach the issue chronologically and relate the discussion of the experimental findings and their interpretation to the surrounding social context.

We really only need refer to two distinct periods of time and a transitional stage between them: the periods before, during and after the struggle for civil rights and socio-economic equality, and the growth of black consciousness. Until that social movement was well established there was little debate as to the significance of the research on black children's identification. Goodman's[144] interpretation, cited earlier, was typical of many in suggesting that misidentification was an index of a basic ambivalence on the part of black children concerning their identity, a psychological barrier to wholeheartedly identifying themselves with figures that were so negatively viewed by the majority culture. For her this was not a superficial matter, restricted to the experimental situation, but encapsulated the real, everyday experience of the child living at the receiving-end of racism. The eminent black psychologist, Kenneth Clark[70], eloquently expressed this point of view when he wrote:

> Human beings who are forced to live under ghetto conditions and whose daily experience tells them that almost nowhere in society are they respected and granted the ordinary dignity and courtesy accorded to others, will, as a matter of course, begin to doubt their own worth. Since every human being depends upon his cumulative experiences with others for clues as to how he should view and value himself, children who are consistently rejected understandably begin to question and

139

doubt whether they, their family and their group really deserve no more respect from the larger society than they receive. These doubts become the seeds of a pernicious self- and group-hatred, the Negro's complex and debilitating prejudice against himself. . . . Negroes have come to believe in their own inferiority'.

Clark clearly interpreted his own and other 'misidentification' studies as signifying more than the incorrect choice of a few more or less life-like dolls; rather, here was evidence of the early emergence of a whole complex of identity and personality problems. And while this might seem to go beyond the evidence of the doll studies alone, he and other theorists could draw upon wider data which pointed in the same direction. Deutsch[89], for example, had studied black and white nine- to eleven-year-olds and found that:

> . . . a relatively high proportion of the white lower-class children in this sample have negative self-responses, but not nearly as many as in the Negro group. . . . The Negro group as a whole is affected by lowered self-esteem.

As a result of this negativity in their self-conceptions they were also more passive, morose and fearful. Lowered self-esteem in black children was also identified by Butts[55]; Palermo[292] found that black children suffered more anxiety than whites, and Mussen[282] showed that they perceived the world as more threatening and hostile than did their white counterparts. In this context, misidentification on the doll tests was seen as the tip of an iceberg, the outward symptom of a far more profound malaise, involving identity-conflict, lowered self-esteem, perhaps even personality disorder.

It is not difficult to see how this conclusion was reached, given the prevailing picture of black *adult* psychology; it was inevitable that any evidence which might suggest childhood identity confusion would be seen as the early antecedents of adult problems, as they were currently conceived. Here it is necessary to digress somewhat in order to see how this account of black adult personality was developed by psychologists, and how it provided a persuasive context into which black children's responses were set.

Black mental health: early perspectives
Though not a psychologist, W.E.B. Du Bois, one of the earliest and most prolific contributors to black literature, had an acute and intui-

tive understanding of 'Negro' psychology. He described how black men had become ashamed of their own colour because white society had forced them to accept its own appraisal of them. In 1903 he wrote:

> . . . [the] American world . . . yields him no self-consciousness, but only lets him see himself through the revelation of the other world. It is a peculiar sensation, this double consciousness, this sense of always looking at oneself through the eyes of others, of measuring one's soul by the tape of a world that looks on in amused contempt and pity.[105]

He saw the antidote in the attainment of an independent sense of self, a process of 'dawning self-consciousness, self-realization, self-respect'. James Baldwin took up the same theme some sixty years later: 'There was not, no matter where one turned, any acceptable image of oneself, no proof of one's existence.'[16] Elsewhere[15], he said of his brother: '. . . he was defeated long before he died because, at the bottom of his heart, he really believed what white people said about him.' Baldwin realized that at the time he was writing, acceptance by white society entailed acceptance of that society's portrayal of blacks; and 'One of the prices an American Negro pays for what is called his 'acceptance' is a profound, almost ineradicable self-hatred.'[16]

Until the 1960s the solitary attempt at a black psychology by psychologists was Kardiner and Ovesey's *The Mark of Oppression*.[206] Published in 1951, its authors used a psychodynamic approach, gathering material from life-histories, accounts of daily life, and so on 'through the agency of free associations, dreams and reactions to the interviewer'. Twenty-five people were studied, twelve of whom were patients in psychotherapy, weighting the account towards the extreme or abnormal modes of adjustment. But they concluded that for any black person:

> The central problem of . . . adaptation . . . is the discrimination he suffers and the consequences of this discrimination for the self-referential aspects of his social orientation. In simple words it means that his self-esteem suffers . . . because he is constantly receiving an unpleasant image of himself from the behaviour of others to him.

Kardiner and Ovesey felt confident that their account revealed the 'basic personality' of 'the Negro'. This personality was essentially an unhappy stressful one, suffering more and enjoying less than white people. The need for vigilance and personal control was ever-present, which was 'distractive and destructive of spontaneity and ease . . . it diminishes the total social effectiveness of the personality'. The remedies seemed clear:

> Obviously Negro self-esteem cannot be retrieved nor Negro self-hatred destroyed, as long as the status is quo. What is needed by the Negro is not education but re-integration. It is the white man who requires the education. There is only one way that the products of oppression can be dissolved and that is to stop the oppression.

Of course, a study of twenty-five people, many in therapy, is hardly a satisfactory basis for typifying the 'basic personality' of an entire human group. Is Kardiner and Ovesey's account verified by more objective information, like relative mental illness rates for blacks and whites? This is not easy to answer because *actual* incidence rates are notoriously hard to discover. For some time estimates were made from a simple statistic: mental hospital admissions. On this basis, the incidence of psychosis among black Americans appeared to be approximately twice as high as among whites[223]. However, these figures came from state mental hospitals; as the white population can more frequently afford private treatment, they seriously underestimate the white rates, and one study[185] which took account of private hospitals as well found the admission rates to be *lower* for blacks. Add to this self-selection factors which might differentiate between the races, like attitudes towards mental illness, recognition of symptoms, willingness to report and confine oneself etc., and it becomes obvious that the statistic is not a satisfactory basis for comparison of the races. These considerations apply with even greater force to the milder psychoneurotic disorders. Here there has been even less differentiation between black and white incidence rates, but if anything, tending to show a higher rate for whites.

Inter-racial comparisons on the basis of admission rates, then, have become somewhat discredited. As Dreger and Miller[102] have pointed out:

> Such comparisons have very appropriately decreased, being obviously of limited value . . . attempts to talk about the 'true'

incidence of mental disturbance among races on the basis of those in treatment is questionable even without considering the many definitional problems that exist.

However, their survey of the entire literature concerning mental health diferences between the races, including research with personality tests, clinical studies and survey techniques concluded: 'It does appear that Negroes more frequently experience psychiatric difficulties, particularly of a severe nature.'[101] They found that blacks more often received diagnoses of:

> . . . schizophrenia, alcoholism, paresis, mental deficiency, drug addiction. The following diagnoses are more likely to occur among whites: senile psychosis, chronic brain syndrome, arteriosclerosis, psycho-physiological and autonomic visceral disorders and the various depressive reactions. Again these differences are associated with the lower socio-economic groups regardless of race . . . [although] overall there are some consistent differences between Negroes and whites . . . it is our opinion that the evidence over the last five years suggests that these differences are primarily related to class and caste.[102]

In the early perspectives on black mental health there was no suggestion that black people were genetically or psychologically more prone to mental illness of various kinds. Rather their adjustment (or maladjustment) was seen as an accommodation to intense material and psychological privations. So that H.V., one of Kardiner and Ovesey's subjects, who was preoccupied with violence in all his thought and behaviour, is described as 'about as "normal" an individual as it is possible to be. He has effected a successful adaptation to his social situation. . . . His preoccupation with assertion is not neurotic, it is entirely a projection of the social realities which confront him.'[206] In other words a variety of reactions which would be classified as 'abnormal' in other contexts, are only normal reactions to miserable and degrading conditions of life. And of course, to classify them as mental illness or disturbance locates the pathology in the individual rather than the society, what Ryan[330] called 'blaming the victim'.

Beyond the social and material conditions of black life, there was another even more influential strand in the argument about black mental health, to which we have already alluded: the issue of racism and black identity-conflict.

Black identity-conflict

The conventional view of black psychology suggested that racism created the conditions for identity conflict and that this was central to an understanding of the black personality. This view can be stated as follows: living within a culture dominated by whites and their values, black people to some extent introject white attitudes which hold them to be inferior. Feelings of inferiority are entirely natural for the role that black people are required to play, and the way in which this is conceived by the majority and depicted in literature and the mass media simply *is* an inferior one. Moreover, the social and material environment they inhabit gives further cause for such feelings:

> . . . many Negroes . . . accept in part these assertions of their inferiority . . . when they employ the American standards of success and status for judging their own worth, their lowly positions and relative lack of success lead to further self-disparagement.[297]

This image of their race makes for difficulties in identification with a low-status, socially-rejected group. They may identify with their own group, but then it is difficult to escape the implications of this derogatory group-identity for their own self-image. Alternatively they may identify with whites, which denies their true identity, is unrealistic and fraught with anxiety. The problem is presented as a choice of evils; it may be resolved in one direction or the other, or the individual may stay in a state of conflict, but in each direction there lies anxiety and lowered self-esteem.

We shall pass on without comment to examine the implications of these different modes of identification, according to this view. Identification with one's own group is the 'normal' pattern as we have seen in Chapter 3; however, this was said to cause problems for black children, both in terms of identification with a socially rejected group, and specific identification with parents, who embody the group and are themselves affected by its inferior status. Oppressed minorities have little power with which to resist the imposition of a derogatory identity. The journalist I.F. Stone characterized the black American's condition as 'a unique case of colonialism, an instance of internal imperialism, an underdeveloped people in our very midst'.[363] The analogy is a profound one, for colonial and neo-colonial societies are cemented by the inferiorization of the subject peoples. Frantz Fanon[114] has described the pyschological oppression of the colonized thus:

> the feeling of inferiority of the colonized is the correlative to the European's feeling of superiority. Let us have the courage to say it outright: it is the racist who creates his inferior. This conclusion brings us back to Sartre: 'The Jew is one whom other men consider a Jew; that is the simple truth from which we must start. . . . It is the anti-Semite who makes the Jew.'

This was never more powerfully expressed (nor more eloquently) than by Fanon himself when he wrote:[114]

> All round me the white man, the sky tears at its navel, the earth rasps under my feet, and there is a white song, a white song. All this whiteness that burns me . . .

Indeed, Jahoda[186], writing of Ghanaians before independence, described how elements of inferiority enter into the Africans' conception of themselves. Through European-inspired schooling, Africans encountered a system of values which in many ways contradicted their own. There were strong pressures to accept these values, for in doing so, both the social prestige of education and the material benefits it brings accrued to them. As a result the African:

> now comes to look at Africans and African culture to some extent through the eyes of those European educators who determined the manner and the content of the teaching he received; but the price he often pays for this partially enlarged vision is psychological inferiority.

The implication is clearly that identification with the in-group, where that group is inferiorized, leads to damage to the self-image. Logically, of course, there should be a perfect correlation betwen the individual's feelings towards the group as a whole, and his/her feelings towards the self, as a member of that group. Psychologically, things may be rather different. It seems that it is possible for individuals, while disparaging their group as a whole, to protect their self-esteem by distinguishing themselves from the rest of the group at least subjectively, and avoiding the opprobrium heaped upon them. Jahoda[186] found evidence of just this process:

. . . one of the most remarkable mechanisms was that people were apt to talk about the faults of 'Africans' in a way which implied that they were excluding themselves. Sometimes it was evident from the context that they were referring to another group, (for example) literates would be speaking about illiterates; but occasionally it seemed to mean 'all Africans except myself'.

Obviously, then, there is not a simple one-to-one correspondence between group-attitudes and self-attitudes. But while there is no *necessary* relation between the two, it seems unlikely that there will be no relation between them. Certainly it has conventionally been argued that negative attitudes towards one's group was likely to involve some degree of self-disparagement, even if these conceptions were not wholly derogatory.

The alternative to this self-damage through identification with the in-group, as it was seen, was hardly more attractive or less damaging. Identification with whites was altogether less realistic, but it offered some escape, if only in fantasy, from the predicament we have just described. It was not just misidentification on doll tests which suggested this strategy was sometimes followed. Brody's[45] interviews with young black boys and their mothers confirmed:

. . . that many of these Negro boys do have significant conflicts involving anxiety or guilt-laden wishes to be white rather than Negro. . . . Some seem to have little ambivalence or uncertainty, and clearly noted their wish to be white and their depressed feelings about being dark-skinned.

In the same vein, Dai[80] wrote of black children like 'Alice' whose:

transformation from black into white through the process of identification is certainly an ingenious psychological manoeuvring, but it only enhances [her] lack of the sense of belonging; she strives to be acceptable to both white and coloured groups, but ends by belonging to neither.

It must be remembered that these observations and interpretations are drawn from an era which pre-dates the growth of black consciousness. Lighter skin was still a passport to higher status; white hairstyles and fashions were the desired ones and black magazines contained more advertisements for hair straighteners and skin

146

bleaches than practically anything else. Malcolm X, one of those most responsible for the first black advances, described how he himself had aped the white ideal in his earlier hustling days:[155]

> I endured all of that pain, literally burning my flesh with lye, in order to cook my natural hair until it was limp, to have it look like a white man's hair.

Later he described how this denial of blackness and desire to be like whites was transmitted from parent to child:

> As anti-white as my father was, he was subconsciously so afflicted with the white man's brainwashing of Negroes that he inclined to favour the lighter ones, and I was his lightest child. Most Negro parents in those days would almost instinctively treat any lighter child better than they did the darker ones. It came directly from the slavery tradition that the 'mulatto', because he was visibly nearer to the white, was therefore better.

James Baldwin described similar experiences[16]:

> One's hair was always being attacked with hard brushes and combs and Vaseline: it was shameful to have 'nappy' hair. One's legs and arms were always greased, so that one would not look 'ashy' in the winter time. One was always being scrubbed and polished, as though in the hope that a stain could thus be washed away — I hazard that the Negro children of my generation, anyway, had an earlier and more painful acquaintance with soap than any other children anywhere. The women were forever straightening and curling their hair, and using bleaching creams. And yet it was clear that none of this effort would release one from the stigma and danger of being a Negro; this effort merely increased the shame and rage. . . . One had the choice of 'acting just like a nigger' or of *not* acting just like a nigger — and only those who have tried it know how impossible it is to tell the difference. . . . And the extraordinary complex of tensions thus set up in the breast, between hatred of whites and contempt for blacks, is very hard to describe. Some of the most energetic people of my generation were destroyed by this interior warfare.

147

Sartre[333] described a comparable predicament — that of the 'inauthentic' Jew', one who has been persuaded by anti-Semitic propaganda and lives in fear that his/her actions will conform to this despised portrayal of the group. Thus any spontaneity of action is poisoned by attempting to always monitor behaviour and to contradict the notion (absorbed from the oppressor) of the Jewish nature:

> For him it is not a question of recognizing certain faults and combating them, but of making clear by (his/her) behaviour that (he/she does) not possess these faults.

This deliberate self-consciousness destroys personal authenticity; it arises because 'he knows he is watched . . . (and therefore) takes the initiative and tries to look upon himself with the eyes of others'. The price that must be paid for this is anxiety at the possibility of rejection by everyone; for these actions imply a denial of his/her true group membership, which must antagonize its authentic members, while the view of the self through the eyes of the majority is a picture of a Jew or a black trying to 'make it' or 'pass'.

We have devoted some time to these early accounts of the psychological predicament of black people. Their implication is that blacks find themselves in a heads-you-win-tails-I-lose dilemma. By identifying with whites they are insecure, vulnerable to acute anxiety and mental illness; by identifying with blacks they incorporate within their own self-image disparaging elements which damage self-esteem and may lead to emotional disturbance. This simplification verges on parody, but a reading of the earlier literature gives the impression that the entire black population is embroiled in this 'Catch-22' situation, where to identify in either direction almost ensures psychological difficulty. Where, then, were the normal, well-adjusted black people, who were identified with their group but had sufficiently resilient psychological resources to withstand the imposition of inferiority on their selves? While the emphasis on the destructive consequences of racism was a necessary one both for clinical and ideological reasons, it all but obscured the mass of black people, whose lives were undoubtedly difficult and sometimes degraded in their contacts with whites, but not necessarily pathogenic.

Undoubtedly a section of the black population has suffered psychological disorder (with racism as a contributory factor) and will continue to do so, but they have been represented as though they were typical of the whole group. It is ironic that liberal psychologists

148

whose concern with racism and its effects should attune them to the dangers of stereotyping, should nevertheless themselves contribute to a somewhat negative image of black people through such a gross over-generalization.

The partial character of the 'conventional view' of black identity and mental health was not its only serious shortcoming; its longevity ensured that it remained a static and ultimately dated picture, unable to come to terms with any of the revolutionary changes in the conditions of black people in the last two decades. For the period has seen a 'great leap forward' which has transformed the picture. As important as the tangible gains of desegregation, Civil Rights legislation and socio-economic development, are the psychological gains. As the Civil Rights movement emerged, so too did the beginnings of a new identity; all the successors of that movement have fostered black consciousness in different ways so that the contemporary 'image' of black Americans bears no relation to the deferent slave-like stereotype that preceded it. Who would have agreed that black is beautiful thirty years ago? Who would have predicted that black people would *choose* to identify with their African roots? As Baldwin wrote[16]:

At the time when I was growing up, Negroes in this country were taught to be ashamed of Africa. They were taught it bluntly, as I was, for example, by being told that Africa had never contributed 'anything' to civilization. Or one was taught the same lesson more obliquely, and even more effectively, by watching nearly-naked, dancing, comic-opera cannibalistic savages in the movies. They were nearly always all bad, sometimes funny, sometimes both. If one of them was good, his goodness was proved by his loyalty to the white man.

Friedman[130] suggests that this denigration of Africa was in itself an important and negative part of black identity:

. . . the Negro's acceptance of the white man's image of himself has been inextricably intertwined with the Negro's acceptance of the white man's image of Africa . . . the first in the long series of Negro denials and self-denial was the denial of the African heritage.

These images were not remote from the ordinary black American for they were retailed by their Churches (raising funds to civilize

African savages), by the mass media and by their schoolbooks:

> In the fourth grade those pictures of the races of man . . . with a handsome guy to represent whites, an Indian with a feathered hat, a Chinese, and an East Indian, and then a kinky-haired specimen. That was me, a savage, a cannibal; he was at the bottom. That picture in the book was the picture of where and what I came from. I carried that idea round with me for years. . . . If you can imagine inverting the biases consciously or unconsciously at work in this process, you might then see the white race represented . . . by . . . a mugshot of Al Capone, or, to make the selection on purely aesthetic grounds, someone with the looks of Charles Laughton.

Friedman[130] argues that the worldwide development of black people has come to provide the black American with an alternative positive identity:

> With the emergence of Africa on the world scene, the re-writing of African history, and especially the re-evaluation of the pre-European African cultures, the place of Africa in the Negro's mental landscape is in the process of slowly moving from the negative to the positive pole. Black people are exchanging a domestic for an international identity.

There is no question but that this has developed apace since Friedman wrote this in 1969. The significance of colour within the black community has radically changed such that blackness has developed a positive connotation, together with different concepts of beauty, style and above all else, worth. Friedman's emphasis on the international dimension is a necessary one; certainly Nyerere, Kaunda, Biko and the peoples of Mozambique and Zimbabwe, to name but a few, have given black people all over the world an example which they regard as wholly positive, and far outweighs the evils of Amin and Bokassa. And the profound appeal of the African connection could hardly be more dramatically demonstrated than by the 'Roots' phenomenon. But in the domestic context Friedman seems to pass over the changes during the period which have had a far greater immediacy for black Americans, changes which they have effected themselves. Certainly emergent Africa has reminded them of a history, a cultural heritage and a racial pride; but emergent black Americans have forged themselves a new identity from their own experience. Above all, this is an identity of self-respect which has come from individual and group assertion, from standing up and being counted. From the early days of bus boycotts, sit-ins and freedom marches, through the organization of voters in the teeth of violent opposition by whites, even the rioting and looting in the urban insurrections, all were experienced first-hand or via the media as psychologically liberating — liberation from a notion of black people as passive, fearful, even co-operative victims of oppression. The social, political and economic gains that this period initiated are in turn reinforcing these early psychological advances so that respected and successful black people provide positive role-models to an extent which could scarcely have been conceived as little as ten years ago. If the quantity of media portrayal of blacks (see Chapter 4) has not changed as dramatically as was hoped, the type of portrayal has evolved from Amos 'n' Andy, through Angela Davis to something approaching a realistic and unremarkable picture of black people on a par with whites. If this picture is more optimistic than the reality, it is probably less harmful than the stereotypical denigration which preceded it.

It is important not to exaggerate the extent of these changes: it is still nearer the beginning of the story than the end. But the fact that change has taken place must be acknowledged and any account of black identity development must take account of this. What is clear is that the earlier view of black identity has been palpably outdated for some time; as a static model it could not help but be overtaken by a dynamic process. Friedman put this cogently: 'Social science was caught flat-footed when the 'mood-ebony' appeared. . . . Now theory must follow newspaper headlines.'

Social psychology and black identity

It would be wrong to suggest that social psychology has completely ignored those headlines; that there has been no recognition of the developing black identity. In fact the earlier view has come increasingly under fire, and the last five years have seen a swing of the theoretical pendulum which has not only sought to embrace these new developments, but also to sweep away those which went before them. Earlier notions of black identity-conflict have been labelled, at worst, as racist, and, at best, as simply wrong. The new appraisal is welcome and long overdue; what is less welcome is that some history is being re-written in the process. The debate is controversial and, perhaps inevitably, sometimes acrimonious. Much of it centres on our original concern, the issue of racial identity in black children. There are two strands to the argument: firstly it has been suggested that the 'traditional' findings on black misidentification were in some sense artifactual, or at least unimportant; secondly that the 'related' findings of low self-esteem in black children were equally suspect.

Some of the criticism of the early research has been purely methodological; later criticisms have been methodological in form, though more ideological in nature. In the first category was Greenwald and Oppenheim's argument that the choice between simply two dolls, black and white, on identification tasks unduly restricts the child.[152] In their own study they added 'mulatto' dolls and found considerably less identification with the out-group among black children than other studies had found. There are a number of methodological criticisms that can be levelled at the study; in addition, their results could be interpreted quite differently. The authors divided their sample of children into dark, medium and light groups on the basis of their skin colour. A majority of all groups indicated the *dark* doll to be the one who 'looked most like a Negro'. In fact 22 per cent of the 'light' children and 50 per cent of the 'medium' children actually selected this figure as 'looking most like them' on the identification test. In this context it could be argued that the other children, who identified with either the 'mulatto' doll or the white doll were misidentifying to an extent. So that although the sheer number of children identifying with the white doll was less than in other studies, the proportion of children *not* identifying with the figure who they had maintained was most like their group, was very much the same. In any case we should expect a reduction in the numbers of children choosing either the black or the white doll in this experiment, simply through the provision of an extra figure.

Another source of criticism of the doll and picture studies concerned the race of the tester. When we consider Dreger and Miller's reviews[102,103] of comparative studies of blacks and whites across the whole realm of psychology, and we see how influential is the race of the tester in, for example, intelligence testing, then it is difficult to see how it could not be a factor in the senstive area of racial attitude testing. And of course it has proved to be influential in some studies — and not in others, the balance if anything inclining towards the latter. Where this 'experimenter effect' (i.e. the unwitting influence of the tester) has occurred it has been in the predictable direction, operating to produce responses from the children which are more favourable to the experimenter's own ethnic group. Jahoda and his colleagues[188] found this in their work with Asian settler children in Scotland, as have a number of American studies.[123,227,367,396] Equally, several studies found no effect or a negligible one that did not attain statistical significance.[152,182,272,273,274] Sattler[334] reviewed all the available evidence and came to the conclusion that 'young black and white children do not appear to be affected by the experimenter's race in their preference for dolls which vary in skin colour'. This seems too emphatic a conclusion, given the fine balance of evidence; it is important to acknowledge that this unintentional experimenter effect may operate under certain conditions, but we cannot yet specify precisely what they are.

It can be argued that these criticisms do not detract from the validity of the misidentification findings, for in neither case do modifications of the experiments (either with regard to providing extra stimulus figures, or own-race experimenters) *substantially* affect the phenomenon. And against these criticisms of its validity, we must also weigh other kinds of evidence which give it some credence. Within the same context the children's responses to 'ideal' identity tests ('if you could be one of these two dolls, which one would you rather be?) are far more white-oriented than are their responses to the straightforward identification question. In other words, when the literal question, 'Which one looks most like you?', with its 'requirement' of accuracy is supplemented by a pure *preference* question, 'Which one would you rather be?' a substantially greater amount of white-orientation emerged — almost as though in the former question it was there, but deterred by the implicit demand for a correct answer.

Beyond the testing situation there were many instances of real-life behaviour which pointed in the same direction. Teachers often reported examples of black children depicting themselves as white in self-portraits, painting their actual skin with white paint or covering it in chalk, or even attempting to scrub themselves white. Painful as these images are, it is difficult to escape the conclusion that they are simply the childhood correlates of the skin bleaching and hair straightening that James Baldwin, Malcolm X and others testified to earlier; and that all these reactions represented at some level a desire to change the stigmata of colour.

Thankfully, this is now largely a matter of history (though an important historical period, as we shall show later). For the picture has radically changed during the last ten or so years, such that the earlier pattern of black children's preferences for whites has virtually reversed. At the beginning of the 1970s the first indications of this were apparent: Hraba and Grant[182] and Fox and Jordan[121] recorded a marked decline in misidentification and white preference in their black subjects, and this was generally interpreted as reflecting the growth of black consciousness in the black community. To be sure, if blackness had acquired a newly positive connotation, there was no need to identify with whites. Other studies in the US confirmed the trend further,[318, 352] and Vaughan[408] found equivalent changes in New Zealand.

All in all this indication of wider social changes manifest in these 'artificial' tests is further evidence of their validity (in the light of which Teplin's[381] earlier suggestion that these methods have been unresponsive to changes in the socio-cultural milieu, seems misplaced). However, other critics have seized upon the new chapter of research findings and somehow contrived to use it to revise the story which went before. Banks[21], for example, has gone back to re-examine some of the earlier studies of racial identification, and taken together with more recent studies, concluded that 'white preference in blacks has not, in fact, been convincingly demonstrated'. He indicates a number of factors which he feels might undermine the validity of the measures employed like the novelty and attractiveness of the stimulus figures (see also Brand, Ruiz and Padilla[42]). More importantly, though, he questions whether black children's responses as a group have departed significantly from 'chance' levels of white choices.

It is arguable whether the studies he cites are fully representative of the whole body of work in this area, in that he overlooks some of the earlier studies where out-group choices were more prevalent, and draws more heavily on studies conducted since the phenomenon had diminished, which is nudging the scales of evidence. He also omits reference to any of the studies conducted outside the US which are congruent with the earlier American findings and give them further credence. However, it is his contention that, amongst the studies he has cited, 'the predominant pattern of choice behaviour among blacks towards white and black stimulus alternatives has conformed to simple chance' which shows extraordinary tunnel vision. It is perhaps literally correct, but it disguises more than it reveals. 'Chance' implies a random, arbitrary kind of choice, at a level biased in neither one direction nor the other. But unless one can show that the nature of the task is ambiguous and misunderstood (and the evidence is decidedly to the contrary), then choosing across racial lines (*particularly* on identification tasks, thus contradicting objective reality) is obviously a more deliberate choice than 'chance' implies. This is not after all, a 'heads' or 'tails' situation, but one where 'heads' is being called *as* 'tails'. If these choices were truly operating at or about the chance level, and were affected by no other factors, then we would expect the same pattern of choices amongst white children (i.e. a random, 50–50 kind of choice that was racially unbiased). This is manifestly not the case; white children's choices clearly mirrored adult racial values amongst the dominant majority-group. While black children's choices were less white-oriented, bringing them down near the 'chance' level numerically speaking, they departed hugely from the white results in terms of a positive orientation towards one's own group. It is when we go beyond the numbers to make *interracial* comparisons of their implications that we see the fallacy in Banks' analysis, as indeed Williams and Morland[423] have pointed out.

Identity and self-esteem
Some of the force behind the arguments of Banks and other critics comes from their misgivings about the simple equation that has conventionally been made between 'misidentification' on doll and picture tests and low self-esteem. They are right to point out that very few studies have measured both simultaneously, and that the relationship between them has never been reliably established. Turning to the earliest studies they show that 'lowered self-esteem among black children' was frequently an 'interpretive' finding; it was based on nothing more than an interpretation of the doll tests (and in a few cases, for example Goodman[145], additional interview material), rather than self-esteem tests *per se*. We have already described how the traditional views of adult black mental health made this kind of over-interpretation more likely.

Where evaluation of self-esteem did take place it was in this specifically racial context, as an adjunct to the doll and picture tests. In contrast, the later studies of black self-esteem embraced a broader range of subjects (adolescents as well as young children) and employed standardized measures of *overall* self-esteem (that is, tapping the individual's general feelings of self-regard, not just *vis-à-vis* whites). Most of these studies were conducted in the 1960s and early 1970s and demonstrated comparable levels of self-esteem in blacks and whites (for reviews of this literature, see Rosenberg and Simmons[321], Silverstein and Krate[350], Taylor[380], and Porter and Washington[302]). The strands of the argument appear to draw apart because of the difficulties in comparing different studies of different subjects using diferent methods at different times. They are brought together somewhat in a study by Ward and Braun[414] which combined a conventional doll test of racial preference and a standardized self-concept test. With seven- to eight-year-old black children they found a majority favouring the black figures, *and* higher self-concept scores amongst those children, as against the lower self-concept scores of the children who were more white-oriented in their preferences. These findings are in line with *both* the studies showing increasingly black-oriented racial preferences, and those showing higher levels of self-esteem than previously, and they suggested a relationship between the two. As the children who were more orientated towards whites also had lower self-concept scores, there is also the implication that the earlier generation of doll studies may have been right: that there was lowered self-esteem in a significant minority of blacks, even if they went beyond the evidence in saying so. As ever, things are not quite so simple, given McAdoo's[253] study showing little correlation between racial attitudes and overall self-esteem.

It is impossible to reconcile all findings from all studies but some kind of resolution can be attempted. First of all there are clear indications that we have to make a distinction between a child's *overall* self-esteem, and that aspect of self-esteem which pertains specifically to *race*. Simmons[351] argues that:

> . . . an individual's positive or negative attitude towards himself is influenced less by the larger society and more by the opinions of significant others in his immediate environment. The black, particularly the black child, tends to be surrounded by other blacks. Thus, those persons who matter most to him — parents, teachers and peers — tend to be black and evaluate him as highly as white parents, teachers and peers evaluate the white child. In addition, although his race, family structure or socio-economic status may be devalued in the larger society, in his immediate context most others share these characteristics. Comparing himself to other disprivileged blacks, the black child does not feel less worthy as a person on account of race or economic background . . . encapsulated in segregated environments as are most urban black children, they may be less aware of societal prejudice than is assumed. Even if aware, they may attribute the blame to the oppressor rather than themselves. Militant black ideology is aimed at just this end, encouraging the disprivileged to externalize rather than internalize blame for their low societal rank and thereby protect their self-esteem.

Simmons is perhaps too optimistic about the amount of insulation against prejudice provided by segregated backgrounds, given the influence of the mass media and racism institutionalized within the education system. Nevertheless there is a lot to commend her argument. It suggests that those aspects of self-esteem which derive from the child's day-to-day interaction with parents and other blacks may indeed be positive, and this will be reflected in test situations where *overall* self-esteem is being measured. It also allows that in other contexts there may enter into the child's conception of him or herself some more negative elements as a result of interracial comparisons with whites. These may not taint overall self-esteem, either because these situations and comparisons play a minor role in the child's life, or because of the increasing social support for externalizing blame as Simmons describes.

What is more, this picture can also be reconciled with the earlier conceptions, because it describes a relatively recent state of affairs: firstly, as many black writers have testified, parents' own ambivalence about identity and self-esteem may well have been less supportive of the child's self-esteem in the period before black consciousness took root. Secondly, and related to this, the strategies that can now be used to avoid internalizing blame and to resist negative self-conceptions were far less prevalent. In other words, in the pre-black-consciousness era, there simply were less positive resources of self-esteem, whether from significant others or from pro-black ideology in the wider community.

Once again we are drawn to the conclusion that the early studies of black children's identity and self-esteem may well have been valid even though, as their critics rightly point out, they were too reliant on interpretation rather than conclusive data. They probably also exaggerated both the amount of psychological damage black children suffered (as they were too heavily influenced by the prevailing 'pathological' view of black psychology) and the sheer proportion of the problem, implying that all black children were more or less affected, thereby compounding the stereotyping process. Nevertheless, now that we can evaluate these studies from a distance, it is possible to disregard the excesses of interpretation surrounding them, and retrieve the core, namely the valuable insights they have given us into the inferiorizing pressures of racism. Inferiorization is not just a problem for blacks, but for other oppressed minorities too. We need to retain the concept and our understanding of its consequences. We cannot do this if history is to be re-written to fit current facts, beside which earlier stages are felt to appear demeaning. For in doing so we deny the evidence of *change*, which reflects nothing but credit on the emergent minority, and we replace one static model by another one.

We need dynamic models which account for the revolutionary psychological and social changes that have taken place, and a number of theorists have been working in this direction. Hall *et al.*[157], Crawford and Naditch[75], Sherif and Sherif[346], Cross[78], and Thomas[384], have all proposed models (or hypotheses) concerning black identity transformation that are process-oriented (and do not require any denial of the more negative picture of black identity that went before). A more ambitious formulation, which speaks not only to black identity development and change, but embraces the whole range of reactions to minority-group status — and locates them within a general theory of inter-group relations — has been proposed by Tajfel and Turner [376]; aspects of their theory have already been described in Chapter 2.

A new theory of minority identity development
Tajfel and Turner's theory, it will be recalled, attempts to go beyond the simple 'realistic group conflict theory' ('RCT') of, for example, Sherif[342] as an explanation of negative inter-group attitudes. This latter kind of theory viewed conflicts of interest and competition for scarce resources as the determinant of both negative *inter*-group attitudes and concomitant positive *intra*-group attitudes; Tajfel and Turner emphasize the need to create and maintain a positively-valued group identity *vis-à-vis* other groups, and their theory spells out the related processes of social categorization, social comparison and inter-group attitude development through which this can be achieved, as already described.

Clearly, RCT theories cannot cope with precisely those situations we have described in this chapter: where a minority group (or a proportion of its members) at a particular point in its history manifests not hostile attitudes towards the competing, dominant group, but in a sense, overly positive ones. Now as we have seen, these attitudes have in turn been replaced by newly positive in-group attitudes (and more negative out-group ones?) among blacks in the 1960s and 1970s, but:

> . . . these developments do not rescue the RCT in its original form. The very suddenness with which the scene has changed effectively rules out objective deprivation and therefore *new* conflicting group interests as sufficient conditions for the 'subordinate' group ethnocentrism. On the contrary, there is often

less 'objective' deprivation than there has been in the past. An active and new search for a positive group identity seems to be one of the critical factors responsible for the re-awakening of these groups' claims to scarce resources.[376]

But this is not the first stage in the process:

. . . when social identity is unsatisfactory, individuals will strive either to leave their existing group and join some more positively distinct group and/or make their existing group more positively distinct.

Clearly, individual mobility may be constrained by any number of individual and social factors; as an alternative to *real* social mobility, the person may opt for individual 'psychological' mobility by dissociating him/herself subjectively from the group. It is this distancing or disidentification that may be evident in embryonic form in the misidentification responses of black children described earlier.

Given the contradictions and discomforts this strategy involves, whether for adult or child, it can hardly provide a viable way of being for the mass of individuals in the long term. The alternatives are *group* strategies which essentially change the group's social identity. Tajfel and Turner[376] suggest that groups may follow a strategy of *social creativity,* for example, involving one or more of the following processes:

(a) comparing the in-group to the out-group on some new dimension, which is often intimately bound up with:
(b) changing the values assigned to the attributes of the group, so that comparisons which were previously negative are now perceived as positive. The celebration of blackness, including the re-evaluation of previously-disparaged physical characteristics like skin colour and hair, together with the cultivation of roots and all things African, are clearly examples of these strategies.
(c) Changing the out-group (or selecting the out-group) with which the in-group is compared. For example, for blacks in the US this might take the form of comparisons with 'poor whites' or Mexican-Americans, or any group with whom the comparison is likely to be favourable to the in-group.

The argument, then, is that these group strategies emerge when the individual strategies prove fruitless. Clearly in the case of black

Americans, individual mobility has been severely restricted by the millstone of prejudice, discrimination and limited educational/ occupational opportunity; even beyond these obstacles black Americans have not been able to 'pass' into the mainstream in the same way as other disadvantaged but 'white' minorities (such as Jewish Americans) have done. And everything we have argued in this chapter underlines the ultimate futility of the alternative individual strategy: 'psychological mobility' through identification with the out-group.

Then, say Tajfel and Turner, the only salvation for the individual and the group is *collective* action to alter the social valency of the group, using the variety of strategies already outlined. As a descriptive theory of minority-group identity development it rings true, but in terms of explanation it has one significant shortcoming. This is its failure to specify how the transition from individual to group strategies is made. Is it that the material (or relative) deprivation of the group becomes too flagrantly apparent, or its inferiorization too demeaning to bear? Although these material and psychological factors are clearly both involved, in a complex relationship, we cannot be satisfied with the implication that under some unspecified conditions of adversity they magically coalesce and are articulated in collective social action. Otherwise the theory is open to the same charges of reductionism that have been levelled at earlier theories (for example, the frustration-aggression hypothesis), when they implied (by omission) that the dispositions of masses of individuals aggregated spontaneously into group behaviour.

It may be, however, that there are not typical conditions which can be identified and generalized. When Victor Hugo wrote of the irresistible force of 'an idea whose time has come', he spoke to this very situation; but why should the *idea* of, for example, black power have come and flourished in the 1960s and not in the 1950s; and more particularly, *how* did it do so? We have acknowledged the material and psychological factors; there is clearly also a complicated relationship between the exhortation of charismatic leaders in the community (in both the local and national sense) which must find a resonance throughout their constituency, and the real or apparent possibility of tangible social and psychological advances. In other words, the appeal of group strategies and the commitment of individuals to them will depend to some extent on the perceived likelihood of their success, for history is littered with examples of social movements which have withered without the sustenance of any recognizable progress. In that connection, the role of models (like African national liberation movements) is crucial in providing external evidence of the possibility of successful advancement. The precise chemistry of imposed inequality (both material and psychological), aspiration, ideology, leadership, social organization, successful models and feedback from actual social progress, remains to be defined. Perhaps at this stage we have to be content, not with an answer but at least with an appreciation of the complexity such an answer will involve.

Black British identity development

Some of these generalities and abstractions may be more meaningful if we can illustrate them from experience; it seems, to the present author, that the course of black British children's identity development over the last decade encapsulates much of the debate in this chapter.

It will be recalled that Milner's[263] first study revealed a degree of white-orientation in black British children on a par with the earlier era of American findings. Within five years a further study showed a substantial decline in 'misidentification' (see Chapter 8 and Appendix), and most recently, Davey and Mullin[81] have shown that by the end of the 1970s the phenomenon had almost disappeared. During the same period, Britain's black communities were subjected to ever more extreme racism via the propaganda and provocation of overtly fascist political groups, out and out physical intimidation through racist attacks on people and their homes, while continuing to endure the day-to-day individual and institutional racism which circumscribes their life-chances. On the positive side, black consciousness has grown, black social and political organizations have flourished and black culture has evolved a specifically 'British' variant, all of which has given black children and youth an alternative, acceptable image of their group with which to identify. Both the good and the bad developments over the period can have left black children with little doubt (and little alternative) as to their identification. And this is surely what the doll studies have reflected, the progression of 'blackness' from the negative towards the positive pole.

It should be abundantly clear by now that the present author is not one of those who wishes to consign the earlier 'misidentification' findings (including his own) to the dustbin of history, on methodological or ideological grounds. In this connection it is difficult to forget that immortal comment on another exercise in self-justification. 'Well, he would say that, wouldn't he?'. Nevertheless, more objective observers might agree that the identification tests revealed a crucial stage in minority-group identity development — corresponding to Tajfel and Turner's individual strategy of 'psychological mobility', at a childhood level. Indeed it is our contention that this was not simply a crucial stage, but revealed the *psychological* dynamic behind black identity development — both for individuals and for the group.

If we accept that there *are* psychological consequences of racism, oppression and inferiorization, which are demeaning, even painful, then we go some way towards explaining the emotional impetus behind the transition from the first to the second generation of doll test results, *and* the transition from Tajfel and Turner's 'individual' to their 'group' strategies. We do not have to 'buy' the whole conventional package of emotional disturbance, mental illness or even lowered self-esteem. We need only attend to the ways in which it has been increasingly possible (not to say appropriate) for blacks to externalize blame for their predicament onto whites, rather than internalize it. Neither do we have to rely solely on doll and picture studies for our evidence of these processes. Malcolm X's evolution from a 'light' black who enjoyed his consequent status, through his education in racial power relations during his prison years, to become one of his race's most forceful and militant champions is a case in point, and no less significant a piece of evidence for being a literary account.[155]

Oppressed peoples will always rise against the power structure that contains them, by virtue of their objective, material deprivations; the argument here is that racism compounds this oppression with subjectively-experienced psychological devaluation, and it is the emotional imperative to deny and transcend that attempt at inferiorization which may be quite as important in giving strength to black people's struggle for racial justice as material disprivilege. To put it another way, when we look at the news film of black youths involved in the inner-city riots of 1981, who could say which dolls they would have chosen ten years before?

As yet only a minority of black British youth has expressed its grievances on the streets. There are also other indications of a collective re-definition of group identity in positive, assertive terms which involves a far greater proportion of black youth. In this process, the Rastafarian movement has been one pole of influence which is out of all proportion to its numbers or its importance in Jamaica (see, for example, Owens[291]). In its original context it is not a major political force; but translated into the British situation, its outlaw/outcast image, its celebration of blackness and the African connection, and the hard-edged rejection of whites and their values which is bound up in its own brand of reggae music, have all combined to make the Rastas quasi-political totem figures for young blacks, a reference group of sorts. The Rastas are reflected in their music and clothes, their values and lifestyles — if in diluted form (see also Cashmore[61] and Hebdige[165]). If there has been a single force which has typified black youth culture in the past decade it has been reggae, in all its variants. Troyna[397], for example, has shown its influence in providing a focus and a voice for low-achieving blacks in schools: it is felt to express their common predicament, and is an important factor underlying the stronger in-group identity shown by this group.

One final cautionary note on black identity: while the basis of a more positive identity has perhaps been retrieved, the millennium has not yet arrived, and we should not assume that all black people are invulnerable to the negative consequences of prejudice. The positive developments in identity should not distract attention from the paucity of material improvement in blacks' social position. Recall that in the first doll-studies the vast majority of black children said they would 'rather be' the white figure. This may have been a diluted form of misidentification or simply a recognition that to be white in this society is to be (relatively) valued and privileged. In any event, while misidentification itself has virtually disappeared over the course of the 1970s, this expressed 'wish to be' the white figure has not declined to anything like the same extent. Still in the late 1970s, around half the black children in Davey and Mullin's study[x1] were choosing the white figure. The contrast with the increased accuracy in self-identification is marked. It suggests that black children are now quite clear about their racial identity and view it positively, but are also very clear about the racial pecking-order in society. As Davey[x3] wrote:

> It is in this crevice between the heightened sense of personal worth and the sharpened perception of relative status that the seeds of inter-group hostility will germinate.

* The crucial factor, of course, is status, not considerations of numerical majority or minority.

7
Race and education

Race + class = underachievement

Until now we have only been concerned with the processes of social learning by which children acquire racial attitudes and identity. At this point we turn to consider how this learning may affect other, more general, learning in the education process. The focus of this chapter is black children's underachievement in schools. At the simplest level this has sometimes been couched in terms of the effects of prejudice in the education system. But this is where the purely psychological level of analysis breaks down for clearly, the educational plight of black children cannot simply be explained as a consequence of 'prejudice' and 'discrimination' by teachers and other children. Rather, as argued in the Introduction, we have to take on board the concept of racism (more properly 'racialism'. Strictly speaking, 'racism' is the ideology, 'racialism' the practice, but since Carmichael and Hamilton's[60] distinction between individual and institutional *racism* has become the accepted usage, the term will be retained here.) Thus we can begin to consider a number of less obvious factors which (while they may sometimes surface in the day-to-day exchanges between individuals) are built into the structure of the institution. In other words, while the overt expression of prejudice by teachers and peers undoubtedly affects black children adversely, these incidents are rather infrequent; there are more fundamental but less obvious influences which shape the child's educational experience. These influences are a reflection of the fact that the implicit racism of a culture will inevitably find expression within its institutions, particularly those whose express purpose is to transmit that culture.

There is another dimension, too. Many black people in Britain and America, probably the majority, are *relatively* poor. This is often an even more crucial determinant of their educational experience than their racial membership, and it is a predicament they share with many whites. Thus we have to consider the effects of both urban poverty and racism, separately and in interaction.

Urban poverty and education

There is no shortage of research material on the educational problems of the poor; in total it amounts to an encyclopaedia of deprivation and inadequacy, but it is a partial one in both senses of the word. For the moment we will simply synthesize this material, without comment, into a profile of 'the lower-class child' as depicted in the literature. From the moment of conception the lower-class child is said to be disadvantaged; it has been shown that nutritional factors can produce disorders in pregnancy, spontaneous abortion and infant disability, and these are all found more frequently at the lower socio-economic levels[293]. There is also more prematurity, involving neurological abnormalities and later retardation of development[288].

In infancy the child suffers handicaps in developing perceptual abilities:

> The slum child is more likely than the middle class child to live in a crowded, cluttered home. . . . There is likely less variety of stimuli in the home, and less continuity between home and school objects. Where money for food and basic clothing is a problem, there is little for children's play things. . . and for decorative objects. . . . Where parents are poorly educated, there is likely to be less verbal interaction and less labelling of objects (or of the distinctive properties of stimuli). . . . There is less stress on encouraging the production of labels by the child, and on teaching him the more subtle differentiations between stimuli (for example, knowing colour names and identifying them) . . . as a result he could be expected to come to school with poorer discrimination performance than his middle-class counterpart.[88]

Indeed it has been demonstrated that lower-class children do perform less well on auditory discrimination tasks[87]. This may well contribute to both speech and reading difficulties.

The beginning of speech is more likely to be delayed in lower-class children[194]. Apparently the 'shaping' of a child's speech sounds is more persistently practised by middle-class parents than lower class ones. In addition, the lower-class home provides a high level of 'noise' through which discriminations must be made and which distracts both parent and child from satisfying interaction. In Bernstein's[31] early work it was argued that the language the lower-class child acquires is different from middle-class language. It was

165

called a 'restricted' code, signifying a more informal, concrete, immediate and need-oriented mode than the 'elaborated' code of the middle-class. The latter was portrayed as more formal, abstract and concept-oriented; as a nearer approximation to grammatical written language, it put the child at a considerable advantage in dealing with reading materials and teachers at school. As language and thought are in many ways interdependent, the lower-class child would experience more difficulty with abstract problems and with concept-formation.

In what other ways is the lower-class home apparently deficient in preparing the child for school? Lower-class children, it seems, have fewer family-centred activities than middle-class children[251]; they have less interaction with parents and seek information from them less often[90]. They have fewer books in the house, are read to less and speak less with parents at mealtimes. They also have more physical punishment[266]. Parental aspirations for their children are lower in the working class[358]; the children themselves have less achievement motivation[320]. They learn more quickly for material incentives than for non-material ones such as praise or satisfaction, while the reverse is true for middle-class children[383]. Apparently, lower-class children also have a time-perspective which is more immediate than middle-class children. These last two factors fit them badly for a school system in which rewards are abstract and long term.

Deutsch sums up this background to learning in the following way:

> The lower-class child enters the school situation so poorly prepared to produce what the school demands that initial failures are almost inevitable, and the school experience becomes negatively rather than positively reinforced.[90]

After two to three years of age, social class differences on measures of intelligence appear and increasingly diverge with age in favour of middle-class children[103]. In school, lower-class children do worse on arithmetic concepts tests[269], IQ tests, reading scores and problem-solving[74]. High status children score higher than low-status children on all tests of conceptual ability[349]. On comparisons of overall IQ and achievement scores of lower- and middle-class children, 'groups of pupils from higher-income families scored higher on all cognitive measures, even when these were ostensibly "culture-fair"'[107]. Lower-class children receive a disproportionate share of lower grades[1]; and in one study of eight-year-olds, lower-class children were eight months behind middle-class children on vocabulary, nine months on reading comprehension, six in arithmetic, and eleven in problem solving[172].

Lower-class children make more modest estimates of their own ability than middle-class children[428], show greater maladjustment[74], are more aggressive and competitive[257], participate less in extra-mural activities[74], and drop out more[36].

Collating even a small sample of the relevant studies in this way produces a profile of the lower-class child which gets very close to caricature. Educationalists have apparently felt free to make broad generalizations about children according to their class, and while acknowledging that there are variations within groups, nevertheless assume that sufficient homogeneity exists to permit this kind of 'summary portrait of the disadvantaged child'. There are, of course, all kinds of problems in this sort of approach: comparability of samples, of class criteria, of methods, and so on. Beyond these, there is the inescapable problem that the frame of reference within which the lower-class child is considered is a highly evaluative one; and that this evaluation is made by educationalists and researchers who do not share the same social class background. There is, then, a kind of implicit bias against modes or levels of performance which deviate from the ideal-type middle-class norm which, for many people, undermines the objectivity and validity of these studies. However, there is another aspect to this which retrieves some value for this kind of work: the unintentional bias in researchers' values is also one which is present in the education system as a whole, and therefore these studies give us quite an accurate picture of how the child's performance is likely to be perceived in the school. And whether it is really valid or not, it may be more important to ask whether this kind of picture of 'the disadvantaged child' is *believed* by teachers, and influential in shaping teaching practice.

The teacher's perspective
The teacher is not the only arbiter of the child's educational experience, but is perhaps the most important one. Certainly in the business of evaluating the child's performance the teacher has more influence than any other person; therefore the perspective which he or she brings to the task, and the assumptions, beliefs and standards of comparison which colour this perspective, will crucially influence the outcome of the evaluation. In the primary (or elementary) school, the class teacher will probably spend more hours of the day

with the child than the child's own parents; he or she has to fulfil many of the parents' roles, not only in teaching about the world (and as we have argued, simultaneously transmitting attitudes and values) but also in caretaking and providing emotional support and comfort. The teacher rapidly becomes one of the most significant 'others' in the child's life. Where this relationship is successful there can be a good deal of identification with the teacher. The affection and respect that a good teacher engenders underwrites two important dimensions to the teacher-child relationship: one is the extent to which the child will take the teacher as a model and internalize the standards and values that he or she embodies; the other concerns the emotional and evaluative tenor of feedback *from* the teacher, which may support or undermine the child's feelings of self-worth.

There are indeed angelic teachers who are able to give unqualified approval and support to all their charges. But teachers, in the main, are also human beings and can hardly be blamed for simply liking particular children more than others. That is entirely natural and most of us have struggled with the problem of even-handedness in our treatment of disagreeable or uncooperative students; all of us can recall the discomfort of being on the receiving-end of a teacher's failure to disguise the fact that their evaluation of us is lower than our own.

Faced with thirty new faces at the beginning of the school year, the teacher is confronted with a very complex social situation. It is impossible to hold so many individuals' special characteristics and needs in mind simultaneously. Some means of simplification is necessary, some differentiation of the mass, some kind of categorization, in just the same way as we have to simplify and categorize in every other kind of perception of the world. The criteria which are used for categorizing pupils may be quite idiosyncratic to a particular teacher: performance, behaviour, attractiveness or a host of other features. What concerns us here is whether there are regularities across different teachers, perhaps even across the whole profession, precisely because there are accepted ways of categorizing children, according to criteria which are believed to predict the child's performance; these proven categories would simplify both the present and the future, in guiding the teacher's approach to the child and his or her expectations of performance. For example, Goodacre[143] did a very detailed study of the ways in which teachers categorize their children according to home background. What emerged was an overall use of the terms 'good' or 'poor' homes, poor not necessarily referring to socio-economic status. The good home was one which, through motivating the child and instilling the importance of reading, made the teacher's task easier. Some of the supposed characteristics of the good home were quite revealing. Along with the emphasis on cultural and motivational factors, things like 'good conversation and manners', religious faith, and a mother who does not go out to work, were counted as important.

This simple categorization is a very credible one, though the question arises as to how the children are allocated to each group. In other words, what evidence do the children present or does the teacher discover which allows them to be classified in this way. This will be explored in greater detail later, but for now we wish to look at some far simpler and more obvious criteria for categorization, namely racial characteristics. Here are existing social categories which are immediately visible, and which carry potent evaluative connotations. It is indeed difficult for the teacher to be unaware of these ready-made categories or ignore them. What we have to additionally consider is that these categorizations not only imply a great deal about home circumstances that might well fit in with the 'good/poor' scheme of things; they also bring with them a legacy of beliefs about intelligence and achievement.

Race, class and IQ
We have already seen, in Chapter 1, how the early psychologists and other social theorists conceived of the relationship between race and intelligence, and between intelligence and social class. Their belief in black intellectual inferiority has survived them and continued to influence educational and social policy throughout this century. Periodically the issue has re-surfaced as a controversial debate between their descendants and more liberal social scientists who have contested their views. Each party to the debate has been well aware of the profound social implications of their arguments and therefore the necessity to make their views prevail if various social evils are to be avoided. This is not an ideal recipe for scientific debate, and consequently this running contest has been quite as much a confrontation of values as of objectively-appraised scientific facts. It seems to the present author that a truly value-free position on this issue is probably unattainable; however, this has not unduly detained the majority of contributors to the debate who have been happy to represent their evidence and arguments as scientific facts, rather than reflections of their values, when the truth of the matter invariably lies between the two. This was never better illustrated

169

than in the title of an article by Sherwood and Nataupsky[347] in 1968; it was called 'Predicting the conclusions of Negro-white intelligence research from the biographical characteristics of the investigator' and the authors were able to show that, indeed, various background characteristics of the researchers were good predictors of the kind of results and conclusions they would arrive at on this issue.

By the same token, neither can this chapter be objective and value-free. However, it is to be hoped that intellectual dishonesty can be avoided if, without a detailed biography, the author makes clear his own position on the issue. At this point in this book, it is perhaps stating the obvious to say that I do not concur with the view that heredity overwhelmingly determines intelligence, nor that there are genetic differences between racial groups which predicate differences in intelligence. The rationale for this position will be spelled out in the course of this chapter.

The heart of the matter is the false dichotomy which has been created between heredity and environment, as determinants of intelligence. It was Galton who first posed 'nature' against 'nurture' as though they were adversaries and, of course, for him they were, for heredity promised the survival of the *status quo*, while environmental factors opened the door to unthinkable social changes. Contemporary scientists are still unclear as to what is really implied when we say that, for example, a particular human trait is determined more by heredity than by environment. As soon as we indicate that both factors are involved, we have to specify the nature of the relationship between them. Do they act independently, or if not how do they combine? Does heredity set the limits, by predicating a range of possibilities, like a hand of cards, while environment dictates how the cards are played? Or is the *interaction* of the two factors more than the sum of their individual contributions? The honest answer to these questions is that we do not know; we only know that both are involved.

In this context it is, to say the least, absurd to pretend that our state of knowledge is sufficiently advanced for us to be able to put precise numerical weights on the two factors — to actually specify their proportional influence on intelligence. And yet Eysenck[111] tells us that, '. . . individual differences in intelligence — that is, IQ — are predominantly attributable to genetic differences, with environmental factors contributing a minor proportion of the variance among individuals. The heritability of the IQ . . . comes out at about 80 per cent, the average value obtained from all relevant studies now reported.' One may wonder whether the *irrelevant* studies concurred with these estimates, when amongst the 'relevant' studies are those of Sir Cyril Burt, whose entire output has come under a cloud of suspicion since evidence of his fabrication of data has emerged.

Much of the hereditarian case rests upon a foundation of empirical studies of identical or monozygotic twins. MZ twins develop from a single zygote (fertilized ovum) and thus have identical genetic structure. They should also have identical levels of intelligence, if the hereditarians are correct, and indeed they normally show a high correlation of IQ scores, though not a perfect one. Of course, under normal circumstances they also have *nearly* identical environments, which could also, theoretically, account for this correlation (with the slight differences in their treatment accounting for the departure from perfect correlation). Very infrequently we find cases of identical twins separated at birth and reared apart; this provides a 'naturally' occurring controlled experiment, for heredity is held constant but is subjected to different environments. Leaving aside the highly unusual (and therefore atypical) nature of identical twins, particularly those reared apart, it is clear that if there were high correlations in IQ scores, this would be powerful evidence for hereditary factors alone. And indeed, there are a number of studies of MZ twins reared apart which show very high correlations in IQ. But from Kamin's[205] masterly re-analysis of this work, in particular the studies of Burt[54] and Shields[348], it is clear that very substantial 'experimenter effects' influenced the outcome of the data, and certainly its interpretation. Within Shields' data, for example, there is neglected but equally powerful evidence of environmental influences which are submerged in the thrust of the hereditarian argument. And in Burt's work, Kamin identifies all manner of unwarranted assumptions, methodological short-cuts and plainly biassed interpretations of the data which undermined their validity, some time before the data themselves were revealed as fabrication[139], and his fraudulence conceded by even his (formerly) staunchest adherents[431].

Although the dispute will certainly continue, as much because of its social implications as its scientific value, it is arguably anti-scientific in its premises because it asserts the polarity of two kinds of influences which clearly act together. To argue for the supremacy of one factor over another is a little like saying that the area of a field is determined more by its length than its breadth. Nor is the relationship necessarily a multiplicative one, as that would imply. Alice Heim[166] described the problem quite well in her quotation from D.H. Lawrence: 'Water is H_2O, Hydrogen two

171

parts, Oxygen one, but there is also a third thing that makes it water, and nobody knows what that is. . . .' To take the analogy a little further, supposing the 'formula' for intelligence were H_2E, which is more important: heredity, because there are two H atoms, or environment, because only one E atom equals two H's? Either the question is meaningless or the answer must be 'neither' because both depend on the other's presence.

The environmentalist case (or interactionist case — for few environmentalists deny the interaction of environment with heredity) is more diffuse, more all-embracing and less quantifiable. It rejects the idea that heredity is destiny and points to the infinite variety of human behaviour that results from the same genetic stock. Human beings are less mature at the point of birth than almost any other mammals; this means that a great deal of our physical maturation and psychological development takes place in constant interaction with our environment. It is precisely because we are so malleable that we have been able to adapt our behaviour to most climates and circumstances and achieved pre-eminence over all other species. The capacity for complex learning, together with the ability to communicate that learning in symbolic form, has enabled us to benefit from the learning of previous generations; our cognitive complexity allows us to even anticipate future contingencies and adjust our strategies accordingly. In other words, so much of our behaviour stands in dialectical relation to the outside world — the environment — that it is difficult to accept that much of our behaviour is driven or limited by our 'internal' genetic inheritance. If the ability to learn and change is what characterizes the species, then it must also shape the individual members. In the case of intelligence there are myriad factors which lead to a person being assessed as having a particular level of mental ability. Some, like creativity or motivation, may also have some 'internal' origin, and these are not even measured by IQ tests*. Others, like home circumstances, nutrition, stimulation, learning opportunities, interaction with others, early school experiences and sheer, unadulterated good fortune, will equally shape the person's abilities. Are all these factors really 'a minor proportion' of the intelligence story? The simple fact is that we do not have a direct line to the 'intelligence genes': we cannot measure native intelligence *apart from* these environmental influences. We can only measure certain kinds of performance — like performance on IQ tests — and this is as much a product of our experience as our innate potential. (It should be noted that an analysis of the practice of IQ testing would properly require several chapters to itself. The general reader is advised to consult Heim[166], or Ryan[329], for introductory discussions of the problems of IQ testing.)

The main social implication of the hereditarian view is that education will only marginally affect the social structure, as this structure is founded upon innate differences in ability between the social classes. Over the course of this century, the hereditarian case (and the evidence adduced in its support) has served well the interests of those who wished to resist social change; Sir Cyril Burt, a latter-day Eugenicist, was highly influential in the framing of the 1944 Education Act, which effectively shored up the existing class structure through its provision of different kinds of education for different social groups: academic grammar schools for middle-class children and varieties of technical education for the future manual workers of the 'lower classes'. It is ironic that hereditarians have sought to defend this kind of system so tenaciously against comprehensive education for all, when logically this should not threaten the supremacy of genetic influences; perhaps there *is* evidence to persuade them that the horse should be backed both ways.

The issue of race and intelligence has had a similar longevity. Though it has sometimes receded, it tends to regain momentum at times when the racial *status quo* is threatened. Thus, at the height of the debate over desegregation of American schools in the 1960s came Arthur Jensen's[195] committed restatement of the genetic inferiority of blacks, shortly followed by Eysenck's[111] similar contribution to the debate over the education of the children of black settlers in Britain. Jensen's argument was founded upon two planks: (1) comparative studies of black-white intelligence have frequently found a gap of 10–15 IQ points between the two groups, on average; (2) the millions of dollars expended upon compensatory education programmes in the US did not result in any appreciable narrowing of this gap, therefore it must have a genetic basis, not an environmental one. He concluded that the abilities of the two groups were both quantitatively and qualitatively different, and therefore required different kinds of education.

The facts of the first argument are incontrovertible, though open to widely different interpretations than Jensen's as to the cause of the gap. The magnitude of the difference is put in perspective when we consider that since the 1930s, studies[59] have shown that with a *black* tester, black students score six points higher than with a white tester, that is, around half the hypothesized discrepancy between the groups. It goes almost without saying that the effects of environmental influences in producing this gap are given a minor role in

Jensen's thesis. Where they are acknowledged, it is principally in terms of *current* environmental differences between the groups, and then to demonstrate that when socio-economic status is equated between samples of blacks and whites, differences in IQ still persist. This ahistorical stance ignores four hundred years of slavery, oppression, and inferiorization and compares their cumulative effects on blacks with those on the beneficiaries of a similar period of privileged superiority, on the basis that both now receive a similar dollar income. Eysenck, however, enlists history in support of the hereditarian case to explain how genetic differences have come about[111]:

> If, for instance, the brighter members of the West African tribes which suffered the depredations of the slavers had managed to use their higher intelligence to escape, so that it was mostly the duller ones who got caught, then the gene pool of the slaves brought to America would have been depleted of many high-IQ genes. Alternatively, many slaves appear to have been sold by their tribal chiefs; these chiefs might have got rid of their less intelligent followers. And as far as natural selection after the shipment to America is concerned, it is quite possible that the more intelligent negroes would have contributed an undue proportion of 'uppity' slaves, as well as being much more likely to try and escape. The terrible fate of slaves falling into either of these categories is only too well known . . . in the plantations . . . intelligence would have been counterselective. Thus there is every reason to suspect that the particular sub-sample of the negro race which is constituted of American negroes is not an unselected sample of negroes, but has been selected throughout history according to criteria which would put the highly intelligent at a disadvantage. The inevitable outcome of such selection would of course be the creation of a gene pool lacking some of the genes making for higher intelligence.

This passage is really beyond comment (and belief) but it is an important example of the extraordinary lengths to which people are prepared to stretch the name of science in order to rationalize their convictions.

Jensen's second principal argument is equally specious. Even the most radical re-organization of the entire American educational system could not realistically be expected to countermand this history of disadvantagement within several generations. To charge a

174

variety of disparate and piecemeal compensatory education programmes with failure to achieve this social revolution is frankly bizarre. The generic term 'compensatory education programme' embraces so many different initiatives that it is impossible to generalize about them. Even within any one programme (like, for example, Project Head Start) there was immense variation in the objectives, methods and expertise involved in local projects. However, an important characteristic of many of these projects was that they did nothing to fundamentally alter the children's day-to-day experience in the schools; they were out-of-school activities, extra-mural 'enrichment' programmes, or pre-school projects lasting a few weeks or months designed to prepare the child better for the educational hurdles ahead. Again, we cannot do justice to the evidence here, but the consensus of opinion on these initiatives was that their peripheral influence on children's educational experience, their heterogeneous methods and uncertain objects (described by one commentator as 'a crash course in Western infancy, to raise the disadvantaged child to the level of the Spock-raised one, between now and next Autumn'[2]) could never make serious inroads into the black-white discrepancy in achievement. In fact, Jensen's reliance on the early reports of, for example, Project Head Start's failure turned out to be misplaced; later analyses[259] showed that there were long-term benefits attributable to the programmes.

Jensen's early arguments have been contested by biologists, statisticians, psychologists, sociologists and educationalists, amongst many others (it is interesting to note that the more recent changes in his views[196], and particularly their educational implications, have attracted much less attention than his original treatise). The exchanges between the two sides have not always been edifying, nor illuminating. Of all these contributions, perhaps Flynn's[118] point-by-point analysis is the most nearly objective, and the most telling, precisely because it does acknowledge the force and coherence of Jensen's arguments, as opposed to his followers' less reputable efforts. Flynn presents a highly technical but persuasive case for environmental influences which undermines the Jensenist case, without rancour or slur. He suggests a number of research strategies which would likely provide the kind of direct evidence necessary to clinch the argument, and it behoves social scientists to follow his lead and collect the data in a similarly scrupulous way.

We have frequently referred to the conflicts of value and ideology which have obscured, sometimes intentionally, the scientific facts of the issue. It is important to stress that the indictment of 'racism' has

175

not been made, by and large, for the purpose of vilifying individuals, but rather to indicate the *effects* of their theories. It is unfortunate that these debates are not confined to senior common rooms or learned journals. They have direct consequences in society at large, precisely because the aura of scientific respectability adds intellectual weight to the arguments of politically-motivated interest groups. As Martin Webster, one of the leaders of the avowedly fascist National Front movement, wrote:

> The most important factor in the build-up of self-confidence among 'racists', and the collapse of morale among multi-racialists was the publication in 1969 by professor Arthur Jensen in the Harvard Educational review.[416]

Similarly Eysenck's views have frequently been quoted in the literature of racist organizations. The magazine of the National Party, *Beacon*[29], even boasted an interview with him. Eysenck later denied giving this interview and, adopting the stance of the 'pure' scientist, wrote that 'the devil can quote scripture, and malevolent people can always misquote factual evidence. . . .'[112] But supposedly scientific findings on race and IQ are not published in a social vacuum, and as Billig points out[33], one can deny having sympathy for the devil, but some might feel it is naive or disingenuous to do so if one also furnishes material for his scripts.

The question remains as to the influence of these theories of race and intelligence on the public in general and the education system in particular. Eysenck is the best known of all British psychologists and his views on, for example, crime, smoking and even astrology have received prominent coverage in the national press. This does not mean that the public is persuaded by his ideas on race and intelligence, but given the widespread popular belief in black intellectual inferiority we have identified in British culture, it seems likely that his views have not been rejected out of hand. This would be difficult to determine empirically; in the same way as people are sufficiently aware of liberal norms to play down their prejudices towards black people when interviewed, so would this diminish the avowal of racist beliefs on the intelligence issue. Probably this effect would be even more marked were we to interview members of the teaching profession on the matter. But two factors point to a somewhat wider currency of these beliefs than a straightforward survey would reveal. One is the long-standing influence of the British psychometric tradition in the education system. It is only comparatively recently that

176

the critiques of intelligence testing have threatened the supremacy of the IQ test. It was an important component of the 11+ examination and still plays a part in the assessment and 'banding' procedures of many schools and education authorities. Belief in the validity of the instrument, allied with 'folk-psychological' beliefs in the inheritance of intelligence and biological differences between the races, make the Eysenckian thesis a plausible one. And secondly, if that is too speculative a connection, let us approach the matter from the other end. Teacher unions and organizations are rightly anxious to protect their membership's good name. They have actively intervened to influence if not suppress the publication of material which levelled accusations of racism against members of the profession[176]. And yet, in the same period the National Union of Teachers published a pamphlet, *Race, Education, Intelligence: a teacher's guide to the facts and the issues*[285]. This was a simple but reasoned analysis designed to correct racist misconceptions, and one may genuinely wonder why this was necessary if the Jensen-Eysenck thesis enjoyed no support among teachers.

However, let us suppose for the moment that the education system as a whole feels more persuaded by the environmentalist view and go on to consider the consequences for the evaluation and assessment of black children which flow from that perspective.

Cultural deprivation vs cultural difference

The term 'cultural deprivation' was coined in the early 1960s in America; despite its shortcomings, it caught the imagination of educators and others, gained a momentum of its own and entered the language of educational theory. It continues to influence our conception of black and working-class environments and their effects on the educability of the child. It originally provided a convenient shorthand by which to summarize all those background factors believed to handicap children in their commerce with the education system. But it has become much more than that, it has been reified. Now it connotes a syndrome, a pathology of background, with cognitive and linguistic symptoms in the child which require therapy.

Logically, and in its most literal sense, the term is a nonsense. Every group has a culture, a way of life, and cannot be 'deprived' of that. As Keddie[217] wrote:

It appears therefore that the term becomes a euphemism for saying that working-class and ethnic groups have cultures which are at least dissonant with, if not inferior to, the 'mainstream' culture of the society at large. Culturally deprived children, then, come from homes where mainstream values do not prevail and are therefore less 'educable' than other children. The argument is that the school's function is to transmit the mainstream values of society and the failure of children to acquire these values lies in their lack of educability. Thus their failure in school is located in the home, in the pre-school environment, and not with the nature and social organization of the school which 'processes' the children into achievement rates.

A related idea is that of the 'culture of poverty'. This recognizes differences in the lifestyles of urban blacks and middle-class whites, but rather than according black culture the respect that anthropologists give to alien cultures abroad, it is seen as a 'deprived' and 'disorganized' version of white lifestyles. This is based upon a long tradition of viewing black existence as unstable, an amoral disintegration of 'normal' life, a picture which is drawn from the statistics of illegitimacy, father-absence, social welfare dependence, crime and drug addiction. Valentine[402] has presented a devastating critique of this model. He shows, for example, how theorists have been so concerned with *dis*organization and chaos in black family life that they resent the opposite when it does appear. He quotes Frazier, the sociologist:

> The behaviour of Negro deserters, who are *likely* to return to their families even after several years of absence, often *taxes the patience* of social workers whose *plans for their families are constantly disrupted*.[122] [italics added]

And because of the 'culture of poverty' concept, Valentine argued, poverty was seen as a disabling way of life rather than an involuntary adaptation to an inequitable income distribution. This had the effect of locating the causes of deprivation somehow 'in' the minority and its 'chosen' way of life, not in the economic and social forces to which it was subject. And this self-inflicted plight would continue into future generations through ignorant and ineffective child-rearing practices. This was therefore one of the intellectual parents of the idea of 'cycles of deprivation', in which poverty is seen as a self-perpetuating and particularly vicious circle. The remedy for all of this would be to reach further and further back into the child's life-history to deal with the 'inefficacious' socialization practices of the mothers and the lack of stimulation in the home; the logical extension would be to introduce specialists 'into the home who would not only provide the missing stimulation to the child, but also teach the mother how to raise her children properly'[25]!

This pathological model was highly influential in shaping compensatory education programmes in the US. Pre-school enrichment projects and extra-mural cultural activities were mounted in the hope of making up some of the deficits the child suffered, for:

> . . . he is essentially the child who has been isolated from those rich experiences that should be his. This isolation may be brought about by poverty, by meagerness of intellectual resources in his home and surroundings, by the incapacity, illiteracy, or indifference of his elders or of the entire community. He may come to school without ever having had his mother sing him the traditional lullabies, and with no knowledge of nursery rhymes, fairy-stories or the folk-lore of his country. He may have taken few trips — perhaps his only one the cramped, uncomfortable trip from the lonely shack on the tenant farm to the teeming, filthy slum dwelling — and he probably knows nothing of poetry, music, painting, or even indoor plumbing.[47]

This is arguably one of the most stereotyped and class-centred descriptions of cultural deprivation ever written, but it illustrates vividly the assumptions behind the programmes that introduced Harlem children to the Metropolitan Museum. The other consequence of this emphasis on pre-school and cultural enrichment programmes was to leave the school itself untouched. All the problems of ghetto education, of resourcing, of teacher turnover, of curricula, were removed to the periphery; racism and poverty also receded as explanations of the child's condition. The home and its disabling consequences for the child's abilities were centre stage. Compensatory education thus conceived was a little like ministering to the casualties of a battle, while assuming that they arrived on the battlefield by chance, and that their wounds were self-inflicted.

Of course, many compensatory education programmes involved far more than 'cultural enrichment', but most held the common assumption of the cultural deprivation of their constituents and tried to cater to the linguistic and cognitive 'deficits' that it caused. Ameliorating these was the key to the child's success in school. As Baratz and Baratz wrote[25],

> Because of their ethnocentric bias, both the social pathologists

and the genetic racists have wrongly presumed that linguistic competence is synonymous with the development of Standard English and, thus, they incorrectly interpret the different, yet highly abstract and complex, non-standard vernacular used by Negroes as evidence of linguistic incompetence or underdevelopment.

The gulf of misunderstanding separating black language and white educationalists is well illustrated in a study cited by Forbes[119], which revealed that slum children in Pittsburgh, 'used 3,200 words, including idioms, not recognized by their teachers or by educational tests'. Labov's[230] work has effectively demonstrated the fallacy of black linguistic 'deficits' and this undermines the basis of cognitive deficits, too. Ginsburg has also offered explanations of racial and social class differences in not only language development but also cognitive skills and IQ which contest the notion of the deprived and inadequate lower class child: he concludes that, 'While poverty is not a desirable state and while it may not ennoble those who live in it, it also does not produce serious retardation of their thought-processes.'[140]

Cultural difference viewed as deficit has been the keynote of compensatory education, and it has added considerable weight to the idea of black intellectual inferiority; indeed, the very notion of compensatory education itself implies that there is an inadequacy or deficit to be made up. Even though the more florid excesses of 'cultural deprivation' have been superseded, the core notion of deficit has proved to enjoy a longer life-expectancy, at least at the popular level. It is analogous to the career of Bernstein's 'elaborated' and 'restricted' codes; long after the original formulation has been modified by criticism and even the author's own work, the attractive simplicity of the original has guaranteed its survival in popular discussion. Similarly, 'cultural deprivation' is still bandied around, and cultural difference is still viewed less often in a positive light than a negative one, which adds to the 'problems' of 'these children'.

However we conceive of these issues, the fact remains that background factors *do* disadvantage children in their intercourse with the school. For the child who is poor and black there is a legacy of beliefs and expectations about his/her intellectual performance which must colour the teacher's perceptions, for *both heredity and environment appear to be stacked against the child.*

Teacher expectations and pupil performance
We have given some time to looking at the raw materials from

180

which teachers' expectations may be formed; what of the effects of these expectations? In the 60s Robert Rosenthal became interested in 'experimeter effects' in psychological research, that is, the ways in which experimenters may unwittingly influence their subjects to produce certain kinds of behaviour in accordance with the experimental hypothesis. This was not a deliberate tampering with the results but an unconscious process by which the researcher, perhaps non-verbally, communicated to the subjects the kinds of responses that were 'required' from them[322]. Rosenthal and Jacobson[324] then took these ideas into the educational arena in a study which has become a modern classic, 'Pygmalion in the Classroom'.

In a particular school several classes of children were given a non-verbal intelligence test, which was *said* to be measuring their potential for intellectual growth. A proportion of each class were designated as academic 'spurters' and their names were given to their new class teachers at the beginning of the next school year. All the classes were re-tested on the same test twice more at four-month intervals. Overall, the 'spurters' showed considerably greater gains in IQ during this period than did the rest of the children. This might seem unremarkable, were it not for the fact that these 'spurters' had originally been chosen as such *not* on the basis of the tests but in a completely random way. In the words of the authors, 'When teachers expected that certain children would show greater intellectual development, those children did show greater intellectual development.' But it was not only in intellectual performance that these children made gains; they were also judged by their teachers to be more likely to succeed, 'as significantly more interesting, curious and happy. There was a tendency, too, for these children to be seen as more appealing, adjusted and affectionate and as lower in the need for social approval.' So the children who were expected to gain intellectually not only did so, but were more favourably regarded by their teachers in the process.

None of this bodes well for those children who are heir to expectations of a more lowly kind; the pressure is on to fail for they are surely not expected to succeed. There are particular problems for those children of high ability, who have nevertheless attracted low expectations perhaps because of their background. Rosenthal and Jacobson showed that the *contradiction of expectation* is not easily accepted by the teacher. They showed that those children who were not expected to gain intellectually not only showed less gain than those who were, but were regarded less favourably by their teacher when they did gain: 'These may be hazards to unexpected intellectual growth. Classroom teachers may not be prepared to assimilate the unexpected classroom behaviour of the intellectually upwardly mobile child.'

Naturally these findings aroused a great deal of anxiety among educationalists, for they had profound implications for the classroom. They also prompted close methodological examination and criticism (see, for example, Thorndike[387], and Snow[355]), and a wealth of further studies. We cannot review this literature here but a couple of studies have particular relevance for us. Leacock[237] looked at four schools, two in poor neighbourhoods and two in middle-income areas. One of each was nearly all-black and one all-white. She first interviewed the teachers on their attitudes towards the children, and found much more negative feeling towards the children in the poor neighbourhood than the middle-income schools, and more negativity towards the black children than the whites. When she looked at the children's IQ scores, there was a very strong relationship between them and the teachers' positive or negative feelings towards the children. In the middle-income group, the children (black or white) with the high IQs tended to be those that teachers felt most positively about. Interestingly, it was a different story in the low income group: the higher IQ children attracted the most *negative* feelings from the teachers, particularly the high IQ black children. It was as though the teachers resented those children who were highly intelligent, but who, on grounds of class or race, they would expect not to be.

Rubovits and Maehr[327] did a more controlled study of the racial aspects. They studied black and white children of comparable ability, but half of whom were represented to the teachers as 'gifted' and half as 'non-gifted'. They then observed the teachers' actual behaviour during lessons with these children. The white gifted children were treated best of all; they were given more attention, called on more, praised more — and also criticized more. They were also chosen more often by the teachers in subsequent interviews as 'the most liked student', 'the brightest student', 'the leader of the class', and so on. When we look at the effects of race *per se*, we find that the black students were given less attention, praised less and criticized more than the whites. But again, there was an interaction between 'race' and the label 'gifted' or 'non-gifted': it was the gifted blacks who bore the brunt of the most negative reactions from the teacher, even when compared with the non-gifted blacks. It should be stressed that these were all white teachers, but in the Leacock[237] study there were similarly negative attitudes towards the black students found among the black teachers.

The Rubovits and Maehr study is useful because it does not simply point out the existence of the teacher-expectations effect, it also looks at how it operates in the teacher-child interaction — at what behaviour exactly is producing the effect. After about two hundred and fifty extensions and replications of his original work, Rosenthal[323] decided to survey the field and extract more of that kind of information. The factors which he put forward are only those which have been identified in a number of different studies, and which fewer than 20 per cent have contradicted. There are four categories: climate, feedback, input and output. *Climate* is really warmth, attention and emotional support given to the 'gifted' child. It is evident in tone of voice, mood, smiling, and a variety of non-verbal gestures and signals. *Feedback* is acknowledgment and praise in response to the pupil's behaviour. With large classes many pupils are necessarily ignored even when they have their hands up for the right answer; gifted students are seldom ignored in this way and get more praise when they are called on. *Input* refers to the fact that teachers teach more material directly to the gifted child — and more difficult material. *Output*, which is closely related to feedback, is the fact that teachers give the gifted child more opportunity to contribute — call on them more, ask them harder questions, give more time for an answer and prompt them more towards a correct answer.

It should be stressed that teacher expectations are not automatic, and neither do they inevitably affect children's progress. Of the studies he surveyed, Rosenthal found that about one-third provided substantial evidence of the expectations effect, and we do not know what distinguishes the situations where it was found from those where it was not. So we have an ambiguous situation, where we have evidence of a very damaging, though unevenly distributed phenomenon. We might speculate that these effects are more likely to operate where there are a wealth of cultural expectations attaching to particular categories of children, rather than the contrived labels of experimenters, but that case remains to be proven. In any event, teachers' expectations are not the sole explanation of black under-achievement, and we have to consider some other factors involved.

Race in the classroom
Here we are really considering the social psychology of the classroom, and there is not a lot of direct evidence on the racial aspects

of this situation. Teachers interact with children and both come to this exchange with expectations and preconceptions which will help to structure their perceptions of the other's behaviour. While they are not prisoners of their stereotypes, they may have little control over their behaviour being viewed in that light. To a degree, the classroom is a microcosm of society, and their relationship will inevitably reflect some nuances of the relationship between the social categories they embody, in the wider society — in terms of race, class and sex. The same applies to the interaction of child and child.

Irwin Katz[209] has done some important research into inter-racial situations. He maintains that:

> . . . low expectation of success is an important detrimental factor in the peformance of minority children attending integrated schools. The evidence is strong that Negro children have feelings of inferiority which arise from awareness of actual differences in racial achievement, or from irrational acceptance of the white group's stereotype of Negroes.

In his studies of interracial work situations, blacks were found to 'display marked social inhibition and subordination to white partners' in group tasks. In co-operative problem-solving tasks they 'made fewer proposals than did whites and tended to accept the latter's contributions uncritically'. When actually displaying equal ability on tasks, blacks still rated whites' ability higher than their own. Again, blacks 'tended to accept passively the suggestions of their white companions' even when these were actually wrong answers to problems.

In another experiment[208], although black students performed an 'eye-hand co-ordination task better with a white tester than a black one, when the same task was described as a test of IQ, their performance with the white tester was depressed markedly and elevated slightly with the black tester. Eye-hand co-ordination, says Katz, is not an ability which blacks are stereotyped as lacking. On the IQ test, however, where potent expectations do exist, particularly in the minds of whites, performance suffered in the presence of the white tester.

Obviously one would hesitate to translate these findings from a different situation in a different era directly into the contemporary classroom. But they do bring out into the open some of the ways in which the lowered expectations of all parties reinforce one another in a self-fulfilling spiral. For example, it is very difficult for black students to transcend their own and others' lowered expectations, if even evidence of equal or superior ability is under-rated.

For the present author, there is still a credibility gap between the abstract discussion of social psychological processes and their illustration in experimental situations, on the one hand, and the day-to-day business of teaching and evaluating black children in the classroom. A classic study by Rist goes some way towards bridging that divide.[316]

Rist made a very detailed study of a Washington school, and over a period of three years he intensively studied the actual behaviour of teachers and children in the classroom. What he looked at was the social organization of the classroom: how the teacher distributed the children through the geographical space of the room. He thought this might reflect the teacher's attitude towards the various children *and* affect their experience, through the amount of access they had to her, how well they could hear her lessons and generally participate. He first looked at the information the teacher had on each child before they entered the class; each parent had filled out a registration form giving a lot of detail about the home, area and general status of the family. Then there were social workers' reports on problem children and problem families; two days before the beginning of term the mother and child were interviewed to get the child's medical history and also information about behaviour; finally there were reports on older brothers and sisters from teachers who had already taught members of the family. Now strictly speaking, none of this information is directly relevant to the educational performance of any particular child, but Rist shows how it was *made* relevant, because together with the teacher's reactions to the children in the first few days, it was made the basis for deciding where the children would sit in the classroom.

The children placed on table 1 differed from the children put on the other two tables in a number of obvious ways. They were better dressed, their clothes were generally newer, cleaner and better looked after. Rist also noticed that the table 2 and 3 children were generally less clean, some smelled of urine, and although there was not a clear gradient of skin colour, there was a greater predominance of darker skinned children on the lower tables. The behaviour of the children was very different, too. The natural leaders and the ones who talked most had been grouped on table 1 and their pre-eminence was clear from the beginning; they continued to dominate the interaction with the teacher, effectively pushing the others out to the periphery, without any discouragement from the teacher.

Table 1 children were given all the major tasks of responsibility. They also used far more Standard American English, compared to the greater use of black dialect on the other tables, which favoured them in the question-and-answer sessions with the teacher.

Rist felt that the teacher had not consciously used the background information to arrange the children according to social class; rather that she had a certain reference group herself, of educated middle-class blacks, and the children were evaluated for their 'goodness of fit' to that ideal, in a simple attempt to predict scholastic performance. Quite early on the teacher told Rist that the table 1 children were 'fast learners' while the rest 'had no idea of what was going on'.

The teacher devoted a hugely disproportionate amount of her time to table 1. She would always use them to exemplify what the class should be doing or how they should behave. In storytelling or relating experiences outside school they would invariably be picked to stand up and talk. After a while this was beginning to handicap the lower tables, because apart from the implicit discouragement, they simply were not getting their fair share of instruction from the teacher. Rist noticed that in May of that year, in one hour-long observation period, the teacher addressed no remarks directly to tables 2 and 3, except for two commands to the children to sit down.

Now of course the children themselves were not passive in this situation; they attended to what was going on and behaved accordingly. The children on table 1 clearly identified with the teacher and modelled their behaviour on hers; they began to belittle and disparage the other children and to tell them off when they misbehaved. The major responses of the lower table children were withdrawal and in-group hostility. Sometimes the withdrawal was physical, in the sense of children leaving the classroom, but mostly it was psychological, the child drifting off into a world of her own that might be more satisfactory than the reality around her. Not surprisingly, these children simply learned far less than the table 1 children by the end of the year.

When the class came to move on to the next year, exactly the same kind of geographical sorting process went on. But for the new teacher, there was not only background information and the teacher's report on each child, there was also 'objective' evidence of attainment from the child's recorded academic progress, or lack of it. And so the story went on; by the following year, the children's paths were firmly established, and each new teacher had more and more objective information by which to evaluate them: reading scores, IQ scores, evaluations from speech teachers and so on. But essentially the bandwagon had started in the first week of school-life with the teacher's first evaluation based on background. By the time two or three years had passed, this was no longer important because the process had taken on a momentum of its own: by treating the children differently, they had indeed progressed at different rates and by then appeared to deserve the labels that had attached to them.

Clearly, this is an extreme example and, perhaps significantly, it dates from a time (in the late 1960s) before much was generally known about teacher expectations. But it would be wrong to assume that it has no relevance as a result. One would not have to spend very long in British staffrooms to discover that the 'good'/'poor' home classification is alive and well, and although it may not materialize in classroom organization and discriminatory teaching in the same way as in Rist's study, it is unlikely that it has *no* effect on teacher expectations and pupil performance.

West Indian children and under-achievement

It has *not* been the purpose of this chapter to argue that teachers' lowered expectations of West Indian children alone account for their under-achievement in schools. We have been concerned to emphasize these factors in order to correct what is seen as an imbalance in previous explanations, where they have received relatively little attention. Nearly every other conceivable factor has been considered at one time or another, from the cultural backgrounds, home-circumstances, child-minding experiences, general health and welfare, linguistic and cognitive 'deficits' or differences, behaviour problems, through to the resourcing of the schools, their overt and 'hidden' curricula and national and local education policy. They have been extensively evaluated by, for example, Essen and Ghodsian[110], Tomlinson[392] and Taylor[378], and there is little purpose in yet again reviewing these summaries. Teacher attitudes and expectations have had only limited coverage in these analyses, primarily because so little is known about them. As Taylor[378] writes, although a few studies indicate 'that teachers may well have negative attitudes towards ethnic minority pupils. . . . Whether this is really the case on a large scale and to what extent it influences day-to-day contact and perpetuates the cycle of under-achievement by negative labelling and low expectation is difficult to estimate.'

Other writers have been less circumspect; from her survey of teacher attitudes, Brittan[44] argued that:

There was evidence in the many comments on these items that in the teachers' eyes the cause of difficulties with black children lay principally in their upbringing, in their home environment, in innate characteristics or in the disruptive effects of immigration itself. In contrast there was little reference to the possibility of any adverse factors either originating in or being exacerbated by schools.

The items mentioned specifically concerned West Indian pupils: they elicited a high degree of consensus from the teachers on the children's academic and social behaviour, which the majority evaluated negatively. Brittan suggests that the generality of these kinds of responses amounts to a stereotype. A considerably smaller-scale study by Edwards[106] also suggested that student teachers may have somewhat negative and lower expectations of black pupils. And Rex and Tomlinson[313] found that among head teachers, '. . . there was a strong feeling . . . that the learning process was slower for West Indian children, that they lacked the ability to concentrate for any length of time, and that they would tend to under-achieve and be "remedial".' Partial though this evidence is, it must be remembered that it has been drawn from questionnaires, whose purposes are usually rather transparent. It therefore probably underestimates both the extent and the extremity of these attitudes in the teaching profession, as most respondents would naturally not wish to present themselves in the unfavourable light of appearing 'prejudiced' against black children.

On the basis of evidence submitted to them, the Rampton Committee on ethnic minority education was persuaded of the dangers of teacher attitudes and expectations about black pupils. In their interim report, 'West Indian children in our (*sic*) schools', they say that:

> We are convinced from the evidence that we have obtained that racism, both intentional and unintentional, has a direct and important bearing on the performance of West Indian children in our schools. . . . Teachers who hold explicitly racist views . . . are very much in the minority. We have, however, found some evidence of what we have described as unintentional racism in the behaviour and attitudes of other teachers whom it would be misleading to describe as racist in the commonly accepted sense . . . For example, there seemed to be a fairly widespread opinion among the teachers to whom

we spoke that West Indian pupils inevitably caused difficulties. These pupils were, therefore, seen either as problems to be put up with or, at best, deserving sympathy. . . . low expectations of the academic ability of West Indian pupils by teachers can often prove a self-fulfilling prophecy. Many teachers feel that West Indians are unlikely to achieve in academic terms. . . .[310]

While it is difficult to gather empirical evidence of the entire process whereby teacher attitudes are translated into expectations and thence pupil achievements, Green[151] has recently illuminated some of the steps along the way. In an ingenious and complex study of classroom interaction in seventy multiracial classes he has related teacher ethnocentrism and teaching style to pupil self-concepts. Compared to the highly 'tolerant' teachers in his sample, the highly intolerant teachers directed far less individual attention to West Indian students, and considerably less than would be expected if time were divided equally between ethnic groups; perhaps as a result:

Those [students] who receive the most individual attention from the highly tolerant teachers, boys of West Indian origin, also have more positive self-concepts than boys of the same ethnic group taught by highly intolerant teachers.

The same kind of imbalance existed in the amount of 'didactic' teaching directed at the different ethnic groups, the West Indians receiving less than their fair share from the highly intolerant teachers. The West Indians fared a little better in terms of oral questioning by intolerant teachers, and while they received more than their fair share of negative criticism from both kinds of teachers, the tolerant teachers directed this more to individual children while the intolerant teachers addressed it to the group as a whole. This is not clear-cut evidence of racial discrimination in schools in general, particularly as highly intolerant teachers will hopefully be a small proportion of the profession, but it does illustrate the likely effects of ethnocentric attitudes and teaching styles on pupils' self-concepts — and possibly achievements.

A consumer's-eye-view of teachers' expectations of black pupils is provided by Riley[315] in her conversations with black senior girls in a London school. Audrey and Angela vividly describe how they felt the teacher divided them up into the more academic O-level stream and the lower-status CSE group:

Audrey: It's who she likes. If you are a big mouth who
            likes to back chat her, she chucks you in the CSE
            and if you're a softy, you know, listen and don't
            talk a lot, she puts you in the O-level. . . .
Angela: Every time you talked, you know, 'Hey, so and
            so'; you know, we couldn't talk because we were
            split up. CSE couldn't talk to O-level and O-level
            to CSE.

Riley notes that the girls had not perceived this as racist, although
her 'own count of who had been placed in each of the groups
suggests that most of the black girls had been placed in the CSE
group'. Furthermore, 'there was one area, careers advice, in which a
number of the girls suggested that less was expected of them
because they were black':

Audrey: She sort of puts you off . . . . instead of encourag-
            ing you to do something she puts you off. That's
            why most of the girls don't go to her for advice
            about jobs. . . .
Isatou: She puts everyone off. She's another one pre-
            judiced, isn't it? She seems like she wants you
            to end up in Tesco's packing beans. . . .

Cashmore[62] has recently suggested that another way teachers' expectations become a reality is through the channelling of black pupils
into sporting rather than academic pursuits, and indeed the
Rampton Committee[310] commented that teachers:

May have high expectations of [West Indian pupils'] . . .
potential in areas such as sport, dance, drama and art. If these
particular skills are unduly emphasized there is a risk of establishing a view of West Indian children that may become a
stereotype and teachers may be led to encourage these pupils
to pursue these subjects at the expense of their academic
studies.

There are two other dimensions to this issue which must be taken
into account. Firstly, teacher expectations are not simply important
for their own sake, but also for the added meaning they give to all

190

the other factors mentioned. That is, they create a climate of evaluation around black pupils within which all the other factors may be interpreted. To give just one example, *given* a set of beliefs about West Indian intellectual abilities, it was altogether more likely that the children's language would be interpreted as 'deficient' rather than different. The central role of the teacher in the child's educational experience makes teacher attitudes and expectations the very fulcrum on which that experience pivots.

Secondly, we have to acknowledge the role of the teacher's experience as well as his/her pre-existing attitudes and beliefs. Self-fulfilling prophecies have two consequences in all of this: they result in lowered achievement for the pupils *and* they confirm their own validity for the teacher. Thus they are not only self-fulfilling, but also self-sustaining. And teachers not only have direct experience of West Indian underachievement, they can also read and learn; this issue has received such extensive coverage in the press and educational media that few teachers can be unaware of the association of 'under-achievement' with 'black children'. The terms have become almost synonymous (with 'behaviour problems' following closely in their wake) — so that even with the most impeccably fair-minded attitudes and beliefs, teachers can hardly help but be influenced by the substantial empirical evidence of black failure in the schools. As Taylor wrote[378], '*Depressing* though it is to relate, it appears inescapable that by any standard of comparison the pupil of West Indian origin is under-achieving' (italics added). There is an unfortunate *double-entendre* here, in that the 'depression' may be of black achievement levels. It is ironic that scientific evidence of underachievement, gathered as a necessary preliminary to ameliorative action, itself may provide a further twist to the story — by reinforcing lowered expectations, and thus achievement. Perhaps some optimism can be drawn from the studies of Driver[104] (with its acknowledged flaws), and more recently Rutter[328]. Both provide some evidence of some circumstances in which some West Indian children are not blatantly underachieving. It will be entirely constructive if the media coverage given to this kind of information helps to turn the tide of teacher expectations, while not undermining the pressure for fundamental structural changes, without which black underachievement will continue.

8
Education for equality

A rationale for multiracial education

This is not the place for an all-embracing discussion of the aims of education. Multiracial education in Britain, however, illuminates particular problem areas within that general body of discussion. For example, the issue of how far education is, or should be, an agent of social change and a vehicle for achieving social equality, is one which has taxed educational theorists and policy-makers for many years. But insofar as enlightened multiracial education policy was successful in creating racial equality within the schools, so would it contrast with (and begin to undermine) the racial inequality in the society at large. It would be a naive optimist who argued that social equality could simply be achieved in this way; nevertheless, to the extent that the school, in the process of pursuing its 'ordinary' educational objectives, fosters values or expectations which conflict or comply with the existing social structure, then it becomes a term (however minor) in the social equation. It therefore becomes impossible to consider multiracial education in a vacuum, for it is either an agent of social change or of social stability.

If we were to specify the ideal objectives of multiracial education, they would be best expressed as the attainment of racial equality. The problem with such a utopian formulation is that either disbelief must be unreasonably suspended, or the idea is relegated to the long term (along with 'world peace' and other millennial goals) while we get on with more 'realistic' day-to-day expedients. But, as Keynes said, in the long run we are all dead, and it hardly needs to be stated that today is also part of the future. Racial equality may well be elusive, but even the authors of the Black Papers pay lip-service to 'equality of educational opportunity', and so long as multiracial schools effectively deny that cardinal principle, we have a mandate for change.

There are two principal dimensions to racial inequality in education, themes which have recurred constantly throughout this volume; they help us to define what the objectives of multiracial education should be, as follows:

192

1 *The creation of an educational environment in which black minority children are not systematically disprivileged.* There is abundant evidence that black children are generally not realizing their full intellectual potential in British schools, as we have discussed. Social justice, at one extreme, and the integrity of the system at the other, require that this situation is rectified as our most imperative priority.

2 *The creation of an educational environment which not only embodies racial and cultural diversity, but also actively fosters positive inter-group attitudes and behaviour.* Much of this volume has attempted to tease out the direct and indirect effects of racism upon children, both black and white. Sivanandan once wrote that 'Children are the continuing measure of our humanity and we stand or fall by what we do to them.'[354] We might add that we also stand or fall by what we encourage them to do to each other. We cannot seriously pretend to any ideals of racial justice in society if we do not attend to their foundation in childhood.

We cannot here aspire to a definitive account of the relationship between school and society. We can acknowledge that it is a complex relationship and a dialectical one; it is clearly not the case that one single institution, like the education system, can unilaterally change the social structure around it. This reality has persuaded many people that the press of economic, social and political forces upon such an institution must inevitably circumscribe its effects. This argument would contend that the idea of education-led social change is an illusion and that it is rather the wider society that calls the tune and requires the education system to perform certain functions which will guarantee social stability. In its more extreme form this position views educational institutions as processing devices designed to prepare people for pre-determined roles in the social and occupational structure. Even in its milder form it depicts school and society in a chicken-and-egg relationship, though one in which educational change must wait upon social change rather than the other way round. Invariably this argument is accompanied by a regretful hand-wringing over the problems of initiating social change, with the inevitable conclusion that the cycle cannot be broken. This counsel of despair is one of the more effective sources of resistance to educational change.

It has to be said that the hard evidence for education leading social change in Britain is not very persuasive, and it is this rather than any ideological position which counsels realism on the issue of multiracial education and its effects. One does not have to be a Marxist to appreciate that, whatever the 'push' factors, black immigration to the UK was actively encouraged in order to meet the demand for unskilled and semi-skilled labour in the British economy, and that for many years it has been in the interests of the economy that black immigrants should remain thus employed. Racism has certainly assisted that process, and in the minds of the most Machiavellian politicians it would assist their repatriation, should unemployment continue to rise and the new technologies make the predicted inroads into the labour force. On the other hand it can be argued that mass repatriation is neither politically nor economically feasible, let alone morally defensible, that the new industrial society of automated industry and information technology will require more highly-skilled operatives than we are currently producing, and that it will need quite as much social stability as currently obtains, so that an alienated and embittered black population rising to demand its due must be avoided at all costs.

A cogent argument could be made for either scenario, but with quite opposite predictions as to whether education for racial equality would be 'in the interests' of the system. There are, of course, other considerations beyond 'government policy' and crude 'economic forces' which will determine the course of multiracial education: public opinion is one (and opinion within the educational establishment). There is evidence in recent years that both are more favourably inclined towards positive initiatives in this area, no doubt reinforced by the vivid images of inner-city riots (and despite official assurances that these were 'not racial').

In any event, whether it is supported or countermanded from outside, there is latitude within the education system which can allow a substantial degree of change. Of course it can be limited by resourcing decisions, or by increasing centralized control over the curriculum, as we have seen. But it remains the case that the majority of what goes on in the school and in the classroom is still determined by teachers themselves, and thus a favourable climate of opinion within the teaching profession is probably the most important single factor in the success or failure of multiracial education. This itself is not unproblematic, as we shall discuss, but the necessary flexibility is potentially there.

There is a further issue which is worth mentioning here, and it relates to our second objective. While the first objective is undeniably 'educational', at least in the narrowest sense of the word, the second is arguably so. Many people would maintain that it is not the business of the education system to foster a particular set of values especially where these may conflict with values current in the wider society. Related to that is the feeling that educationalists should not be self-appointed arbiters of children's attitudes in a democratic society. These are not simple issues to resolve, but we can spell out their implications. If we do not encourage a value-system in this way, or at least offer it to our children as an alternative, then we must accept that the school will be, by default, a vehicle of *status quo* values, and we will have to live with the consequences of racism endlessly reinforced and recreated through succeeding generations. The education system is not the only arena for these debates; other opinion-formers have fewer scruples about their effects on their constituencies; the fourth estate and the media in general are cases in point, and they may be even less representative.

We are all aware that innovation, whether social or technological, has often proceeded from the ideas of a minority in conflict with prevailing beliefs. It is the means by which the minority attempts to gain a wider currency for its views that determines whether the progression is democratic or not. There are even precedents for 'anti-democratic' strategies to speed social reform which we have largely accepted without query. Successive governments have abolished capital punishment and maintained that stance while knowing that the majority of the electorate opposes this policy and have not mandated them to oppose their wishes. This is not a principle which is generally defensible, but it has become more common since the 'liberal hour' of the 1960s saw substantial reforming legislation which was 'in advance' of public opinion.

We have so far considered aspects of the complex and diffuse relationship between educational policy and society. If the future of multiracial education seems uncertain, it may be clarified by considering it in historical context. We move to a brief evolutionary history of multiracial educational policy and practice in Britain.

'Education for coloured immigrants'

In the early 1960s the substantial black immigration of the previous few years was stemmed by legislation. As in other areas of society, the education system was presented with a relatively sudden influx of people for whom it was quite unprepared. Because this new population was concentrated in the major conurbations, in already deprived areas, the existing difficulties of urban education were both illuminated and to an extent exacerbated by the new arrivals. Thus, from the outset, black children in British schools were seen in a 'problem' context. Viewed in retrospect, the system's response to this new situation was initially naive. Though the children were termed 'the children of coloured immigrants', it was their recent immigration rather than their colour which was the focus of attention. Despite the racial disturbances in Nottingham and Notting Hill, sociologists gave less emphasis to 'colour prejudice' than to the 'immigrant-host relationship'[294], the class connotations of colour[245], and the problems of 'archetypal strangers' in a xenophobic society[23]. Educationalists were encouraged to believe, therefore, that racism was not a major factor, and the image of Britain as a 'tolerant' society that had welcomed and assimilated countless waves of immigrants over many centuries still held good. The problems were therefore couched in terms of cultural differences, adjustment, language and behaviour, and these could clearly be ameliorated in time through accommodation and assimilation. There was envisaged a relatively temporary period of special provision which would iron out these obstacles to smooth integration.

Naturally, as the new element in the situation, the children themselves were in the spotlight. Because teachers had to deal with problems as the children manifested them, there was an inevitable tendency to see the problems as *in* the children. It therefore became a question of what we could do to or for them: they were, in effect, seen as 'problem children' rather than children presented with enormous problems.

The culture-shock of passing from rural Jamaica or Mirpur to a classroom in Brixton or Bradford in the space of a few days was often immensely numbing. It was partly cushioned by reception centres and reception classes in ordinary schools, but it rapidly became apparent that language problems were the major barrier to the children's entry into the mainstream education process. This became the prime focus of special provision for the immigrants, and within a relatively short time, English as a Second Language teaching (of an elementary kind) was provided by withdrawing Asian pupils into language classes, centres and individual or group tuition with peripatetic language teachers. At this point a basic error was committed in the diagnosis of West Indian language problems which has reverberated throughout the discussions of this issue ever since. Simply stated, the fact that West Indian children spoke a variety of English seemed to obviate the need for special language training. It was clear that the children's dialect was radically different from the Standard English medium of instruction in the school. But here we see a direct consequence of the confusion of 'difference' and 'deficit' discussed in the last chapter. For in a climate where expectations of the black child were low, and stereotypes abounded, it was all too easy for the different West Indian dialects to be seen as 'bad' or 'broken' English, which simply required correction. As Townsend wrote[394]:

> In class [the West Indian child] finds his teacher partly intel-
> ligible, he is frequently corrected for speaking bad English
> although this is the way he and his parents have always spoken
> their language, and he receives little in the way of special help,
> although the Asians in his class disappear every day for extra
> English lessons.

The idea of linguistic deficit brought with it the notion of cognitive deficit. There was a growing suspicion of general backwardness, and this was reinforced by observation of children who were silent and withdrawn or who alternatively responded with disruptiveness. It was a classic case of an ethnocentric and *situational* analysis of children's language, which need not have misled educationalists had they not had pre-conceptions about intellectual abilities, or had they listened to the children's language outside the classroom. It would have then been apparent that the children were quite as articulate and productive as any others, in a dialect which was descriptively rich and complex, but with a lexis, syntax and phonology which differed significantly from Standard English. As it was, West Indian children were doubly disadvantaged: they did not receive the systematic language training that they required to comply with the linguistic demands of the classroom, and the very lowered evaluation of their intellectual abilities which contributed to the misdiagnosis of their language difficulties, *itself* produced depressing effects on their performance, which in turn further lowered expectations. The reader is referred to Edwards[106] for a fuller discussion of this topic.

It is not difficult to imagine the situation of a child who daily experiences this devaluation, together with many others. It is entirely unsurprising that many children reacted with hostility and resentment, and equally unsurprising that these reactions also reinforced teachers' negative perceptions of black children. On both intellectual and behavioural grounds many black children found themselves in special classes and special schools. Coard[73] wrote anecdotally but powerfully about this traffic, and the hugely disproportionate allocation of black children to ESN schools became a highly controversial issue (see also Tomlinson [391, 393] for a more recent analysis).

Integration and 'dispersal'

Through the 1960s the 'problem' connotation of multiracial schools became more firmly entrenched in the public consciousness. Anxieties about educational ghettoes and falling standards, however misplaced, were never very far from the surface of the debate, and one solution was sought in the compulsory integration of black and white pupils. Government policy attempted to satisfy conflicting demands from the electorate by both closing the door on further black immigration and trying to do its best by those settlers who were already here. As a result, it passed the most explicitly racialist legislation ever to reach the statute book in order to restrict the entry of East African Asians, while simultaneously outlawing incitement to racial hatred, and some forms of racial discrimination, in the Race Relations Acts. Roy Jenkins, then the Home Secretary, eloquently described the liberal side of this coin; he defined the kind of integration that government hoped to encourage as 'equal opportunity, accompanied by cultural diversity, in an atmosphere of mutual tolerance'. The ideal of integration was inspired by a transatlantic analogy with American social policy, which had recognized that *de jure* and *de facto* segregation was not only racially divisive, it also discriminated against black children via the *quality* of schools they attended. Effective desegregation of the schools and an improvement in the quality of black education could only be achieved by wholesale movements of population, and realistically this was not a viable strategy. However, a compromise could be struck by integrating the children on a daily basis in the schools. Thus, racial mixing by busing huge numbers of children between schools in the black ghettoes and the white suburbs was actively pursued and became a liberal article of faith.

The principle of busing had its enthusiasts in England, too. The DES had laid the groundwork for such a policy in its circular 7/65 which had advised that the proportion of 'immigrant' children in any schools should not exceed 30 per cent. This was partly justified as a response to immigrant language difficulties, and the need to spread the load of extra teacher-attention needed to meet them. However, there were indications in the circular that other considerations had influenced the policy:

It will be helpful if the parents of non-immigrant children can see that practical measures have been taken to deal with the problems in the schools, and that the progress of their own children is not being restricted by the undue preoccupation of the teaching staff with the linguistic and other difficulties of the immigrant children . . . it is to everyone's disadvantage if the problems within the school are allowed to become so great that they cause a decline in the general standard of education provided.[86]

This suggested that the policy was designed as much to assuage white anxieties as anything else. Several local authorities initiated 'dispersal' policies but they were not an unqualified success. The fact that 'immigrant' children were dispersed, irrespective of whether they were recently immigrant or not, irrespective of whether they had language difficulties or not, and this included some West Indian children (who, in contrast to what we now know, were then thought *not* to have language difficulties), reinforced the more cynical interpretation of the policy. It seemed that 'colour' rather than 'language difficulties' lay nearer the root of the policy. The political repercussions of this realization led to its ultimate demise. Kirp[220] argues that the British way of 'doing good by doing little', of dealing with race and education by 'benign stealth' (i.e. do not *mention* race) has been altogether more effective, and that it was precisely the 'racial explicitness' of the dispersal policy which carried the seeds of its own destruction. However, there is a distinction to be made between racially explicit and explicitly racialist, and it was the latter which determined the fate of the policy. (See also Dorn and Troyna[99] for an analysis of 'the absence of a coherent and explicit national policy on multiracial education despite the DES's stated commitment to producing such a policy as long ago as 1971').

Certainly this era saw racialism become more explicit in every area of public life. The PEP Report[295] uncovered racial discrimination on a massive scale in housing, employment and service industries. Enoch Powell, in his infamous 'rivers of blood' speech, predicted a calamitous future of race riots and urban insurrections of a kind that were currently raging in the US. More significantly, he amplified and reinforced white hostility towards blacks, giving racialism a new respectability. His single-minded pursuit of political capital towed the locus of the debate significantly to the Right and helped to set the stage for the emergence of overtly fascist political groups whose views on repatriation, 'voluntary' or otherwise, seemed hardly more extreme than his own.

The new *zeitgeist* was not lost on British children; over a period of five or six years, several studies showed that they were quite as aware of race as their American counterparts, and that the rudiments of prejudice were developing from the pre-school years onwards[262, 304, 314]. This was not a comfortable discovery: it was only slowly accepted within the education system, and then only by a minority of teachers. Racialism was not obvious in the classroom, and as we have discussed, the idea that primary school children could in any way reflect the complex and divisive attitudes of the adult world was anathema. In any case, the principal responsibility must lie with the parents, and they were largely outside the teacher's sphere of influence. If the early analysis of the school's contribution was over-simple it was also understandable in that analysis and criticism was directed towards the overt curriculum, and its most tangible manifestation in the form of books and materials. While the revision of outdated and ethnocentric children's literature was long overdue, it was rapidly apparent that it would not be achieved without opposition. 'Racism in children's books' quickly became a media issue which simultaneously over-exposed and trivialized the discussion. Irate correspondents to the serious press assured their readership that a childhood spent in the company of *Little Black Sambo* and *The Three Golliwogs* had had no detrimental effects, witness their own 'tolerant' attitudes towards 'coloured people'. More authoritative educationalists played a part in depicting the critics of racist books as humourless, politically-motivated, literary philistines who sought to deprive the children of their cultural heritage. Ten years on, the debate continues: as this is written, the BBC's 'World at One' programme carries an interview with the author of *Mary Poppins* who has recently decided that her classic story would benefit from the revision of the chapter on exotic peoples; if we can disregard the satirical tone of the item, we can assume that some progress has been made on the issue.

Teaching Race and Black Studies

Two priorities stood out from the growing disquiet about the intrusion of racism into the schools: one was the need to educate white children against prejudice, while the other stressed the importance of fostering a positive sense of racial and cultural identity among black children. Initially, for the reasons we have discussed, these aims were pursued at the secondary school level, when

200

it was assumed that adolescent children would be sufficiently mature to cope with the complexity of the issues and to make more adult judgements. The question of white children's prejudices was taken up by the Schools Council Humanities Curriculum Project, as part of a more general investigation of appropriate teaching methods and materials for social education programmes. Along with kits of materials on 'Poverty', 'The Family', 'Relations between the Sexes', 'Education' etc., the project produced what came to be known as the 'Race Pack' (Hipkin[174, 175]). This was a collection of background materials on various aspects of race relations and prejudice, in the form of literary extracts, poetry, political speeches, personal testimony and interviews, and it was accompanied by a teacher's handbook which gave guidance on the use of the materials in the classroom.

The 'Race Pack' came under fire from the very beginning; objections were raised to some of its contents which were felt to be potentially inflammatory and counterproductive, for example an extract from *Mein Kampf*. The criticism acquired some force in the context of the suggested ways of using the materials and, in particular, the role of the teacher in discussions. That is, rather than directly teaching about racism and race relations in an instructional mode, the teacher was envisaged as a neutral chairperson who would supervise a general discussion of the issues which would 'protect divergence of views among participants, rather than attempt to achieve consensus'. This low profile, *laisser faire* approach seemed to many people to be fraught with danger: without more active intervention from the teacher it seemed quite as likely that the discussion would move the participants towards greater prejudice as in the desired direction. Together with the more enlightened contents of the pack, a platform was being provided for some palpably racist material, which would apparently pass unchallenged by the teacher. And the pupil's reactions in discussion would be unpredictable and depend upon the existing attitudes and beliefs. These were not unreasonable suppositions; there was already evidence from elsewhere that race relations teaching programmes could backfire badly. Miller[260] set up courses in race relations for teenage apprentices on day release at a Further Education college, the courses included films, books, group discussions and visiting speakers and lasted for one to three hours per week. Overall, there was a significant *increase* in prejudice amongst the students; any doubt that this was a result of the programme was removed by the discovery that prejudice increased in proportion to the amount of race relations teaching received. Three hours a week produced more prejudice than two hours and so on; only in the control group who had no such teaching was there no change in attitudes.

While the pessimistic conclusion to be drawn from Miller's study is not what it first appears, the study illustrates well the point about the initial attitudes of the students helping to determine the direction of attitude change. In fact, over half of Miller's subjects had registered maximum scores on the attitude scale measuring prejudice before the programme. They were not the best candidates for attitude change, perhaps, and certainly not on the basis of such a short programme.

Presumably the originators of the 'Race Pack' philosophy hoped to avoid the kind of boomerang effect that may well lie behind the Miller findings (that is, the idea that these highly-prejudiced students resented the stereotyped liberal perspective on race and became more firmly entrenched) and at the same time avoid the opposite extreme of teacher-as-successful-indoctrinator. However, the middle, neutral course they advised found little favour, and the potential pitfalls of the approach caused a lot of controversy, which eventually submerged the Pack, unpublished. It should be said that this was on the basis of speculation about its effects, not evidence; the evidence ultimately pointed the other way. Bagley and Verma[13], for example, tested the 'Race Pack' materials in a two month teaching programme for two to four hours per week, with fourteen- to sixteen-year-olds. Even with the 'neutral chairperson' approach, they found a 'small but significant change' in prejudiced attitudes in a more positive direction. The boys, who were initially more hostile to black people than the girls, were noticeably less hostile after the programme. The girls, though less hostile from the outset, changed their attitudes even more in the course of the work. Even after the programme some 43 per cent of the boys were still highly prejudiced, so there could only be some cautious optimism about the results, but one encouraging finding was that there seemed to be some carry-over from the teaching into the children's expressed choice of friends. There was an increase in inter-ethnic choices on a sociometric test after the programme, while there was no shift at all in a control group who had not been exposed to race relations teaching.

There are clearly many reasons which could account for the relatively small changes in attitudes recorded in studies like these. The bulk of the research material in this book would argue that the age of the children concerned was a critical factor. In other words, it may well be that by adolescence these attitudes are too firmly established and rationalized to respond to rather low-key teaching programmes, relegated to the periphery of the child's educational experience. However intrinsically valuable, they come at the end of a long period of learning in the family, the school and the outside world which may encourage contrary beliefs. In that context, a marginal, small-scale and uncertificated input on race appears to be too little and too late.

At the beginning of this section we referred to a growing consciousness of the need to foster a positive sense of racial and cultural identity among black children. Again, this was initially restricted to the secondary school level where Black Studies courses were mounted in response to demands from the children, the black community and progressive educationalists who recognized the absence of curricular material which would give black children any sense of their origins. It was an uneven development which took place in a minority of schools with little to guide it except the American precedent and a keen sense of the ethnocentric imbalance in the existing curriculum. That it was first and foremost directed towards black children made for political difficulties which probably limited its widespread acceptance; many schools and individual teachers viewed it as likely to increase racial divisions and were firmly opposed to the development.

The emphasis in these courses lay in the historical, geographical and cultural origins of Afro-Caribbean peoples, the history and development of Africans and black Americans, and to a lesser extent with the circumstances of contemporary black Britons. The concern with cultural 'roots' was regarded as a very necessary foundation for a positive identity, and research[263] had suggested that the more prominent sense of traditional culture enjoyed by the Asian children might afford them a degree of insulation against the worst excesses of devaluation by the prejudice they encountered. It is difficult to evaluate the success of these courses (though they were certainly popular among the children) because there was no formal assessment of their effects. Giles[135] provides some anecdotal material on Black Studies in a number of London schools and concludes that 'there was no clear expression of the purposes of the courses or how to achieve them'. No doubt this would be regarded as overly critical in a school like Tulse Hill which had pioneered such courses and refined them over a considerable period. In retrospect, more telling criticism might be made of the effects of Black Studies in taking the spotlight away from the mainstream curriculum and the reforms that were necessary there, but equally, many teachers who were involved in these efforts gained an awareness of the wider implications of 'black' curriculum material which they contributed to later developments.

Education for a multiracial society

The recognition of racism as an issue for schools signalled the end of the 'education for coloured immigrants' era. This cannot be precisely dated, but in the early to mid-1970s black children themselves became no longer the sole focus of the debate. Racism, after all, was 'in' whites and evidently took root in early childhood. The implication was clearly that the whole education process had to be examined for the contribution it might make. It also meant that the emphasis switched from the cognitive to the affective aspects of racial learning. Whereas the model with adolescent pupils had been to confront prejudice with factual and rational argument, primary school children were clearly not basing their feelings on a sophisticated appraisal of social facts, they were merely reflecting the affective content of adult attitudes in its simplest form: black=bad, white=good. But the question arose as to how the primary school could engage with this process within the limitations of an elementary level curriculum.

One solution was to begin to revise the conventional books and materials to which children were exposed. In only a minority of British classrooms was there any tangible recognition of the multiracial society. The treatment of black people in the majority of children's literature and educational materials was characterized by omission and stereotyping. Black people were largely invisible, and when they did appear in stories or factual books, it was invariably in a somewhat negative light or in a stereotyped role. Correcting these biases was seen to promote two beneficial effects: white children, it was hoped,would be less likely to have their prejudices reinforced, while black children would have positive black models with whom to identify, and would simply benefit from the recognition of their group in print and picture within the school. The strategy could be justified in the most conventional educational terms, for it was partly a process of correcting what were factual errors; it also involved the broadening of the children's educational experience through the introduction of new materials. The kind of new materials to be used was predicated by several factors: firstly, the goal of fostering cultural identity in black children and the emphasis on 'roots'; secondly, the tendency to try to confront 'prejudice' with 'fact', and thirdly, the continuing reluctance to confront racism head-on in the classroom. All pointed in the same direction, and together with the simple lack of availability of material which dealt with black people in Britain today, ensured that the greater proportion of the new input was concerned with the cultural backgrounds of the 'immigrants'.

It is useful to divert from the narrative at this point and consider the efficacy of this kind of approach, in contrast to some American studies with wider terms of reference. One of the most ambitious of these studies was one of the earliest. Trager and Yarrow[395] mounted a programme of 'inter-cultural education' for elementary school children which, having established that prejudiced racial and religious attitudes did exist, attempted to influence them through two types of teaching philosophy, methods and teaching materials:

> One experimental condition was designed to support democratic inter-cultural values, the second to maintain or foster group prejudices common in our culture.

The second condition was not so unethical as it appears: it amounted to a programme based on the *status quo*, which assumed that the development of prejudice was the norm; so it was less a deliberate intervention to increase prejudice than the continuation of methods in widespread use which did little to prevent prejudice developing. Exposure to these different programmes was achieved by forming 'clubs' of children who were withdrawn from the body of the class for particular activities:

> The neighbourhood was chosen as the curriculum area for the experimental material of both clubs. . . . The neighbourhood was particularly suitable for the purposes of this experiment since it was within the first-hand experience of the children and offered a good possibility of interpretation from either point of view. How people live, the work they do, how they celebrate holidays, worship, get along with neighbours etc., were learned through real and make-believe trips, stories, recordings, dramatizations, parties, painting pictures, meeting people, of their own or other neighbourhoods.[395]

The following is a small selection of the specific objectives of a number of the sessions, and the precise ways in which they were pursued. The objectives and methods listed are only those of the 'tolerance teaching programme'.

Objectives	Methods
To help the children perceive the neighbourhood as multi-cultured, to accept the people who live in it . . . (regardless of differences). To challenge the Jewish stereotype.	Construction of map, location of shops and personalities on it, exchange of information about people and places. Storytelling about 'Mr Cohen' and other minority figures
To help the children know that people do different kinds of work . . . that all work and all workers are important.	Role-playing in different jobs. Discussion of how each one helps the neighbourhood — illustrated by describing what happens when anyone stops. Visits to work places. Conversations with workers, etc.
To challenge the children's stereotype of Negro people. To prepare children for a successful social experience in which racial differences will not be a source of hostility and conflict. To provide (that) experience on the the occasion of Thanksgiving. To demonstrate acceptance and friendliness of Negro and white adults (teachers and parents) in a social situation.	Storytelling with incidental Negro characters. Preparation for inter-racial party with black guest of honour. Black and white adults at party behave non-sterotypically and with friendliness. Post-party group discussions.
To provide a situation in which (a) conflicts over colour differences are acknowledged and (b) good human relations in spite of colour differences are also acknowledged.	Symbolic story telling in terms of brown and white animals. Link made with humans. Further discussion of children's feelings about party and plans for another.

Even this very abbreviated version makes it clear that here was an attempt to deal with the issues of race, culture and religion directly, through the study of the neighbourhood where they all coalesce. As the authors pointed out, the study of the locality is a common theme in early schooling, so the related issues could be introduced in an unremarkable way. Although the language in which the objectives are couched is now rather dated, the researchers clearly had a sophisticated idea of what might be achieved with young children, and the results bore out their optimism. On before-after tests of the children's racial attitudes, the proportion of the experimental group who responded to blacks in hostile terms decreased from 46 per cent to 23 per cent and there were similar trends in their attitudes towards Jews. This compared with movement in the reverse direction for the 'prejudiced', *status quo* comparison group and small random changes in the control groups. The programme did not result in a large number of children totally accepting blacks; rather the main trend was from hostility to ambivalence, but in a short programme occupying little of the school day more dramatic changes would be unlikely if not suspect.

In a more recent study, Litcher and Johnson[243] looked at the effects of multi-ethnic reading books on children's attitudes, compared with control groups who used more traditional readers over a four month period:

> The results of this study dramatically indicate that the use of multi-ethnic readers in an elementary school will result in more favourable attitudes towards Negroes. The data . . . indicate that the reader decreased the preference for one's own racial group over the other. . . . The multi-ethnic reader resulted in a reduction of the amount of social distance placed between the white and Negro racial groups . . . the children in the experimental groups were less likely to exclude a child on the basis of race than were the controls . . . [and] . . . were less likely to attribute negative traits to Negroes and positive traits to whites.

Other studies have focused more upon black children. David Johnson[198] looked at the effect of teaching black history to a group of black American children of eight to thirteen years of age in a 'Freedom School' in Harlem. The children attended the school for two hours each Saturday morning over a period of four months, learning about both African history and the history of black people in America. Johnson reports that:

> The Freedom School . . . seemed to have some effect on the boys in the areas of self-attitudes, equality of Negroes and whites, attitudes towards Negroes, and attitudes towards civil rights. That is, they became more confident in themselves,

more convinced that Negroes and whites were equals, more positive towards Negroes, and more militant towards civil rights.

The same changes were found among the girls, though less strongly. The parents of these children were all involved in the civil rights movement, so the children were probably more disposed towards accepting these beliefs than other children, but equally, as the parents would have encouraged these attitudes long before the children's attendance at the Freedom School, the *change* in attitudes it produced is more remarkable.

Other studies have produced similar changes in self-concept and attitudes towards blackness with much younger black children both in elementary schools (Bunton and Weissbach[53]) and in the pre-school years (Golin[142]). One study, though a small-scale one, is particularly important because it not only demonstrates that these effects can be achieved in racially-mixed situations (as opposed to exclusively black projects) but also that the effects can carry through to the children's behaviour. Belle Likover[239] worked with a group of girls on an interracial summer camp which they attended daily. By concentrating on a small group, twenty-six girls in all, it was possible to observe the effects of her programme on the children's interaction with each other. Only half of them participated in the experimental programme, the other half serving as a control group for comparison. In the first week of the camp the programme was the same for both groups, the theme being Jewish holidays. Subsequently:

Black history was introduced to the girls in the experimental group at the beginning of the second week through many program forms including stories, dance, song, art and discussion. The counselor, with help from the camp director, translated the historical material to a level appropriate for six- to seven-year old girls. Using the camp's general theme for the second week, independence and freedom, the experimental group concentrated its attention on the struggle of blacks for freedom. During the third week . . . the girls explored the contributions that blacks have made to American society under the program theme, 'great Americans'. Biographical material about Negro heroes (like Martin Luther King and John Henry) was presented.

During the same period the control group dealt with issues of freedom of speech and American heroes in a more general way without the emphasis on black people. However, the race issue was not avoided:

> Discussion of the girls' feelings about race were stimulated by the introduction of two picture books, *In Henry's Backyard* and *Your Skin and Mine*. Both books present classical anthropological concepts about race in a form that elementary school children can understand.

The effects of the programme were assessed by three measures: a measure of the extent to which each child behaved positively towards members of the other race, as rated by counsellors and a non-participant observer, at the end of the first and fourth weeks of camp; daily records of each child's behaviour towards children of the other race, and interviews with the girls' mothers to find out what racial attitudes the children relayed at home as a result of their daily experiences. Each of the interaction measures showed a significant increase in cross-racial contact and friendship in the experimental group, compared to a minimal change in the control group. These changes were corroborated by the mothers' accounts of their children's comments and reactions to the experience. The black mothers recognized an increased self-confidence and self-respect in their children, and none of them were informed as to the nature of the study until the end of the interview.

Finally we turn to one of the more recent studies in this area, conducted by the present author in the mid-70s[264]. It combined many of the principles and practices already discussed here, in an attempt to influence the course of young children's racial attitude development through a year-long educational intervention programme. It was directed at both majority and minority-group children simultaneously, in mixed classes, with the emphasis placed on the modification of their ordinary school experience, rather than supplementary race-related teaching tacked on to the normal curriculum. Two innovations provided the main stimulus: (1) the introduction of multiracial, multicultural literature and curricula, and (2) the introduction of minority-group class teachers. The rationale for the first of these need not be rehearsed here; in the second instance, it was obvious that there was an absence of black personnel in the schools, except in ancillary roles as cleaners, kitchen staff etc., and it was felt that black teachers might exert a significant influence on the children's attitudes. A good relationship with a black person in this familiar role might, for white children, generalize into a more positive attitude towards black people as a group. Similarly, for black children, the presence of a black person in this status position would constitute a recognition of their group's worth, a contradiction of stereotypes, and a model with whom they could identify.

The target group for the study was drawn from schools in two large English cities with substantial minority populations. The children were all in the five to eight years age range; it was felt that these influences should be brought to bear at the earliest opportunity so that elementary attitudes would not be too firmly established to be modified. Pre-testing of the children's attitudes at the beginning of the school year showed that while there had been some changes since the author's earlier study[263], there remained ample scope for influence in a positive direction. A majority of the white children still consistently favoured the white figures on the tests, and rejected the black and brown figures, though often with less explicit hostility than in the earlier study (see Chapter 5). Significantly fewer West Indian children identified with the white figure than before (27 per cent cf. 48 per cent) though the proportion of these children maintaining that they would 'rather be' the white figure had not declined accordingly (78 per cent cf. 82 per cent). Clearly, although their identification had become more realistic, no doubt reflecting the growth of black consciousness in the interim, there remained a kind of ambivalence. At the very least this seems to denote a clear awareness of the correlation of race and privilege in the society.

The material input into each classroom consisted principally of books but also included wall-charts, posters, tape-slide sequences and records, together with reading games, alphabets and number-charts for the younger age groups. The greater proportion of this material had to do with the cultural backgrounds of the minorities, though some dealt with contemporary urban Britain. All of the material featured minority figures in a natural, accepting and non-stereotyped way in a variety of multiracial contexts. In addition to this the teachers developed project work with the children on themes arising out of the materials and these ideas were exchanged between different classes. The twelve classes involved in the study were distributed as shown opposite.

	Age	Race of the teacher		
		English	West Indian	Asian
Conventional	5–6	1	3	5
materials	7–8	2	4	6
Multiracial	5–6	7	9	11
materials	7–8	8	10	12

The top half of the table represents those classes who did not receive any input of materials, but retained their existing materials which were conventionally majority-group oriented. The numerals on the left of the table signify the age range of each class. A limitation to the study was that its scope did not allow the inclusion of more than one class per cell of the table. Thus class '4' was the class of seven- to eight-year-olds with a West Indian teacher using conventional materials, while class '11' was the class of five- to six-year-olds with an Asian teacher using multiracial materials, and so on.

When the children's attitudes were re-tested at the end of the year there were no significant changes in the classes who had white teachers using conventional materials (see the Appendix, section (i)); in fact these were the only classes in which there was the slightest deterioration in attitudes. But in the classes exposed to minority teachers or multiracial materials, or both, there were marked changes. Taking these groups as a whole, there was a discernible shift in the white children's attitudes towards greater acceptance of the minority figures and less hostile rejection of them (see the Appendix, section (ii)). It is significant that all the recorded changes were in the desired direction; no child became more hostile to the black figures, which might normally be expected through chance variation. It was among the West Indian and Asian children, though, that the most dramatic results emerged. Of those who had originally identified with the white figures or maintained that they would rather be the white figure, between one-half and two-thirds of the children had reversed their choices by the end of the year, to identify with and prefer the figures representing their own group (see the Appendix, section (iii)).

The analysis of the results allowed an estimate of the extent to which the teachers, as opposed to the materials, had contributed to these changes. Here it seemed that while the race of the teacher *had* contributed significantly to the changes, the greater part of the changes could be attributed to the effects of the materials (see the Appendix, section (iv)). Care should be taken in generalizing too broadly from these findings, because of the relatively small sample involved (274 children) distributed between twelve classes, with an inevitably wide variation in the ability and the commitment of the teachers concerned; categorical statements of the kind that 'materials are more effective than teachers' would not be justified by the data. Obviously there are all manner of questions about the permanence of the changes and their effects on the children's behaviour which cannot be answered without a further study. However, several of the teachers related how reluctant readers had been 'seduced' into the process by the recognition of children like themselves in the materials, which they had not encountered before. Other teachers described how parents had been delighted to discover the changes taking place in the classrooms, enabling the teacher to gain the confidence of some parents who had previously felt that the school ignored their children's background and experience.

If there was a danger in this kind of approach, it was this: the emphasis on the beneficial effects of multiracial books and materials, while important, could be represented as an easy solution to the problems of multiracial education. To be sure, the replacement of conventional classroom materials would be a costly process, but altogether simpler than the more profound changes in teacher education and attitudes many felt to be necessary. Cynics supposed that many schools would be content to purchase a few 'packs' of approved materials and achieve a token 'multiracializing' of the curriculum while leaving the bulk of the institution quite untouched.

It was misgivings of this kind which led the Schools Council/NFER 'Education for a Multiracial Society' Project into a minefield of controversy. The project's original brief was to develop curriculum materials for a multiracial society, but within a very short space of time the team of researchers opted for a different course. It was not simply a question of not wishing to provide the profession with a neatly packaged 'solution' which would forestall more fundamental reform; it was also the realization that the majority of teachers were simply unaware of many of the issues involved, with the danger that even the best multiracial materials would be unused or misused. In the early stages of the project, it encountered a great deal of prejudice among teachers, not of the most offensive kind, but sufficient to require a good deal of education and sensitization to the issues before they could be reasonably expected to analyse their own curricula and teaching practice. This analysis was undoubtedly correct, and the project developed effective techniques for 'sensitizing' teachers as a pre-requisite for curriculum change. The present author was briefly associated with the project at this time and supported this policy, while having some reservations about the absence of 'hard' empirical evidence of teacher attitudes which would justify the major change in direction the project had taken. There was, after all, only anecdotal data on this, which inevitably appears to be subjective and impressionistic to a wider audience who may not be receptive to the conclusions without unimpeachable objective evidence. When the project's report finally came to be published it was attacked on precisely these grounds. The press trivialized and sensationalized the ensuing argument, proclaiming that the report had made the blanket assertion that 'teachers are racist'. Some representatives of the National Union of Teachers, who had supported the project since its inception, described the report as 'propaganda' and 'a slander against teachers'[176]. Neither did the project's sponsors, the Schools Council, accept the report; it was buried with indecent haste, only to later surface in such a sanitized form that several of the project team dissociated themselves from it.

The whole affair was a telling chapter in the history of multiracial education. Ironically, it illustrated vividly one of the main arguments of the project, that at all levels the education system was unwilling to recognize the reality of racism. It was unfortunate that the teaching profession did not accept the mirror that had been held up to it, and doubly unfortunate that the controversy obscured the very valuable curriculum development work with teachers that the project had achieved.

The project helped to emphasize the importance of three major themes in multi-racial education in the 1970s:

1   The *permeation* of the curriculum with multiracial, multicultural material. The 'packet' or incremental approach, whereby discrete packages of appropriate material could be added on to the existing classroom activities (which would remain essentially unchanged) was firmly rejected in favour of a wholesale permeation which would affect every curriculum area. This principle has never been widely accepted in practice, and although there have been strenuous attempts to make many different subject areas multiracial, from learning to read to mathematics[167,168], the packet approach is still the most usual one.

2   The provision of multiracial education for all schools. In contrast

to the 'education for coloured immigrants' era, the focus was no longer solely the 'immigrants' themselves; white children, whether in inner-city schools or country schools also required conscientious preparation for life in multiracial Britain. Geographical and social mobility would ensure that most people would find themselves in inter-racial contact at some time in their lives, and in any event the multiracial education debate had pointed up the very ethnocentric nature of conventional curricula which required revision on factual grounds if no other. Again, the education system as a whole has been slow to respond to this argument; there is little evidence of substantial curriculum change outside multiracial areas.

3 Teacher education: the implication of a philosophy of permeation and of the extension of multiracial education to 'all-white' areas, was that a wider range of teachers would need a wider range of skills to cope with the demands placed on them.

Teacher education
The development of teacher education in this area has closely mirrored developments in the field as a whole. Initially the emphasis was on preparation for English language teaching, followed by a consideration of the 'immigrants' cultural backgrounds and adjustment problems, and only more recently has the issue of racism been given any weight. The *extent* of appropriate teacher education provision has lagged well behind the need for it, both in terms of the number of institutions offering relevant courses, and the role of those courses within the overall context of the students' studies. The early developments were much more a reflection of individual's or individual college's initiatives than of national policy, so that there was a very arbitrary and uneven emergence of courses over the country, and inevitably concentrated in institutions close to multiracial areas. Until the mid-1970s, then, only a minority of student teachers in initial training were receiving any significant preparation for teaching in a multiracial society. Even where there was provision, it tended to be one of a number of optional courses, usually concerned with children's 'special needs'; this helped to define multiracial education both as a 'problem' area, and one which was not regarded as central to most teachers' concerns.

The picture has improved somewhat since this time, as Giles and Cherrington have shown[136], though it still falls far short of the ideal. We are still far from being able to say that the system as a whole has accepted this kind of provision as a central and vital part of all

214

teacher training. In fact, the Rampton Committee could not identify a single teacher training institution which had 'succeeded in providing a satisfactory grounding in multi-cultural education for all its students'. Of course, since successive governments have cut a swathe through initial training institutions, this sector has declined in its influence, providing only a relative trickle of new entrants to the profession. In-service education has assumed a higher profile as a potential avenue for influencing teacher attitudes and providing the kinds of special knowledge and curriculum development principles we would wish to encourage. While the DES and some local authorities have for a long time provided short courses of this kind for teachers, advisers and inspectors, they have tended to attract those teachers who are already persuaded of the need for these skills, rather than the general body of teachers who would perhaps benefit more (see also Eggleston[108] for a recent survey of in-service provision).

Mention should be made of the few full-time and part-time post-experience diploma courses in multiracial education, such as those at Southlands and Goldsmiths' Colleges. While the number of students able to obtain the necessary funding for secondment (or the necessary motivation for evening study) is inevitably small and has declined as a result of expenditure cuts, these excellent courses have had a disproportionate effect as some of their graduates have risen to positions of higher responsibility and influence. At the same time, the role of the 'specialist' in this area has been a difficult one; in a field in which attitudes are often firmly held and somewhat polarized, it is very easy for those who are highly committed to multiracial education to be isolated within the staffroom as 'the one with the bee in his/her bonnet about race'. Wholesale curriculum change requires the support of the majority within the school and effective leadership and support from head teachers. A great deal of local support has been provided by the National Association for Multiracial Education, which has been the single most consistent voice articulating the principles of multiracial education at both national and local levels.

While the increase in national and local authority in-service provision is welcome, its dissemination outside multiracial areas must be seen as equally important. Similarly, if teachers who have benefited from special training are to be truly effective as a force for change within their schools they will require more institutional support than at present. The development of the 'whole school' approach, originally an initiative within the Schools Council/NFER

Project and later taken up by the Inner London Education Authority, seems to promise the best solution to this latter problem. It involves the immersion of a single school in a major re-assessment of its 'organization, curriculum and materials, and school, parent and community relations'[184], working in concert with an outside development team providing expertise and support services where necessary. This kind of action research, working with teachers while they are teaching, rather than simply equipping them with theory, is one of the more encouraging developments in recent years, not only for multiracial education but also as a model for other curriculum development work.

★

Since the mid-1970s the field of multiracial education has expanded very considerably. There remains a large gap between the greater awareness of the issues and any widespread commitment to action. This partly reflects a policy vacuum created by successive administrations' willingness to commission inquiries like the Rampton Committee, but unwillingness to act upon their recommendations, or even formulate a coherent statement of policy. (However, this is not to denigrate those within the DES, who have actively stimulated awareness of multiracial issues: rather it is to criticize their political overseers, who have circumscribed their efforts.) It is entirely to the credit of those local authorities who have advanced the case for multiracial education within their areas in the absence of support from central government. Little and Willey[244] have provided a survey of local authority provision which confirms the piecemeal and uneven development of policy and practice we have alluded to. One of the more interesting parts of their report deals with the attitudes of examination boards to the issue of assessment and syllabuses relevant to a multiracial society. Few, it seems, had felt the need to review their own practices in this light. These are not institutions with a high profile in the day-to-day business of education, and yet their deliberations crucially affect the kind of curriculum content children encounter. Doubtless this is one kind of 'unintentional racism' the Rampton Committee had in mind.

If there has been a growth area in multiracial education in recent years, it has been in the written word. The reader is advised to consult the contributions of Lynch[250], Hicks[170], Twitchen and Demuth[400], James and Jeffcoate[190] and Tierney[389] for more detailed coverage of the many topics which now fall under the umbrella of multiracial education — and which it would be impossible to review within these pages except in the most superficial generalities. This is not to say that any publications should be read uncritically, nor that all the developments in the field are entirely welcome. It would be quite wrong if we had given the impression that there was a happy consensus as to the directions multiracial education should be taking; there a number of discordant voices in the debate, declaring some fundamental differences of principle which have, in the last two or three years, polarized opinion in the field to a considerable extent. The remainder of this chapter is devoted to reviewing these disagreements in the light of the principles we have discussed; this is perhaps best approached through a critical analysis of some of the 'milestone' contributions which have changed the course of the debate.

Jeffcoate's 'Positive Image'

In 1979, Rob Jeffcoate, who was one of the members of the Schools Council/NFER Project team, published *Positive Image: towards a multiracial curriculum*[191], in which he seemed to retreat from many of the ideas that the project had espoused. His book was heavily criticized, often with justice, but it arguably articulated the feelings of many teachers outside the multiracial education movement, and should be taken seriously for that reason. His views are further developed in later publications[190,192], but *Positive Image* marked the turning point.

Returning to the classroom after his period of educational research, Jeffcoate reports, he discovered that he was a born-again 'child-centred progressivist'. This was problematic for he had previously attacked this ideology, on the grounds that it 'subordinated curriculum content, "mere facts", to classroom processes and learning methodologies'. This 'ain't what you teach it's the way that you teach it' idea seemed to be inimical to more directive kinds of curriculum reform which put more emphasis on content than style of teaching. However, in a matter of weeks after his return to the classroom he defected to this 'enemy', as he had seen it:

> There was no other way I wanted to work with my pupils . . . not only did I want to attach overriding importance to skills and concepts (. . . in the interests of the children becoming autonomous) but I also wanted very much to disown affective goals such as respect for self and others. The curriculum model I [had previously] proposed . . . now strikes me as too

prescriptive and moralistic. . . . Those teachers who feel tentative or ambivalent about objectives in the affective domain are reacting to sound instincts. There are substantial dangers (indoctrination, counterproductive effects, for instance) in schools annexing territory — children's attitudes — which is not by common consent properly theirs. . . . It is. . . arrogant and presumptuous, I would now say, for schools to stipulate as a curriculum target that children should respect other races and cultures. . . . Children's attitudes and opinions are their own affair. . . . I trust it will not be thought that I do not want my pupils to respect themselves and others. Obviously I do. But that is a hope, not a curriculum objective.[191]

Jeffcoate does not really explain his conversion, other than as an idiosyncratic personal reaction and a response to the realities of the classroom. He makes some play in an earlier section of the different perspectives of 'insiders' — teachers at the chalk-face, and 'outsiders' — 'LEA advisers, lecturers, curriculum researchers, community workers and the like (the multiracial education lobby)'. He is probably partly right in suggesting that the former regard the latter as representing those 'who are comfortably removed from classroom reality and presume to compensate for their own earlier failures as teachers by regarding the profession as a suitable case for treatment'. This is tendentious insofar as it remains unclear how far he supports this view; if so, it is a facile exercise in stereotyping which is an injustice to those 'outsiders' with substantial successful classroom experience, and ignores the fact that the bulk of the multiracial education lobby are practising classroom teachers. It might also be said that whereas most educational researchers have been classroom teachers, the reverse is not the case. Jeffcoate is not uncritical of teachers' attitudes and resistance to change, but the reader is left with the impression that it is their perspective which is the most valid. Few educational researchers would quarrel with this, while reserving the right to try to inform this perspective with a wider view.

The main issue, however, is whether child-centred progressivism is really as antithetical to firmly defined curriculum objectives as he maintains (and whether these objectives should include affective goals of the kind we have discussed). There is really no necessary contradiction between the two in practice: teachers not only teach in a certain *way*, they have to teach *something*, and it is in the determination of content rather than style that the multiracial education movement seeks to be influential. Of course the two considerations are not completely independent, and an authoritarian instructional style in which the teacher tells the children what to think is neither child-centred nor progressive. But it really is tilting at 'straw persons' to suggest that such an approach has been advocated. Jeffcoate does describe 'criteria for the selection of learning experiences for a multiracial curriculum', which are unexceptionable in what they include, but which omit anything pertaining to racism. It is here that he finds himself in the greatest difficulty, and where many of the contradictions coalesce.

One of the implications of Jeffcoate's position on teaching styles is that not only should children feel able to express their racism in the classroom discussion, but also that the teacher should avoid adopting a censorious attitude in these cases:

> Young white racists have as much right as anyone else to expect to find attentive adult ears at school . . . [they] for the most part, need support and sympathy, not gagging. . . .[191]

Presumably the child of black militant parents is given the same sympathetic hearing, and there we have it, the perfectly 'balanced' classroom discussion, a BBC studio discussion in miniature, and democracy is safe. But what if our child with the racist background is more persuasive and better liked by other children; what if he promises to bring in some National Front literature to support his case; what if he rises to a position of leadership and responsibility in the school (as in one of Jeffcoate's case-histories)? The outcome may be a happy one, or it may lead to a greater currency for racist views. Jeffcoate's strategy of handling the matter in small group or individual discussions is so tentative that he is unable to predict the outcome. He cites the example of a boy who told him individually that 'I can't stand coloureds', only to be confronted with a girl who said 'You mean you don't like Sandra' (a black girl with whom he enjoyed 'a jibing but strong relationship'). The fact that he replied 'Well, she's all right, I suppose' is cited as the proof that this strategy works, as though this creation of an exception signified a turnabout in the boy's attitudes towards blacks. And what of the feelings of less vociferous black children, or their parents, on hearing of their group being denigrated in the classroom? Because the point about this strategy is that the supportive and sympathetic approach of the teacher is hardly likely to be seen as opposed to

219

these views, except by the teacher, viewing it in the long term. It is ironic that in 1965 the government outlawed incitement to racial hatred in public places, while in the 1980s Jeffcoate is still prepared to countenance the childhood equivalent in the classroom. This is not the intention of the teacher's recommended strategy, but it is probably the effect.

It is not being suggested that white racist children should be 'gagged'; but it is certainly necessary that these views be contested by the teacher if opposition is not sufficiently forthcoming from the other children. Otherwise, the neutral chairperson stance, redolent of the 'Race Pack' issue, will be interpreted as tacit acceptance. Jeffcoate's prescription is designed as therapy for the white racist child who needs to express his/her beliefs in public; this is a very naively psychodynamic analysis, which can only allow one person to 'feel better' at the expense of others feeling worse. If the reasons for the child's attitudes are that they are 'vulnerable white children, — dispossessed, or so they feel, of their corner shops, their cinemas, their housing and job prospects, and now confronted with the possibility of losing the school curriculum', then the expression of some racist sentiments in front of an acquiescent teacher is not going to solve their problems. And if the implication is that their beliefs are firmly entrenched within their personalities, then reasoned opposition to their opinions is hardly likely to exacerbate their extreme views. Jeffcoate cites instances of children with National Front parents making such remarks; it is difficult to see how his strategy is likely to win against such extreme odds, or how an oppositional stance could drive them any further Right.

Jeffcoate's position is inspired by his latter-day conversion to a feeling of opposition to affective goals like self- and inter-racial respect, and by a more general dislike of what he views as political indoctrination in the classroom. The position would seem less contradictory if it were being suggested that children should be taught the principles of revolutionary communism, as opposed to the essentially liberal values that Jeffcoate himself espouses. He approvingly quotes Mary Warnock's reminder that 'Democracy is also a form of politics', but in the classroom democracy he envisages, he will not guarantee that anti-democratic voices are contested.

Maureen Stone's 'Myth'*

In 1981 Maureen Stone, a black academic, published *The Education of the Black Child in Britain: the myth of multiracial education*[364]. It was a critical broadside directed at the multiracial education movement which threatened to slaughter many of its sacred cows. From the premise that the schools had failed black children (with which few would disagree) she developed the thesis that multiracial education was in effect part of the problem rather than any solution. The fault lay partly in the diagnosis of the problem, on which multiracial education (MRE) was based, and partly in the prescribed therapy it had developed.

She suggested that 'since compensatory education — the pouring of more resources into Educational Priority Areas — has failed to make any real impact in reducing educational inequality' it has become necessary to locate the causes of black children's under-achievement in the children themselves, attributing to them lowered self-esteem which undermines their school performance. This extends our concern with the environmental factors surrounding the children while remaining uncritical of the education system itself. The school and the teacher then become forms of therapy to enhance self-esteem (and thus achievement) through various activities which draw upon the child's cultural background. But this therapy — otherwise known as MRE — does not work: firstly because the diagnosis is wrong since black children do not have lowered self-esteem; secondly because the link between self-esteem and school performance is disputed; and thirdly because, Dr Stone believes, MRE projects actually interfere with the proper business of the school (teaching basic skills: literacy, numeracy, etc.) and certainly do not enhance self-esteem. Clearly, then, the schools should return to the very pips of the core curriculum and leave the fostering of cultural identity to 'the community'. That West Indian children can be taught to achieve is, she argues, shown by the success of children in the supplementary schools; that MRE projects do not even promote self-esteem, let alone achievement, is shown by the fact that children in some MRE projects she visited scored no higher on self-esteem measures (and sometimes lower) than children in comparison schools with no MRE projects, or children in supple-mentary schools.

We have already devoted some space to the issue of black self-esteem, and in particular to the changing picture through the 1970s; even before those changes it was never argued that *all* black children, as an undifferentiated group, suffered from lowered self-esteem. Perhaps Dr Stone has performed a service in drawing attention to a mis-reading of the original research findings which may have contributed to such a blanket generalization. But in any event, the view is out of date, and requires no further demolition, and even in its most extreme form it was only part of the rationale for MRE.

At the very least MRE has generally been seen as a realization of every child's right to see his/her background and experience reflected in the school. Maureen Stone represents MRE as an ineffective therapy to repair non-existent damage; others would see it as an educational and human right, an aspect of equal opportunity and basically sound pedagogy. The most extreme accusation she lays at the door of MRE is that it actually interferes with the proper education of children. How could this be true? Only if MRE literally supplanted 'basic' educational activities in the timetable, and indeed on the cover of her book we find the claim that 'In many schools, steel band sessions and West Indian dialect classes *replaced basic skills*' [italics added]. This is a serious charge which should be substantiated with evidence, but it is not. If MRE activities are used as a dumping-ground for less able children, it should be exposed, but information from a wide range of primary and secondary school suggests that this is simply not the case. And as the headmaster of a well-known multi-racial comprehensive school commented, 'If you took away the steel band, it wouldn't be replaced by maths or English, it would be the bloody glockenspiel.' These views, from those who are concerned with the practice of MRE, seem to be quite as valid data as the observations of outsiders.

Dr Stone's view of MRE seems to be a very narrow, even stereotyped one, amounting to steel bands, dialect and black history, hermetically-sealed packages which fit into discrete slots in the timetable or extra-mural activities. It is not only a long way from the kind of wholesale permeation approach that has been advocated, it is precisely the kind of incremental approach that has has long been criticized; it is neither useful nor even accurate to depict this as representative of MRE, and then to charge it with failure. The alternative strategy of more 'basic' education, as practised by the supplementary schools, has some appeal if black children are not to be short-changed by the education system. Of course we need to identify and ameliorate the causes of deficiencies in basic skills where they exist. No argument there, but we would contest the divorce proceedings Dr Stone institutes between basic skills tuition and wider educational objectives, including some affective goals. These objectives are not in opposition to each other and it is a disservice to depict them as such. It seems almost too obvious to say that when we teach a child a basic skill like literacy, we do not do so in a vacuum. And at the very simplest level, it is altogether better that the child's reading skills are honed on non-racist material. Above and beyond that, it seems intuitively obvious that the school and the teacher who have set up within their practice resonances with the child's home and culture are more likely to encourage a general involvement in learning than alienation from it, whether that learning is concerned with numeracy, biology or Caribbean history.

The positive contribution of the book has been to re-open the issue of black under-achievement and dispel any complacency following the Driver[104] findings. If the MRE movement's emphasis on affective goals (though not an exclusive one) had played any part in obscuring that issue, then Dr Stone's contribution has been important and timely. But there is another important issue at stake in the discussion of the purposes and effects of MRE; it is ironic that Dr Stone's book compounds the error for which she berates educationalists. While they are censured for their emphasis on the black child's problems, her book continues the emphasis, and in throwing out MRE as an effective strategy, at least one other baby disappears with the bathwater. Nowhere in the book is the issue of white children's racism confronted, and yet this is a fundamental part of the rationale for MRE. Is MRE to remain for white children while black children get on with basic skills? Dr Stone obviously does not suggest such a separate and unequal system, but the question does require an answer.

If there had been any danger of the MRE movement establishing a new orthodoxy, it was quickly dispelled; criticism rained in from all sides and the movement could have been forgiven a little paranoia. On the one hand Hastie[163] railed against MRE and its critique of, for example, history teaching, claiming that the movement was simply replacing one kind of bias with another. His strictures might have been better received were it not for his intemperate and *ad hominem* argument; for him, MRE is 'divisive, grossly ill-informed and intellectually dishonest', its practitioners are 'cynical careerists', and its consequences are to encourage 'tunnel vision' and resuscitate racism, which 'those of us who survived the Second World War thought that by our victory we had slain'. Tim Ottevanger dubbed the article 'The Empire Strikes Back', and in a way it was predictable that there would be some backlash from MRE's recent progress. And while it was not very surprising that the *New Standard*[286] should deliver an editorial attack on Gillian Klein's work on racism in children's books, a similar criticism from an MRE stalwart[189], invoking the spirit of Stalin to satirize the stereotype-

223

hunting in this work, was even less welcome.

More general critiques of multiculturalism have been spawned within the movement, too. Both Mullard[280] and Dhondy[92,93] have characterized multicultural education as a State strategy designed to defuse and co-opt black resistance in the schools, cooling out the natural anger of black youth at their treatment by giving them enough of their 'own' culture to keep them happy. Some of Dhondy's ideas about black subcultures in schools ring very true; there are also echoes of Hall *et al.*'s[156] analysis of 'cultures of resistance' and 'resistance through language'. But the notion that multicultural education could be an effective form of social control, as it is presently practised, is not a convincing one. It certainly has not worked as such; evidently it did not cool out the young blacks involved in the inner city riots of 1981, and when we consider the rather tepid reality of multiculturalism in the next section, it becomes clear why it could not.

Multiculturalism vs. multiracialism

The most significant part of the recent debates within MRE has concerned the business of defining what multiracial/multicultural/multi-ethnic education actually is; 'all things to all people' was what it had become, the interchangeable nomenclature disguising a multitude of practices and philosophies, if not actually sins. And within the confusion in terminology there had been some subtle changes of emphasis with more than semantic significance. Increasingly the term 'multicultural' became the preferred usage, and it is to a critique of pure multiculturalism that we now turn.

Why had this evolutionary change in terminology come about? It has been a recurrent theme of this book that the education system has been unwilling to confront the issue of racism, or even to accept that it should do so. 'Race' has been a four-letter word, and it has been more comfortable to address the problems in school and society in terms of cultural factors, whether we are talking about black children's roots and identity, or the relations between whites and blacks. This has obviated the need to analyse historical or contemporary social structure, issues of power and privilege, poverty and affluence, in other words the past and present structural determinants of the relations between the races. It has also avoided the embarrassment of finding that an analysis of institutional racism would have a tributary which led right into the middle of the classroom. Political education has always been a contentious issue, and pure multiculturalism, guaranteed free from all harmful racial and political ingredients, has offered a safe path round that particular patch of nettles.

A further reason is related to this, but is more a practical consideration: multiculturalism is much easier. No-one among the children's parents will object to the addition to the curriculum of interesting material on People From Other Lands on an occasional basis, nor will these topics be beyond the capabilities of the staff, with or without special training. In other words, multiculturalism lends itself willingly to the piecemeal approach, and to the token inclusion of unexceptionable topics which are an extension of the existing curriculum, not a modification of it. This is not to defame those sincere multicultural practitioners who *have* achieved a considerable change in their classrooms by adopting a wholehearted multicultural approach; it is simply to draw attention to the consequences of a diluted and half-hearted version which masquerades as curriculum change. Some West Indian dancing this week, some Indian cookery next, and a multi-faith assembly once a term does not amount to multicultural education; and in this scheme of things, this month's project on Jamaica assumes the same weight as last month's project on dinosaurs, and somewhere along the line the point has been lost.

Of course it is not simply a matter of the sheer quantity of multicultural input; it is also a matter of the context in which it is presented, and the philosophy it embodies. One of the abiding problems of multiculturalism is the question of the relation between 'culture' abstracted for classroom presentation and people's actual way of living. Rather often we see the emphasis falling on cultural artefacts and traditional customs, which may be considerably less important to (and representative of) a people's lifestyle than we care to admit — and certainly less crucial in defining their quality of life than their economic position, their political system, their caste status and so on. So there are problems of artificiality when we effectively spell culture with a capital 'C'. Even a lower case 'culture' brings problems of representativeness. How do we convey diversity *within* cultures in simple terms, and how do we avoid the opposite extreme of stereotyping? How would a Venusian multiculturalist design a curriculum to reflect the culture of new British immigrants? Roast beef, Vaughan Williams, morris dancing and religious observance (with some 'dialect' lessons in Standard English)? Or fish and chips, Tom Jones, disco, and church attendance three times per life *per capita*, all lessons to be conducted in Cockney or Scouse dialects? The point is not a facetious one, for what we actually do

225

under the banner of multiculturalism may get perilously close to this kind of pastiche.

More importantly, though, the abstraction of culture in this way is misleading to the extent that it conveys an idealized picture of different racial and cultural groups and the relations between them. It can amount to merely a celebration of the exotic, a 'disinfected' account of inter-group relations, a view of the world from the steps of the Commonwealth Institute. It is as though we were content to teach contemporary world politics using the United Nations Charter as our set text, rather than newsreels of the Lebanon, El Salvador or Poland.

A multicultural perspective is vital to multiracial education; but it should 'start from where the child is' by relating the residues and transformations of the minority cultures in Britain to their roots. Only then can the children directly relate the teaching to their experience, and come to grips with the other major term in the equation. For it is in the confrontation of their cultural and racial backgrounds with racism that many of their experiences are forged. When this book appeared in its first edition it was simply entitled *Children and Race*. It was not called *Children and Culture* for the very good reason that it was not, in the author's view, differences in *lifestyles* which accounted for white people's attitudes and behaviour towards blacks, or which had consigned black people to the bargain basement of the society. Rather it was that the (spurious) categorization of people in racial terms, and the devaluation of black peoples (whatever their culture) through racist ideologies had entered the interstices of British culture over hundreds of years; and that these had been actively excavated for political and economic reasons in the period of contemporary black immigration. To be sure, cultural differences had a part to play: they provided available rationalizations for inter-group hostility. But this is a more superficial and secondary reason for hostility. They may well be the 'reasons' for hostility that people will admit to, for there are no other admissible reasons for racism. However, we would maintain that the reality is one of racial hostility rationalized by cultural differences, rather than hostility engendered by the cultural distinctiveness of peoples who, coincidentally, happen to be black.

In contradistinction to apolitical 'multiculturalism', there has been a growing demand from some teachers and parents for explicitly 'anti-racist teaching'. Others have been deterred by what they fear to be an overly political perspective, but Green's[150] excellent account of an anti-racist teaching philosophy puts the matter in its proper context. It is not about political indoctrination in the classroom, it is about the rights of all children to racial justice in education. As some schools have shown, a public statement of an anti-racist philosophy for the school creates an unambiguously positive racial climate in which all groups can have confidence (and by contrast illustrates the true timidity of the teacher-as-neutral-chairperson approach). With that background of institutional support it becomes far easier for MRE to deliver what it promises: an account of race and racism as well as culture. If we do not embrace these issues within the curriculum then we further alienate those children whose lives are crucially affected by these very forces. We retail a half-truth which allows children to believe that the racial ordering of our society is acceptable, inevitable and part of the natural order of things. And if we are pusillanimous in our approach we create a value vacuum which less scrupulous ideologues are only too anxious to fill. If we wish to equip children to confront racism, then we must set an example in our own classroom practice.

Afterword
We have described a sequence of racial attitude development in children which begins within the family in the first few years of life. The currency of prejudiced racial values in Britain has ensured that the socialization of children has included a racial dimension, such that the majority of children attain an early awareness of race and embryonic racial attitudes that parallel adult attitudes. It seems that black children are similarly aware of the attitudes that surround them, which colour their world and their view of their place within it. This is, however, the beginning rather than the end of the story. Beyond the pre-school years, a variety of other influences figure in the picture. We have indicated how the school can reinforce these attitudes or help to countermand them. The will to realize appropriate educational reform has been, in the first instance, a matter of individual commitment and belief on the part of teachers, but it is clear that a widespread adoption of progressive practice is a matter of political will. It is not only cynics who doubt that this will exists at a society-wide level; many feel that in any case, piecemeal reforms in the education system are fruitless in the face of the economic and social structural determinants of racism; that only wholesale social change will change social attitudes. The implicit recognition in this view of the pressures towards racism is a valid one, and a necessary counterbalance to the naively optimistic picture of the education system as a panacea for all social ills. Others,

however, would see the pursuit of racial equality within the education system as a necessary part of the process of social change, rather than a consequence which must wait upon it.

As Britain copes with a period of deepening economic recession, these issues are thrown into sharper relief. On the one hand the resources necessary to reform, in the education system or outside it, are in short supply and becoming scarcer. On the other, we may anticipate that the consequences of that depression will follow the familiar pattern of social divisiveness, as the heightened competition for a diminishing supply of employment, housing and material goods is articulated in racial terms. While pundits argue about whether the inner-city uprisings have their roots in poverty or race, the black poor understand that for them the two are inseparable. It is difficult to believe that the enduring strain of racism in our society will not be mobilized as white people are encouraged to externalize the blame for their misfortunes on black people, rather than their political leaders. Multiracial education cannot conceivably reverse these processes alone, but to the extent that it can assist in the pursuit of social and psychological equality and create a value system in which such ideologies are unacceptable, it offers more than a token resistance to them.

* Much of this section first appeared as a review of Maureen Stone's book by the present author in *New Community*[265].

Appendix

This appendix contains some further details of the results of the author's research described in Chapter 8. A complete account of the data, analysis and conclusions can be found 'Changing children's racial attitudes: an action research project', Final Report to Social Science Research Council on grant HR1648/2, available from SSRC or the author.

The main data for analysis were the children's responses to 'preferences' and 'stereotypes' questions involving dolls and pictures as described. Previous work suggested sufficient relationship between these sections of the tests for the scores to be combined into a single score per child, elicited before and after the intervention programme, so that this before-after difference was the principal measure of attitude change over the course of the programme. These data were collected in a form suitable for conventional analysis of variance; however, due to the loss of one cell and the resulting imbalance, together with the divergent numbers of subjects of different ethnic groups in the various cells, this was no longer possible and the alternative strategy of analysis of covariance was judged to be the best approach.

In addition, the identification responses were subjected to a separate analysis (see section iii).

Section (i) Classes with English teachers/conventional materials
Even from inspection of the raw difference-score data it was clear that these two classes had manifested very little change over the course of the year. In a subsequent 2-way ANOVA, to allow the inspection of interaction effects as well as the main effects due to teacher's race and materials, there was confirmed a highly significant 'materials' effect ($F=62.87$ 0.1%) and a significant interaction between materials and teacher's race ($F=5.19$ 1%), in the data from the sample as a whole (this was an addition to the main analysis of covariance which had shown significant effects due to materials and teacher's race). It was clear from this analysis that the

229

minority group teachers were considerably more effective in producing attitude change when using conventional materials than were the English teachers (whose classes contained the only pupils whose attitudes changed in a more negative direction).

Section (ii)   Effects of multiracial materials on white children's attitudes
Both the main analysis of covariance and successive single ANOVAs showed that the multiracial materials had contributed significantly to the attitude change that had taken place in the sample as a whole. The data also showed that for the English children, the multiracial materials had significantly more effect than the conventional materials (using Winer's formula, $t = 2.67$ 1%) but that this effect was significantly less than for the West Indian and Asian children.

Section (iii)   West Indian and Asian children's responses to identity tests
Actual identity: In the pre-tests, 27% of the West Indian children and 30% of the Asian children had 'misidentified'. By the post-tests, these proportions had significantly changed to 11% ($\chi^2 = 8.52$ 1%) and 17% ($\chi^2 = 3.84$ 5%), respectively.
Ideal identity: In the pre-tests, 78% of the West Indian children and 81% of the Asian children said they would 'rather be' the white figure. By the post-tests, these proportions had significantly changed to 37% ($\chi^2 = 30.19$ 0.1%) and 41% ($\chi^2 = 19.9$ 0.1%), respectively.

Section (iv)   Effects of materials vs effects of teachers
In the initial analysis of covariance the contribution to the recorded attitude changes made by the multiracial materials was highly significant: $F = 24.353$ (0.1%).

   Successive single covariate analyses were carried out which suggested that the race of the teacher contributed somewhat to the difference score, but that the effect was relatively small compared to the materials effect. Subsequent ANOVA revealed that with the multiracial materials, the relatively minor effect of teacher's race was largely a result of it being masked by the marked effectiveness of two English teachers who recorded the largest attitude changes in their pupils of all groups.

230

References

1 ABRAHAMSON, S. (1952) Our status system and scholastic rewards *Journal of Education Sociology*, 25, 441–50

2 ADAM, R. (1969) Project Headstart: LBJ's one success *New Society*, no. 370, 681–3

3 ADORNO, T.W., FRENKEL-BRUNSWIK, E., LEVINSON, D.J. and SANFORD, R.N. (1950) *The Authoritarian Personality* New York: Harper & Row

4 ALLPORT, F.H. (1924) *Social Psychology* Cambridge, Massachusetts: Houghton Mifflin

5 ALLPORT, G.W. (1954) *The Nature of Prejudice* Cambridge, Massachusetts: Addison-Wesley

6 ALLPORT, G.W. and KRAMER, B.M. (1946) Some roots of prejudice *Journal of Psychology* 22, 9–39

7 AMIR, Y. (1969) Contact hypothesis in ethnic relations *Psychological Bulletin* 71, 5, 319–342

8 AMMONS, R.B. (1950) Reactions in a projective doll-play interview of white males two to six years of age to differences in skin colour and facial features *Journal of Genetic Psychology* 76, 323–41

9 ARCHER and THOMAS (1958) *Eight Children from Near and Far* London: Ginn & Co.

10 ARISTOTLE *Politics*, Book xxx, 1, London: Heinemann

11 ASHLEY MONTAGU, M.F. (1968) *Man and Aggression* New York: Oxford University Press

12 ASHMORE, R.D. and DEL BOCA, F.K. (1976) 'Psychological approaches to understanding intergroup conflict' in P. Katz (ed) *Towards the Elimination of Racism* New York: Pergamon

13 BAGLEY, C. and VERMA, G.K. (1972) Some effects of teaching designed to promote understanding of racial issues in adolescence *Journal of Moral Education* 1, 3, 231–8

14 BAKER, R.S. (1908) *Following the Color Line* Reprinted 1964 New York: Harper & Row

15 BALDWIN, J. (1963) *The Fire Next Time* London: Michael Joseph

16 BALDWIN, J. (1964) *Nobody Knows My Name* London: Michael Joseph

17 BALLARD, B. and KELLER, H.R. (1976) Development of racial awareness: task consistency, reliability and validity *Journal of Genetic Psychology* 129, 3–11

231

[18] BANDURA, A. and HUSTON, A.C. (1961) Identification as a process of incidental learning *Journal of Abnormal and Social Psychology* 63, 311–18

[19] BANDURA, A., ROSS, D. and ROSS, S.A. (1961) Transmission of Aggression through imitation of aggressive models *Journal of Abnormal and Social Psychology* 63, 575–82

[20] BANDURA, A. and WALTERS, R.H. (1963a) 'Aggression' in *Child Psychology* (part I), Chicago: National Society for the Study of Education

[21] BANKS, W.C. (1976) White preference in blacks: a paradigm in search of a phenomenon *Psychological Bulletin* 83, 6, 1179–1186

[22] BANNERMAN, H. (1971) *Little Black Sambo* London: Chatto & Windus

[23] BANTON, M. (1959) *White and Coloured* London: Jonathan Cape

[24] BANTON, M. (1967) *Race Relations* London: Tavistock

[25] BARATZ, S.S. and BARATZ, J.C. (1970) 'Early childhood intervention: the social science base of institutional racism' *Harvard Educational Review* 40, 29–49

[26] BARNES, T.R. (1960) 'Captain Johns and the adult world' in B. Ford (ed) *Young Writers, Young Readers* London: Hutchinson

[27] BARZUN, J. (1965) *Race: A Study in Superstition* New York: Harper & Row

[28] BASTIDE, R. (1967) Colour, Racism and Christianity *Daedalus*, Spring 1967, 312–27

[29] *BEACON* (1977) *An interview with Prof. Hans Eysenck Beacon*, February, 1977

[30] BERGER, P.L. and LUCKMANN, T. (1966) *The Social Construction of Reality* New York: Doubleday

[31] BERNSTEIN, B. (1962) Linguistic codes, hesitation phenomena and intelligence *Language and Speech* 5, 1, 31–46

[32] BILLIG, M. (1976) *Social Psychology and Intergroup Relations* London: Academic Press

[33] BILLIG, M. (1979) *Psychology, Racism and Fascism* Birmingham: Searchlight Publications

[34] BIRD, C., MONACHESI, E.D. and BURDICK, H. (1952) The effect of parental discouragement of play activities upon the attitudes of white children towards Negroes *Child Development* 24, 63–80

[35] BLAKE, R. and DENNIS, W. (1943) The development of stereotypes concerning the Negro *Journal of Abnormal and Social Psychology* 38, 525–31

[36] BLEDSOE, J.C. (1959) An investigation of six correlates of student withdrawal from high school *Journal of Educational Research* 53, 3–6

[37] BLUM, J. (1978) *Pseudoscience and Mental Ability* New York: Monthly Review Press

[38] BOGARDUS, E.S. (1925a) Social distance and its origins *Journal of Applied Sociology* 9, 216–26

[39] BOGARDUS, E.S. (1925b) Measuring social distance *Journal of Applied Sociology* 9, 299–308

232

40 BOGARDUS, E.S. (1928) *Immigration and Race Attitudes* Boston: Heath
41 BOLT, C. (1971) *Victorian Attitudes to Race* London: Routledge and Kegan Paul
42 BRAND, E.S., RUIZ, R.A. and PADILLA, A.M. (1974) Ethnic identification and preference: a review *Psychological Bulletin* 81, 11, 860–890
43 BRIGHAM, J.C. (1971) Ethnic stereotypes *Psychological Bulletin* 76, 15–38
44 BRITTAN, E. (1976) Multiracial education 2: teacher opinion on aspects of school life; Part 2: pupils and teachers *Educational Research* 18, 3, 182–91
45 BRODY, E.B. (1963) Colour and identity conflict in young boys: observations of Negro mothers and sons in urban Baltimore *Psychiatry* 26, 188–207
46 BRONFENBRENNER, U. (1960) Freudian theories of identification and their derivatives *Child Development* 31, 15–40
47 BROOKS, C.K. (1966) 'Some approaches to teaching English as a second language' in Webster, S.W. (ed) *The Disadvantaged Learner* San Francisco: Chandler Publishing Co.
48 BROWN, G. and JOHNSON, S.P. (1971) The attribution of behavioural connotations to shaded and white figures by caucasian children *British Journal of Social and Clinical Psychology* 10, 306–12
49 BROWN, R. (1958) *Words and Things* Glencoe, Illinois: The Free Press
50 BROWN, R. (1965) *Social Psychology* New York: The Free Press
51 BRUNER, J.S. and GOODMAN, C.C. (1947) Values and need as organizing factors in perception *Journal of Abnormal and Social Psychology* 42, 33–44
52 Bulletin of the Council on Inter-racial Books for Children, 1841 Broadway, New York, N.Y. 10023, USA
53 BUNTON, P.L. and WEISSBACH, T.A. (1971) 'Attitudes towards blackness of black pre-school children attending community-controlled or public schools' Mimeograph, Pomona College
54 BURT, C. (1966): The genetic determination of differences in intelligence: a study of monozygotic twins reared together and apart *British Journal of Psychology* 57, 146–151
55 BUTTS, H. (1963) Skin colour perception and self-esteem *Journal of Negro Education* 32, 122–8
56 CAMERON, S. (1971) Prejudice in the printed page *The Teacher*, 19 November
57 CAMPBELL, D.T. (1967) Stereotypes and the perception of group differences *American Psychologist* 22, 817–829
58 CAMPBELL, J.D. and YARROW, M.R. (1958) Personal and situational variables in adaptation to change *Journal of Social Issues* 14, 1, 29–46
59 CANADY, H.G. (1936) The effect of 'rapport' on the IQ: a new approach to the problem of social psychology *Journal of Negro Education* 5, 209–19

[60] CARMICHAEL, S. and HAMILTON, C.V. (1968) *Black Power* London: Cape

[61] CASHMORE, E. (1979) *Rastaman: the Rastafarian movement in England* London: George Allen & Unwin

[62] CASHMORE, E. (1982) *Black Sportsmen* London: Routledge and Kegan Paul

[63] CHADWICK, O. (1958) *Western Asceticism* London: S.C.M. Press

[64] CHEIN, I. and HURWITZ, J.I. (1950) 'The reactions of Jewish boys to various aspects of being Jewish' Jewish Centre Division, National Jewish Welfare Board, New York

[65] Children's Book Bulletin *from* Children's Rights Workshop, 4, Aldebert Terrace, London, S.W.8

[66] CHILDS, C. (1972) Doing what comes naturally *The Guardian*, 14 April

[67] CHRISTIE, R. and COOK, P. (1958) A guide to the published literature relating to the authoritarian personality through 1956 *Journal of Psychology* 45, 171–99

[68] CHYATTE, C., SCHAEFER, D.F. and SPIAGGIA, M. (1951) Prejudice verbalization among children *Journal of Educational Psychology* 42, 421–31

[69] CLARK, K. (1955) *Prejudice and Your Child* Boston: Beacon Press

[70] CLARK, K. (1965) *Dark Ghetto* London and New York: Gollancz

[71] CLARK, K. and CLARK, M. (1939) The development of consciousness of self and the emergence of racial identification in Negro pre-school children *Journal of Social Psychology, SSPSI Bulletin* 10, 591–9

[72] CLARK, K, and CLARK, M. (1947) Racial Identification and preference in Negro children in T.M. Newcomb and E.L. Hartley (eds) *Readings in Social Psychology* New York: Holt

[73] COARD, B. (1971) *How the West Indian Child is made Educationally Subnormal in the British School System* London: New Beacon Books

[74] COLEMAN, H.A. (1940) The relationship of socio-economic status to the performance of junior high school students *Journal of Experimental Education* 9, 61–3

[75] CRAWFORD, T.J. and NADITCH, M. (1970) Relative deprivation, powerlessness and militancy *Journal of Psychiatry* 33, 2, 208–23

[76] CRISWELL, J.H. (1937), Racial cleavage in Negro-white groups *Sociometry*, 1, 87–9

[77] CRISWELL, J.H. (1939) A sociometric study of race cleavage in the classroom *Archives of Psychology*, no. 235

[78] CROSS, W.E. (1970) 'The black experience viewed as a process: a crude model for black self-actualization' Paper presented at the 34th annual meeting of the Association of Social and Behavioural Scientists, April 23–4, 1970 Tallahassee, Florida

[79] CURTIN, P.D. (1964) *The Image of Africa: British Ideas and Action 1780–1850* Madison: University of Wisconsin Press

[80] DAI, B. (1953) Some problems of personality development among

Negro children in C. Kluckhohn & H. Murray (eds) *Personality in Nature, Society and Culture* New York: Knopf

81 DAVEY, A.G. and MULLIN, P.N. (1980) Ethnic identification and preference of British Primary school children *Journal of Child Psychology and Psychiatry* 21, 241–51

82 DAVEY, A.G. and MULLIN, P.N. (1982) 'Inter-ethnic friendship in British primary schools' *Educational Research*, 24, 2, 83–92

83 DAVEY, A.G. and NORBURN, M.V. (1980) Ethnic awareness and ethnic differentiation amongst primary school children *New Community*, 8, 1 & 2, 51–60

84 DAVIDSON, B. (1979) African history in British schools *New Approaches in Multiracial Education*, 7, 3, 1–2, 20

85 DENTON, J. (1976) *The Colour Factory* Kestrel Books

86 Department of Education and Science (1965) *The Education of Immigrants* Circular 7/65, London: HMSO

87 DEUTSCH, C.P. (1964) Auditory discrimination and learning: social factors *Merrill-Palmer Quarterly* 10, 3, 277–96

88 DEUTSCH, C.P. (1968) 'Environment and perception' in M. Deutsch, I. Katz and A.R. Jensen (eds) *Social Class, Race and Psychological Development* New York: Holt Rinehart and Winston

89 DEUTSCH, M. (1960) 'Minority group and class status as related to social and personality factors in scholastic acievement' Monograph 2, New York: Society for Applied Anthropology, Cornell University

90 DEUTSCH, M.P. (1963) The disadvantaged child and the learning process in A.H. Passow (ed) *Education in Depressed Areas* New York: Columbia University Press

91 DEUTSCHER, I. (1966) Words and deeds: social science and social policy *Social Problems*, 13, 3, 235–54

92 DHONDY, F. (1974) The black explosion in schools *Race Today*, February, 1974

93 DHONDY, F. (1978) Teaching young blacks *Race Today*, May 1978

94 DIXON, R. (1972) Racialism in children's literature *Teachers Against Racism Bulletin*, 2, June, 1972

95 DIXON, R. (1977) *Catching them Young (I): sex, race and class in children's fiction* London:Pluto Press

96 DODDRELL, R. (1982) 'A study of racial identity, racial preference and self-esteem in black, Asian and white children' Unpublished dissertation, Polytechnic of Central London

97 DOLLARD, J., MILLER, N.E., DOOB, L.W., MOWRER, O.H. and SEARS, R.R. (1939) *Frustration and Aggression* New Haven: Yale University Press

98 DOMINICK, J.R. and GREENBERG, B.S. (1969) 'Communication among the urban poor: Blacks on TV — their presence and roles' Report no. 8, Project CUP, Dept of Communication, Michigan State University

⁹⁹ DORN, A. and TROYNA B. (1982) 'Multiracial education and the politics of decision-making' Oxford Review of Education, 8, 2, 175–185

¹⁰⁰ DRAGON'S TEETH: Bulletin of the National Committee on Racism in Children's Books, The Methodist Church, 240, Lancaster Road, London, W.11

¹⁰¹ DREGER, R.M. and MILLER, K.S. (1960) Comparative psychological studies of Negroes and whites in the US, 1959–65 Psychological Bulletin Monograph supplement 70, 3, part 2, 1–58

¹⁰² DREGER, R.M. and MILLER, K.S. (1968) Comparative psychological studies of Negroes and whites in the US Psychological Bulletin, 57, 361–402

¹⁰³ DREGER, R.M. and MILLER, K.S. (eds) (1973) Comparative Studies of Blacks and Whites in the United States New York: Seminar Press

¹⁰⁴ DRIVER, G. (1980) Beyond Underachievement: Case Studies of English, West Indian and Asian School-leavers at 16-Plus Commission for Racial Equality, London

¹⁰⁵ DU BOIS, W.E.B. (1908) Souls of Black Folk Greenwich, Conn: Fawcett reprinted 1964

¹⁰⁶ EDWARDS, V.K. (1979) The West Indian Language Issue in British Schools London: Routledge

¹⁰⁷ EELS, K., DAVIS, A., HAVIGHURST, R.J., VERGIL, E. and TYLER, R. (1951) Intelligence and Cultural Differences Chicago: University of Chicago Press

¹⁰⁸ EGGLESTON, J., DUNN, D. and PUREWAL, A. (1982) In-Service Teacher Education in a Multiracial Society: a report of a research project University of Keele

¹⁰⁹ ELKIN, J. (1980) Multiracial books for the classroom Birmingham: Youth Libraries Group of the Library Association

¹¹⁰ ESSEN, J. and GHODSIAN, M. (1979) The children of immigrants: school performance New Community, 7, 3, 422–9

¹¹¹ EYSENCK, H.J. (1971) Race, Intelligence and Education London: Temple Smith

¹¹² EYSENCK, H.J. (undated) Personal communication to M. Billig cited in Billig, M. (1979) Psychology, Racism & Fascism Birmingham: Searchlight Publications

¹¹³ EYSENCK, H.J. (1982) The Listener, 29 April, 2–3

¹¹⁴ FANON, F. (1968) Black Skin, White Masks London: MacGibbon and Kee

¹¹⁵ FESTINGER, L. (1954) A theory of social comparison processes Human Relations 7, 117–40

¹¹⁶ FISHEL, L.H. and QUARLES, B. (1970) The Black American: a documentary history New York: Morrow

¹¹⁷ FISHMAN, J.A. (1955) Negative stereotypes concerning Americans among American-born children receiving various types of minority-group education Genetic Psychology Monographs 51, 107–182

236

118 FLYNN, J.R. (1980) *Race, IQ and Jensen* London: Routledge and Kegan Paul
119 FORBES, J.D. (1971) 'The mandate for an innovative educational response to cultural diversity' in J.C. Stone and D.P. DeNevi (eds) *Teaching Multi-Cultural Populations* New York: Van Nostrand
120 FOSTER, K. (1951) *Dragon Island* London: University of London Press
121 FOX, D.J. and JORDAN, V.B. (1973) Racial preference and identification of black, American Chinese and white children *Genetic Psychology Monographs* 88, 229–86
122 FRAZIER, E.F. (1966) *The Negro Family in the US* Chicago: University of Chicago Press
123 FREEDMAN, P.I. (1967) Race as a factor in persuasion *Journal of Experimental Education* 35, 48–52
124 FRENKEL-BRUNSWIK, E. (1949) Intolerance of ambiguity as an emotional and perceptual personality variable *Journal of Personality*, 18, 108–143
125 FREUD, A. (1946) *The Ego and the Mechanisms of Defence* New York: International University Press
126 FREUD, S. (1924) *Collected Papers*, vol. 4, London: Hogarth Press
127 FREUD, S. (1933) *New Introductory Lectures on Psychoanalysis*, New York: Norton
128 FREUD, S. (1949a) *Group Psychology and the Analysis of the Ego* London: Hogarth Press
129 FREUD, S. (1949b) *An Outline of Psychoanalysis* New York: Norton
130 FRIEDMAN, N. (1969) Africa and the Afro-American: the changing Negro identity *Psychiatry* 32, 2, 127–36
131 GALTON, F. (1883) *Inquiries into the Human Faculty* London: Macmillan
132 GALTON, F. (1869) *Hereditary Genius: an enquiry into its laws and consequences* London: Macmillan
133 GERGEN, K.J. (1967) The significance of skin colour in human relations *Daedalus* Spring, 390–406
134 GIBBES, R.W. (1851) Death of Samuel George Morton, MD *Charleston Medical Journal* 6, 594–8
135 GILES, R. (1977) *The West Indian Experience in British Schools* London: Heinemann
136 GILES, R. and CHERRINGTON, D. (1981) The provision of courses in multicultural education for teachers in the UK: a survey. Paper presented to the Commission for Racial Equality Advisory Group on Teacher Education, Nottingham University Seminar, 3–5 April, 1981
137 GILL, D. (1982) 'Assessment in a Multicultural Society: Schools Council Report: Geography' London
138 GILL, D. (1982) The contribution of secondary school geography to multi-cultural education: a critical view of some materials *Multiracial Education* 10, 3, 12–26

[139] GILLIE, O. (1978) Sir Cyril Burt and the great IQ fraud *New Statesman* 24 November, 688–94

[140] GINSBURG, H. (1972) *The Myth of the Deprived Child* New Jersey: Prentice Hall

[141] GLENDINNING, F. (1971) Racial stereotypes in history text-books *Race Today*, 3, 2, 52–4

[142] GOLIN, S. (1971) Project Self-Esteem: some effects of an elementary school black studies program *Proceedings of the 79th Annual A.P.A. Convention*

[143] GOODACRE, E. (1968) *Teachers and their Pupils' Home Backgrounds* National Foundation for Educational Research, Windsor

[144] GOODMAN, M.E. (1946) Evidence concerning the genesis of interracial attitudes *American Anthropologist* 48, 624–30

[145] GOODMAN, M.E. (1952) *Race Awareness in Young Children* Cambridge, Massachusetts: Addison-Wesley

[146] GOODMAN, M.E. (1964) *Race Awareness in Young Children* New York: Collier Books

[147] GOSSETT, T.F. (1965) *Race: the History of an Idea in America* New York: Schocken Books

[148] GOUGH, H.G., HARRIS, D.B., MARTIN, W.E. and EDWARDS, M. (1950a) Children's ethnic attitudes (I): relationship to certain personality factors *Child Development* 21, 83–91

[149] GOUGH, H.G., HARRIS, D.B. and MARTIN, W.E. (1950b) Children's ethnic attitudes (II): relationship to parental beliefs concerning child training *Child Development* 21, 169–81

[150] GREEN, A. (1982) In defence of anti-racist teaching: a reply to recent critiques of multicultural education *Multiracial Education* 10, 2, 19–35

[151] GREEN, P. (1982) Tolerance teaching and the self-concept in the multi-ethnic classroom *Multi-ethnic Education Review* 1, 1, 8–11

[152] GREENWALD, H.J. and OPPENHEIM, D.B. (1968) Reported magnitude of self-misidentification among Negro children: artifact? *Journal of Personality and Social Psychology* 8, 49–52

[153] GREGOR, A.J. and McPHERSON, D.A. (1966) Racial preference and ego-identity among white and Bantu children in the Republic of South Africa *Genetic Psychology Monographs* 73, 217–53

[154] HAKLUYT, R. (1589) *The Principall Navigations, Voiages and Discoveries of the English Nation* London

[155] HALEY, A. (1968) *The Autobiography of Malcolm X* Harmondsworth: Penguin Books

[156] HALL, S., CRITCHLEY, C., JEFFERSON, A., CLARKE, S., and ROBERTS, B. (1978) *Policing the Crisis: Mugging, the State, Law and Order* London: Macmillan

[157] HALL, W.S., CROSS, W.E. and FREEDLE, R. (1972) Stages in the development of black awareness: an exploratory investigation in R.L. Jones (ed) *Black Psychology* New York: Harper & Row

[158] HARBIN, S.P. and WILLIAMS, J.E. (1966) Conditioning of color con-

notations *Perceptual and Motor Skills* 22, 217–18

159 HARDING, J., PROSHANSKY, H., KUTNER, B. and CHEIN, I. (1969) Prejudice and ethnic relations in G. Lindzey & E. Aronson (eds) *Handbook of Social Psychology* vol. 5 Reading, Mass: Addison-Wesley

160 HARRIS, A. and WATSON, G. (1946) Are Jewish or Gentile children more clannish? *Journal of Social Psychology* 24, 71–6

161 HARTLEY, E.L., SCHWARTZ, S. and ROSENBAUM, M. (1948a) Children's use of ethnic frames of reference: an exploratory study of children's conceptions of multiple ethnic group membership *Journal of Psychology* 26, 367–86

162 HARTLEY, E.L., ROSENBAUM, M. and SCHWARTZ, S. (1948b) Children's perceptions of ethnic group membership *Journal of Psychology* 26, 387–98

163 HASTIE, T. (1981) Encouraging tunnel vision *Times Educational Supplement* 6 April 1981, 20–22

164 HATCH. S. (1962) Coloured people in school textbooks *Race* 4, 1, 63–72

165 HEBDIGE, D. (1975) Reggae, rastas and rudies *Cultural Studies* 7 & 8 (Summer), 135–54

166 HEIM, A. (1970) *Intelligence and Personality* Harmondsworth: Penguin Books

167 HEMMINGS, R. (1980a) Multi-ethnic mathematics *New Approaches in Multiracial Education* 8, 3, 1–4

168 HEMMINGS, R. (1980b) *Multi-ethnic mathematics* Multiracial Education 9, 1, 29–38

169 HICKS, D. (1980) *Images of the World: an introduction to bias in teaching materials* Occasional paper no. 2, Centre for Multicultural Education, Institute of Education, University of London

170 HICKS, D. (1981) *Minorities: a teacher's resource book for the multiethnic curriculum* London: Heinemann Educational Books

171 HICKS, D. (1981) 'Bias in schoolbooks: messages from the ethnocentric curriculum' in A. James and R. Jeffcoate (eds) *The School in the Multicultural Society* London: Harper & Row (& Open University Press)

172 HILL, E.H. and GIAMMATTEO, M.C. (1963) Socio-economic status and its relationship to school achievement in the elementary school *Elementary English* 40, 265–70

173 HIMMELWEIT, H., OPPENHEIM, A.N. and VINCE, P. (1958) *Television and the Child* London: Oxford University Press

174 HIPKIN, J. (1969) The Humanities Curriculum Project and race relations *Institute of Race Relations Newsletter*, April 1969, 183–4

175 HIPKIN, J. (1972) *Race Pack* Schools Council/Nuffield Humanities Curriculum Project. London: Heinemann Educational Books

176 HODGES, L. (1978) Off to a prejudiced start? *Times Educational Supplement*, 24 February, 1978

177 HOGAN, I. (1956) *Nicodemus and His New Shoes* London: Dent

178 HOROWITZ, E.L. (1936) Development of attitudes towards Negroes *Archives of Psychology* no. 194
179 HOROWITZ, E.L. and HOROWITZ, R.E. (1938) Development of social attitudes in children *Sociometry* 1, 307–38
180 HOROWITZ, E.L. (1940) Some aspects of the development of patriotism in children *Sociometry* 3, 329–41
181 HOROWITZ, R.E. (1939) Racial aspects of self-identification in nursery school children *Journal of Psychology* 7, 91–9
182 HRABA, J. and GRANT, G. (1970) Black is beautiful: a re-examination of racial identification and preference *Journal of Personality and Social Psychology* 16, 398–402
183 HUSBAND, C. (1972) The Media *Race Today* 4, 9, 307
184 Inner London Education Authority (1977) *Multi-Ethnic Education* London: ILEA
185 JACO, E.G. (1960) *The Social Epidemiology of Mental Disorders* New York: Russell Sage Foundation
186 JAHODA, G. (1961) *White Man* London: Oxford University Press
187 JAHODA, G. (1962) Development of Scottish children's ideas and attitudes about other countries *Journal of Social Psychology,* 58, 91–108
188 JAHODA, G., THOMSON, S.S. and BHATT, S. (1972) Ethnic identity and preferences among Asian immigrant children in Glasgow: a replicated study *European Journal of Social Psychology* 2, 1, 19–32
189 JAMES, A. (1981) Teacher Education for a Multicultural Society: a perspective on initial training. Paper presented to the Commission for Racial Equality Advisory Group on Teacher Education, Nottingham University Seminar, April, 1981
190 JAMES, A. and JEFFCOATE, R. (eds) (1981) *The School in the Multicultural Society* London: Harper and Row (in association with the Open University Press)
191 JEFFCOATE, R. (1979) *Positive Image: towards a multiracial curriculum* London: Writers and Readers Publishing Co-operative (in association with Chameleon Books)
192 JEFFCOATE, R. (1982) *Ethnic Minorities and Education* Units 13 & 14, Block 4, E354, Educational Studies Course, Ethnic Minorities and Community Relations, The Open University, Milton Keynes
193 JELINEK, M.M. and BRITTAN, E. (1975) Multiracial Education 1: Interethnic friendship patterns *Educational Research* 18, 1, 44–53
194 JENSEN, A.R. (1968) Social class and verbal learning in M. Deutsch, I. Katz and A.R. Jensen (eds) *Social Class, Race and Psychological Development* New York: Holt, Rinehart & Winston
195 JENSEN, A.R. (1969) How much can we boost IQ and scholastic achievement? *Harvard Educational Review* 39, 1–123
196 JENSEN, A.R. (1979) *Bias in Mental Testing* New York: Free Press
197 JOHNS, W.E. (1969) *Biggles Flies South* London: Collins
198 JOHNSON, D. (1966) Freedom school effectiveness: changes in attitudes

of Negro children *Journal of Applied Behavioural Science* 2, 3, 325–30

[199] JOHNSON, N.B. (1966) What do children learn from war comics? *New Society*, 7 July 1966

[200] JOHNSON, N.B. (1971) 'Some aspects of the formation of national concepts in children' Unpublished PhD dissertation, University of London

[201] JOHNSON, N.B., MIDDLETON, M.R. and TAJFEL, H. (1970) The relationship between children's preference for and knowledge about other nations *British Journal of Social and Clinical Psychology*, 9, 232–40

[202] JONES, C. and KLEIN, G. (1980) *Assessing Children's Books for a Multi-ethnic Society* Centre for Urban Educational Studies, London

[203] JONES, E.E. and GERARD, H.B. (1967) *Foundations of Social Psychology* New York: Wiley

[204] JORDAN, W.D. (1969) *White Over Black* Baltimore: Penguin Books Inc

[205] KAMIN, L. (1977) *The Science and Politics of IQ* Harmondsworth: Penguin Books

[206] KARDINER, A. and OVESEY, L. (1951) *The Mark of Oppression* New York: Norton

[207] KATZ, D. and BRALY, K. (1933) Racial stereotypes in one hundred college students *Journal of Abnormal and Social Psychology* 28, 280–90

[208] KATZ, I. (1967) The socialization of academic motivation in minority-group children in D. Levine (ed) *Nebraska Symposium on Motivation* 1967, Lincoln: University of Nebraska Press

[209] KATZ, I. (1968) Factors affecting Negro performance in the desegregated school in M. Deutsch, I. Katz and A.R. Jensen (eds) *Social Class, Race and Psychological Development* New York: Holt, Rinehart & Winston

[210] KATZ, P.A. (1973a) Perception of racial cues in pre-school children: a new look *Developmental Psychology* 8, 295–9

[211] KATZ, P.A. (1973b) Stimulus predifferentiation and modification of children's racial attitudes *Child Development* 44, 232–7

[212] KATZ, P.A. (1976) *Towards the Elimination of Racism* New York: Pergamon

[213] KATZ, P.A. and SEAVEY, C. (1973) Labels and children's perceptions of faces *Child Development* 44, 770–5

[214] KATZ, P.A., SOHN, M. and ZALK, S.R. (1975) Perceptual concomitants of racial attitudes in urban grade school children *Developmental Psychology* 11, 135–44

[215] KATZ, P.A. and ZALK, S.R. (1974) Doll preferences: an index of racial attitudes? *Journal of Educational Psychology* 66, 663–8

[216] KAWWA, T. (1963) Ethnic prejudice and choice of friends amongst English and non-English adolescents Unpublished MA dissertation, University of London

[217] KEDDIE, N. (1973) *Tinker, Tailor . . . The Myth of Cultural Deprivation* Harmondsworth: Penguin Education

[218] KIERNAN, V.J. (1972) *The Lords of Human Kind: European attitudes towards the outside world in the Imperial age* Harmondsworth: Penguin

[219] KINGSLEY, C. (1973) *The Water Babies* London: Pan Books

[220] KIRP, D. (1979) *Doing Good by Doing Little: race and schooling in Britain* Berkeley: University of California Press

[221] KIRSCHT, J.P. and DILLEHAY, R.C. (1967) *Dimensions of Authoritarianism* Lexington: University of Kentucky Press

[222] KLEIN, G. (1982) Resources for multicultural education: an introduction York: Longman for Schools Council

[223] KLEINER, R.J., TUCKMAN, J. and LAVELL, M. (1960) Mental disorder and status based on race *Psychiatry* 23, 271–4

[224] KNOX, R. (1850) *The Races of Men: a Fragment* London: Renshaw

[225] KOCH, H.L. (1946) The social distance between certain racial, nationality and skin-pigmentation groups in selected populations of American schoolchildren *Journal of Genetic Psychology* 68, 63–95

[226] KOZOL, J. (1967) *Death at an Early Age* Harmondsworth: Penguin Books

[227] KRAUS, S. (1962) Modifying prejudice: attitude change as a function of the race of the communicator *Audio-Visual Communication Review* 10, 14–22

[228] KUH, D.Z., MADZEN, C.H. and BECKER, W.C. (1967) Effects of exposure to an aggressive model and frustration on children's aggressive behaviour *Child Development* 38, 739–46

[229] KUYA, D. (1971) in 'Schoolbooks attacked for warped outlook on race' *The Guardian*, 17 April

[230] LABOV, W. (1969) The logic of non-standard English *Georgetown Monographs on Language and Linguistics* 22, 1–31

[231] LAING, R.D. (1961) *The Self and Others* London: Tavistock

[232] LAISHLEY, J. (1971) Skin colour awareness and preference in London nursery-school children *Race* 13, 1, 47–64

[233] LAISHLEY, J. (1972) Can comics join the multiracial society? *Times Educational Supplement*, 24 November

[234] LANDRETH, C. and JOHNSON, B.C. (1953) Young children's responses to a picture and inset task designed to reveal reactions to persons of different skin colour *Child Development* 24, 63–80

[235] LA PIERE, R.T. (1934) Attitudes versus actions *Social Forces* 13, 230–7

[236] LASKER, B. (1929) *Race Attitudes in Children* New York: Holt

[237] LEACOCK, E. (1971) *The Culture of Poverty: a critique* New York: Simon & Schuster

[238] LEWIS, C.D. (1966) *The Otterbury Incident* London: Bodley Head

[239] LIKOVER, B. (1971) The effect of black history on an inter-racial group of children *Children* 17, 5, 177–82

[240] LINNAEUS, K. (1735) *Systema Naturae* cited in P.D. Curtin, op cit

241 LIPPMAN, W. (1927) *Public Opinion* London: Allen & Unwin
242 LIPSET, S.M. (1959) Democracy and working class authoritarianism *American Sociological Review* 24, 482–501
243 LITCHER, J.H. and JOHNSON, D.W. (1969) Changes in attitudes towards Negroes of white elementary school students after use of multi-ethnic readers *Journal of Educational Psychology* 60, 2, 148–52
244 LITTLE, A. and WILLEY, R. (1981) *Multi-ethnic Education: The Way Forward* Schools Council Pamphlet 18
245 LITTLE, K. (1972) *Negroes in Britain* London: Routledge and Kegan Paul (2nd revised edition)
246 LOFTING, H. (1972) *The Story of Doctor Doolittle* Harmondsworth: Penguin Books
247 LONG, E. (1774) *History of Jamaica* Vol II London
248 LOOMIS, C.P. (1943) Ethnic cleavage in the South-West as reflected in two high schools *Sociometry* 6, 7–26
249 LUNDBERG, G.A. and DICKSON, L. (1952) Selective association among ethnic groups in a high school population *American Sociological Review* 17, 22–35
250 LYNCH, J. (ed) (1981) *Teaching in the Multicultural School* London: Ward Lock Educational
251 MACDONALD, M., McGUIRE, C. and HAVIGHURST, R. (1949) Leisure activities and the socio-economic status of children *American Journal of Sociology* 54, 505–19
252 MAKINS, V. (1978) 'Headstart – alive, well and kicking back' *Times Educational Supplement* 17 April, p 5
253 McADOO, H. (1976) 'The development of self-concept and race attitudes of young black children over time' Paper presented to the Conference on Empirical research on Black Psychology III, Cornell University, 1976
254 McCANDLESS, B.R. and HOYT, J.J. (1961) Sex, ethnicity and play preference of pre-school children *Journal of Abnormal and Social Psychology* 62, 683–5
255 McCONAHAY, J. (1978) The effects of school desegregation upon students' racial attitudes and behaviour: a critical review of the literature and prolegomenon to future research *Law and Contemporary Problems* 42, 3, 77–107
256 McDOUGALL, W. (1908) *Social Psychology* London: Methuen
257 McKEE, J.P. and LEADER, F.B. (1955) The relationship of socio-economic status and aggression to the competitive behaviour of pre-school children *Child Development* 26, 135–41
258 MELTZER, H. (1939) Group differences in nationality and race preferences of children *Sociometry* 2, 86–105
259 MIDDLETON, M.R., TAJFEL, H. and JOHNSON, N.B. (1970) Cognitive and affective aspects of children's national attitudes *British Journal of Social and Clinical Psychology* 9, 122–34
260 MILLER, H.J. (1969) The effectiveness of teaching techniques for

reducing colour-prejudice *Liberal Education* 16, 25–31

[261] MILLER, N.E. and BUGELSKI, R. (1948) Minor studies in aggression: the influence of frustrations imposed by the in-group on attitudes towards out-groups *Journal of Psychology* 25, 437–42

[262] MILNER, D. (1971) Prejudice and the immigrant child *New Society*, 23 September 1971, 556–9

[263] MILNER, D. (1973) Racial identification and preference in black British children *European Journal of Social Psychology* 3, 3, 281–95

[264] MILNER, D. (1979) Does multiracial education work? *Issues in Race and Education* 23, 2–3

[265] MILNER, D. (1981) The education of the black child in Britain: a review and a response *New Community* 9, 2, 289–93

[266] MILNER, E. (1951) A study of the relationship between reading readiness in grade one schoolchildren and patterns of parent-child interactions *Child Development* 22, 95–122

[267] MINARD, R.D. (1931) Race attitudes of Iowa children *University of Iowa Stud. Char.* 4, 2

[268] MINARD, R.D. (1952) Race relationships in the Pocahontas coalfields *Journal of Social Issues* 25, 29–44

[269] MONTAGUE, D.O. (1964) Arithmetic concepts of kindergarten children in contrasting socio-economic areas *Elementary Schools Journal* 64, 393–7

[270] MORENO, J.L. (1934) *Who Shall Survive?* Washington: Nervous & Mental Disorders Publishing Co.

[271] MORLAND, J.K. (1958) Racial recognition by nursery school children in Lynchburgh, Virginia *Social Forces* 37, 132–7

[272] MORLAND, J.K. (1962) Racial acceptance and preference of nursery school children in a Southern city *Merrill-Palmer Quarterly* 8, 271–80

[273] MORLAND, J.K. (1963) Racial self-identification: a study of nursery school children *American Catholic Sociological Review* 24, 231–42

[274] MORLAND, J.K. (1966) A comparison of race awareness in Northern and Southern children *American Journal of Orthopsychiatry* 36, 22–31

[275] MORLAND, J.K. (1969) Race awareness among American and Hong Kong Chinese children *American Journal of Sociology* 75, 3, 360–74

[276] MORRIS, M. (1982) Incident at Tommy White's *Guardian*, 6 August

[277] MOSHER, D.L. and SCODEL, A. (1960) Relationship between ethnocentrism in children and child-rearing practices of their mothers *Child Development* 31, 369–76

[278] MOWRER, O.H. (1950) *Learning Theory and Personality Development* New York: Ronald Press

[279] MUHYI, I.A. (1952) 'Certain content of prejudices against Negroes among white children of different ages' Unpublished PhD dissertation, Columbia University

[280] MULLARD, C. (1980) *Racism in Society and Schools: history, policy and practice* Occasional paper no. 1, Centre for Multicultural Education,

244

Institute of Education, University of London

[281] MURRAY, W. (1965) *Ladybird Key Words Reading Scheme* reader 2b, Ladybird Books, Loughborough

[282] MUSSEN, P.H. (1953) Differences between the T.A.T. responses of Negro and white boys *Journal of Consulting Psychology* 17, 373–6

[283] MUSSEN, P.H. (1950) Some personality and social factors related to changes in children's attitudes towards Negroes *Journal of Abnormal and Social Psychology* 45, 423–41

[284] MUSSEN, P.H. (1967) Early socialization: learning and identification in *New Directions in Psychology* vol. 3 New York: Holt, Rinehart & Winston

[285] National Union of Teachers (1978) *Race, Education, Intelligence* NUT, London

[286] New Standard Editorial, 30 April 1981

[287] NORBURN, V. and PUSHKIN, I. (1973) Ethnic awareness in young children: a follow-up study into early adolescence Institute of Education, London

[288] O'REILLY, R.P. (1970) *Racial and Social Class Isolation in the Schools* New York: Praeger

[289] ORWELL, G. (1939) 'Boys' weeklies' in his *Collected Essays* London: Secker & Warburg

[290] OWEN, R. (1980) Third World studies: pitfalls to be avoided *Teaching Geography* January 1980, 116–17

[291] OWENS, J.V. (1978) Literature on the Rastafari: 1955–1974 *New Community* 6 (i/ii), 150–64

[292] PALERMO, D.S. (1959) Racial comparisons and additional normative data on the children's manifest anxiety scale *Child Development* 30, 53–7

[293] PASAMANICK, B. and KNOBLOCH, H. (1961) Epidemiological studies on the complications of Pregnancy and the birth process in G. Caplan (ed) *Prevention of Mental Disorders in Children* New York: Basic Books

[294] PATTERSON, S. (1963) *Dark Strangers* London: Tavistock

[295] P.E.P. (1967) *Report on Racial Discrimination* London: Political and Economic Planning

[296] PETTIGREW, T.F. (1958) Personality and socio-cultural factors in intergroup attitudes: a cross national comparison *Journal of Conflict Resolution* 2, 29–42

[297] PETTIGREW, T.F. (1964) *A Profile of the Negro American* Princeton: Van Nostrand

[298] PIAGET, J. (1928) *Judgment and Reasoning in the Child* London: Routledge

[299] PIAGET, J. and WEIL, A. (1951) The development in children of the idea of the homeland and of relations with other countries *International Social Science Bulletin* 3, 561–78

[300] PORTER, J.D.R. (1963) 'Racial concept formation in pre-school age

children' Unpublished Master's thesis, Cornell University

301 PORTER, J.D.R. (1971) *Black Child, White Child* Cambridge, Massachusetts: Harvard University Press

302 PORTER, J.D.R. and WASHINGTON, R.E. (1979) Black Identity and Self-Esteem: a review of studies of black self-concept, 1968–78 *Annual Review of Sociology* 5, 53–74

303 Press Council (1982) Press Release no. 58335R/1460, 8 October

304 PUSHKIN, I. (1967) 'A study of ethnic choice in the play of young children in three London districts' Unpublished PhD thesis, University of London

305 PUSHKIN, I. (1967a) Personal communication

306 RADKE, M., SUTHERLAND, J. and ROSENBERG, P. (1950) Racial attitudes of children *Sociometry* 13, 154–71

307 RADKE, M. and TRAGER, H. (1950) Children's perceptions of the social roles of Negroes and whites *Journal of Psychology* 29, 3–33

308 RADKE, M., TRAGER, H. and DAVIS, H. (1949) Social perceptions and attitudes of children *Genetic Psychology Monographs* 40, 327–447

309 RADKE-YARROW, M., TRAGER, H. and MILLER, J. (1952) The role of parents in the development of children's ethnic attitudes *Child Development* 23, 13–53

310 RAMPTON, A. (1981) *West Indian Children in our Schools* London: HMSO

311 RANSOME, A. (1941) *Missee Lee* London: Cape

312 RENNINGER, C.A. and WILLIAMS, J.E. (1966) Black-white colour-connotations and race awareness in pre-school children *Perceptual and Motor Skills* 22, 771–85

313 REX, J. and TOMLINSON, S. (1979) *Colonial Immigrants in a British City. A class analysis* London: Routledge and Kegan Paul

314 RICHARDSON, S.A. and GREEN, A. (1971) When is black beautiful? coloured and white children's reactions to skin colour *British Journal of Educational Psychology* 41, 62–9

315 RILEY, K. (1982) Black girls speak for themselves *Multiracial Education* 10, 3, 3–12

316 RIST, R.C. (1970) Student social class and teacher expectations: the self-fulfilling prophecy in ghetto education *Harvard Educational Review* 40, 411–51

317 RITCHIE, J.E. (1963) The Making of a Maori *Publications in Psychology,* no. 15 Wellington: University of Victoria

318 ROBERTS, A., MOSELEY, K. and CHAMBERLAIN, M. (1975) Age differences in racial self-identity of young black girls *Psychological Reports* 37, 1263–6

319 ROSE, E.J.B. *et al* (1969) Colour and Citizenship: a Report on British Race Relations London: Oxford University Press for the Institute of Race Relations

320 ROSEN, B. (1946) The achievement syndrome: a psychocultural dimension of social stratification *American Sociological Review* 21, 203–11

321 ROSENBERG, M. and SIMMONS, R.G. (1972) *Black and White Self-*

Esteem: the Urban School Child The Arnold & Caroline Rose Monograph Series in Sociology, American Sociological Association, Washington

322 ROSENTHAL, R. (1966) *Experimenter Effects in Behavioral Research* New York: Appleton-Century-Crofts

323 ROSENTHAL, R. (1973) The Pygmalion effect lives *Psychology Today* 1, 58–63

324 ROSENTHAL, R. and JACOBSON, L. (1968) *Pygmalion in the Classroom* New York: Holt, Rinehart & Winston

325 ROSS, E.A. (1908) *Social Psychology* New York: Macmillan

326 ROWLEY, K.G. (1968) Sociometric study of friendship choices among English and immigrant children *Educational Research* 10, 2, 145–8

327 RUBOVITS, P.C. and MAEHR, M.L. (1973) Pygmalion black and white *Journal of Personality and Social Psychology* 25, 2, 210–18

328 RUTTER, M. (1982) Report of lecture by Rutter, *The Sunday Times* 10 October 1982

329 RYAN, J. (1972) 'IQ: the illusion of objectivity' in K. Richardson and D. Spears (eds) *Race, Culture and Intelligence* Harmondsworth: Penguin Books

330 RYAN, W. (1972) *Blaming the Victim* New York: Vintage Books, Random House

331 SAINT, C.K. (1963) 'Scholastic and sociological adjustment problems of the Punjabi-speaking children in Smethwick' Unpublished M.Ed. dissertation, University of Birmingham

332 SANFORD, N. (1955) The dynamics of identification *Psychological Review* 62, 106–18

333 SARTRE, J.-P. (1948) *Anti-Semite and Jew* New York: Schocken Books

334 SATTLER, J.M. (1973) Racial experimenter effects in K.S. Miller and R.S. Dreger (eds) *Comparative Studies of Blacks and Whites in the US* New York: Seminar Press

335 SCHWARTZ, M.A. (1967) *Trends in White Attitudes Towards Negroes* National Opinion Research, Chicago

336 SEARS, R.R. (1957) Identification as a form of behavioural development in D.B. Harris (ed) *The Concept of Development* University of Minnesota Press

337 SEARS, R.R., RAU, L. and ALPERT, R. (1965) *Identification and Child-Rearing* Stanford: Stanford University Press

338 SECORD, P.F. and BACKMAN, C.W. (1964) *Social Psychology* New York: McGraw-Hill

339 SECORD, P.F., BEVAN, W. and KATZ, B. (1956) The Negro stereotype and perceptual accentuation *Journal of Abnormal and Social Psychology* 53, 78–83

340 SEGAL, R. (1966) *The Race War* London: Cape

341 SELLTIZ, C. and COOK, S.W. (1962) Factors influencing attitudes of foreign students towards their host country *Journal of Social Issues* 18, 1, 7–23

[342] SHAW, M.E. (1973) Changes in sociometric choices following forced integration of an elementary school *Journal of Social Issues* 29, 4, 143–57

[343] SHERIF, M. (1966) *Group Conflict and Co-operation: their social psychology* London: Routledge & Kegan Paul

[344] SHERIF, M., HARVEY, O.J., WHITE, B.J., HOOD, W.R. and SHERIF, C. (1961) *Intergroup Conflict and Co-operation: The Robber's Cave Experiment* University of Oklahoma, Norman, Oklahoma

[345] SHERIF. M. and SHERIF, C. (1953) *Groups in Harmony and Tension* New York: Harper & Row

[346] SHERIF, M. and SHERIF, C. (1970) Black unrest as a social movement toward an emerging self-identity *Journal of the Social and Behavioural Sciences* 15, 3, 41–52

[347] SHERWOOD. J.J. and NATAUPSKY. M. (1968) Predicting the conclusions of Negro-white intelligence research from biographical characteristics of the investigator *Journal of Personality and Social Psychology* 8, 1, 53–8

[348] SHIELDS, J. (1962) *Monozygotic Twins Brought Up Apart and Brought Up Together* London: Oxford University Press

[349] SILLER. J. (1957) Socio-economic status and conceptual thinking *Journal of Abnormal and Social Psychology* 55, 365–71

[350] SILVERSTEIN, B. and KRATE. R. (1975) *Children of the Dark Ghetto* New York: Praeger

[351] SIMMONS, R.G. (1978) Blacks and high self-esteem: a puzzle *Social Psychology* 41, 1, 54–7

[352] SIMON. R. (1974) An assessment of racial awareness, preference, and self-identity among white and adopted non-white children *Social Problems* 22, 43–57

[353] SINGER, D. (1967) 'Inter-racial attitudes of Negro and white fifth grade children in segregated and unsegregated schools' Doctoral dissertation, Columbia University. Ann Arbor Mich.: University Microfilms, 1967. No. 67–2836

[354] SIVANANDAN, A. (1969) Race: the revolutionary experience *Race Today* 1, 4, 108–9

[355] SNOW, R.E. (1969) Unfinished Pygmalion *Contemporary Psychology* 14, 197–9

[356] SPRINGER, D.V. (1950) Awareness of racial differences by pre-school children in Hawaii *Genetic Psychology Monographs* 41, 215–70

[357] STANTON, W. (1960) *The Leopard's Spots: scientific attitudes towards race in America, 1815–59* Chicago: University of Chicago Press

[358] STENDLER, C.B. (1961) Social class differences in parental attitude towards school at grade one level *Child Development* 22, 37–46

[359] STEVENSON. H.W. and STEWART, E.C. (1958) A developmental study of racial awareness in young children *Child Development* 29, 399–409

[360] STEWART, I. (1970) Readers as a source of prejudice *Race Today* 2, 1, 27–8

248

[361] STINTON, J. (ed) (1980) *Racism and Sexism in Children's Books* London: Writers and Readers Publishing Co-operative

[362] ST JOHN, N. (1975) *School Desegregation: outcomes for children* New York: Wiley

[363] STONE, I.F. (1966) *New York Review of Books* 18 August

[364] STONE, M. (1981) *The Education of the Black Child in Britain: the myth of multiracial education* London: Fontana

[365] STONES, R. A Multi-ethnic booklist Harmondsworth: Penguin

[366] SULLIVAN, H.S. (1955) *Conceptions of Modern Psychiatry* London: Tavistock

[367] SUMMERS, G.F. and HAMMONDS, A.D. (1966) Effects of racial characteristics of investigator on self-enumerated responses to a Negro prejudice scale *Social Forces* 44, 515–18

[368] TAJFEL, H. (1970) Personal communication

[369] TAJFEL, H. (1973) The roots of prejudice: cognitive aspects in P. Watson (ed) *Psychology and Race* Harmondsworth: Penguin Education

[370] TAJFEL, H. (1978a) Intergroup behaviour I: individualistic perspectives in H. Tajfel and C. Fraser (eds) *Introducing Social Psychology* Harmondsworth: Penguin Books

[371] TAJFEL, H. (1978b) *Differentiation Between Social Groups* London: Academic Press

[372] TAJFEL, H., FLAMENT, C., BILLIG, M. and BUNDY, R. (1971) Social categorization and inter-group behaviour *European Journal of Social Psychology,* 1, 149–78

[373] TAJFEL, H. and JAHODA, G. (1966) Development in children of concepts and attitudes about their own and other nations: a cross-national study *Proceedings of the XVIIIth International Congress in* Psychology, Moscow, Symposium 36, 17–33

[374] TAJFEL, H., JAHODA, G., NEMETH, C., RIM, Y. and JOHNSON,, N.B. (1972) The devaluation of children of their own national and ethnic group: two case studies *British Journal of Social and Clinical* Psychology 11, 88–96

[375] TAJFEL, H., NEMETH,, C., JAHODA, G., CAMPBELL, J.D. and JOHNSON, N.B. (1970) The development of children's preference for their own country: a cross-national study *International Journal of Psychology* 5, 245–53

[376] TAJFEL, H. and TURNER, J. (1979) An integrative theory of intergroup conflict in W.G. Austin and S. Worchel (eds) *The Social Psychology of Intergroup Relations* Monterey, California: Brooks Cole

[377] TAJFEL, H. and WILKES, A.L. (1963) Classification and quantitative judgment *British Journal of Psychology* 54, 101–14

[378] TAYLOR, M. (1981) *Caught Between: a review of research into the education of pupils of West Indian origin* Windsor: NFER-Nelson

[379] TAYLOR, M. and HURWITZ, K. (1979) *Books for under-5's in a multicultural society* Islington Libraries, 22 Fieldway Crescent, London, N.1

380 TAYLOR, R. (1976) Psychosocial development among black children and youth: a re-examination *American Journal of Orthopsychiatry* 46, 1, 4–19

381 TEPLIN, L.A. (1974) 'Misconceptualization as artifact? A multi-trait, multi-method analysis of inter-racial choice and interaction methodologies utilized in studying children' Paper presented to the annual meeting of the Society for the Study of Social Problems, Montreal

382 TEPLIN, L.A. (1977) Preference vs prejudice: a multi-method analysis of children's discrepant racial choices *Social Science Quarterly* 58, 390–406

383 TERREL, G., DURKIN, K. and WIESLEY, M. (1959) Social class and the nature of the incentive in discrimination learning *Journal of Abnormal and Social Psychology* 59, 270–2

384 THOMAS, C.W. (1971) *Boys No More* Beverly Hills, California: Glencoe Press

385 THOMAS, W.I. (1904) The psychology of race prejudice *American Journal of Sociology* 9, 5, 593–611

386 THOMPSON, R.H.T. (1953) Maori affairs and the New Zealand press *Journal of Polynesian Sociology* 62, 363–83

387 THORNDIKE, R.L. (1968) Review of R. Rosenthal and L. Jacobson *Pygmalion in the Classroom. American Educational Research Journal* 5, 708–11

388 THURSTONE, L.L. (1931) The measurement of social attitudes *Journal of Abnormal and Social Psychology* 36, 249–69

389 TIERNEY, J. (ed.) (1982) *Race, Migration and Schooling* London: Holt, Rinehart & Winston

390 TITUS, H.E. and HOLLANDER, E.P. (1957) The California F scale in psychological research, 1950–1955 *Psychological Bulletin* 54, 47–74

391 TOMLINSON, S, (1978) West Indian children and ESN schooling. *New Community* 6, 3 ,235–42

392 TOMLINSON, S. (1980) The educational performance of ethnic minority pupils *New Community* 8, 3, 213–34

393 TOMLINSON, S. (1981) *Educational Subnormality: a study in decision making* London: Routledge & Kegan Paul

394 TOWNSEND, H.E.R. (1971) *Immigrant Pupils in England: the L.E.A. response* Slough: NFER

395 TRAGER, H. and YARROW, M. (1952) *They Learn What They Live* New York: Harper & Row

396 TRENT, R.D. (1954) The colour of the investigator as a variable in experimental research with Negro subjects *Journal of Social Psychology* 40, 281–7

397 TROYNA, B. (1978) Race and Streaming: a case study *Educational Review* 30, 1, 59–65

398 TROYNA, B. (1981) *Public Awareness and the Media: a study of - reporting on race* London: Commission for Racial Equality

399 TURNER, J. (1975) Social comparison and social identity: some

prospects for intergroup behaviour *European Journal of Social Psychology* 5, 5–34

400 TWITCHEN, J. and DEMUTH, C. (1981) *Multicultural Education: views from the classroom* London: BBC Publications

401 UPTON, B. and UPTON, F. (1967) *The Golliwog's Bicycle Club* London: Longman

402 VALENTINE, C.A. (1968) *Culture and Poverty* Chicago: Chicago University Press

403 VAUGHAN, G.M. (1963) Concept formation and the development of ethnic awareness *Journal of Genetic Psychology,* 103, 93–103

404 VAUGHAN, G.M. (1964a) Ethnic awareness in relation to minority-group membership *Journal of Genetic Psychology,* 105, 119–30

405 VAUGHAN, G.M. (1964b) Ethnic awareness and attitudes in New Zealand *Victoria University of Wellington Publications in Psychology* no 17

406 VAUGHAN, G.M. (1964c) The development of ethnic attitudes in New Zealand schoolchildren *Genetic Psychology Monographs* 70, 135–75

407 VAUGHAN, G.M. (1972) (ed) *Racial Issues in New Zealand* Auckland: Akarana Press

408 VAUGHAN, G.M. (1978) Social change and intergroup preferences in New Zealand *European Journal of Social Psychology* 8, 297–314

409 VERNON, P.E. (1938) *The Assessment of Psychological Qualities by Verbal Methods* Medical Research Council, Industrial Health Research Board, Report no. 83 London: HMSO

410 WADDINGTON, M. (1967) Education for one world: the teacher's field of action *New Era* 48, 55–62

411 WALTERS, E. (1966) Some factors in the background and experience of West Indian children which may affect their progress and behaviour in English schools. Unpublished paper cited in E.J.B. Rose *et al: Colour and Citizenship* op cit

412 WALTERS, R.H. (1966) Implications of laboratory studies on aggression for the control and regulation of violence *Annals of the American Academy of Political and Social Sciences* 364, 60–72

413 WALVIN, J. (1971) *The Black Presence* Orbach & Chambers

414 WARD, S.H. and BRAUN, J. (1972) Self-esteem and racial preference in black children *American Journal of Orthopsychiatry* 42, 4, 644–7

415 WASHINGTON, B.T. (1945) *Up From Slavery* London: Oxford University Press

416 WEBSTER, M. (1973) in *Spearhead*, April

417 WERNER, N.E. and EVANS, I.M. (1968) Perception of prejudice in Mexican-American preschool children *Perceptual and Motor Skills* 27, 1039–46

418 Westinghouse Learning Corporation and Ohio University *The Impact of Headstart* Maryland: Bladenburg

419 WHITING, J.W.M. (1960) Resource mediation and learning by identification in I. Iscoe & H.W. Stevenson (eds) *Personality Development*

251

in Children Austin: University of Texas Press

420 WICKER, A.W. (1969) Attitudes vs Actions: the relation of verbal and overt behavioural responses to attitude objects *Journal of Social Issues* 25, 41–78

421 WILLIAMS, J.E. (1964) Connotations of colour names among Negroes and Caucasians *Perceptual and Motor Skills* 19, 721–31

422 WILLIAMS, J.E. (1970) Connotations of racial concepts and color names in M.L. Goldschmid (ed),*Black Americans and White Racism* New York: Holt, Rinehart & Winston

423 WILLIAMS, J.E. and MORLAND, J.K. (1976) *Race, Color and the Young Child* University of North Carolina Press, Chapel Hill

424 WILLIAMS, J.E. and MORLAND, J.K. (1979) Comment on Banks's 'White preference in blacks: a paradigm in search of a phenomenon' *Psychological Bulletin* 86, 1, 28–32

425 WILLIAMS, J.E., MORLAND, J.K. and UNDERWOOD, W.L. (1970) Connotations of color-names in the US, Europe and Asia *Journal of Social Psychology* 82, 3–14

426 WILLIAMS-ELLIS, A. (1963) *Round the World Fairy Tales* Glasgow: Blackie

427 WILSON, W.C. (1963) Development of ethnic attitudes in adolescence *Child Development* 34, 247–56

428 WYLIE, R.C. (1963) Children's estimates of their schoolwork ability as a function of sex, race and socio-economic status *Journal of Personality* 31, 203–24

429 ZELIGS, R. (1938) Tracing racial attitudes through adolescence *Sociology and Social Research* 23, 45–54

430 ZELIGS, R. and HENDRICKSON, G. (1933) Racial attitudes of two hundred sixth grade children *Sociology and Social Research* 18, 26–36

431 ZIMET, S. (1976) *Print and Prejudice* London: Hodder & Stoughton

Index

relation to teacher attitudes 182
interracial behaviour 125–7, 201, 208–9
intolerance of ambiguity 31

Jaco, E.G. 142
Jahoda, G. 68, 145–6
Jahoda, G. *et al.* 121, 152
James, A. 223–4
James, A. & Jeffcoate, R. 216
Jeffcoate, R. 217–20
Jelinek, M.M. & Brittan, E. 127
Jenkins, R. 198
Jensen, A.R. 105, 106, 165, 173–5, 177
Johns, W.E. 84
Johnson, D. 207–8
Johnson, N.B. 56, 70, 92
Johnson, N.B. *et al.* 69, 70
Jones, C. & Klein, G. 91
Jones, E.E. & Gerard, H.B. 54
Jordan, W.D. 7, 8, 10

Kamin, L. 171
Kardiner, A. & Ovesey, L. .141–2, 143
Katz, D. & Braly, K. 44
Katz, I. 183, 184
Katz, P.A. 106, 107
Katz, P.A. & Seavey, C. 107
Katz, P.A. *et al.* 107
Katz, P.A. & Zalk, S.R. 130
Kawwa, T. 126
Keddie, N. 177
Keynes, J.M. 192
Kiernan, V.J. 10
Kingsley, C. 78, 79, 80, 82
Kirp, D. 199
Kirscht, J.P. & Dillehay, R.C. 32
Klein, G. 91, 223–4
Kleiner, R.J. *et al.* 142
Knox, R. 11
Koch, H.L. 117, 126
Kozol, J. 78, 79, 80
Kraus, S. 152
Kuh, D.Z. *et al.* 60
Kuya, D. 77

Labov, W. 179, 180
Laing, R.D. 61
Laishley, J. 94, 120
Landreth, C. & Johnson, B.C. 115, 133, 134
language provision 196, 197, 199
LaPiere, R.T. 48
Lasker, B. 23
Leacock, E. 182
Lewis, C.D. 79
Likover, B. 208

Linnaeus, K. 10
Lippman, W. 5
Lipset, S.M. 115
Litcher, J.H. & Johnson, D.W. 207
Little, A. & Willey, R. 216
Little, K. 196
Lofting, H. 81, 82
Long, E. 11
Loomis, C.P. 126
Lorenz, K. 52
Lundberg, G.A. & Dickson, L. 126
Lynch, J. 216

MacDonald, M. *et al.* 166
Makins, V. 175
Maoris, 119, 135
mass media and racial attitudes
    press 97–9
    television 95–7
McAdoo, H. 156
McCandless, B.R. & Hoyt, J.J. 117, 125, 126
McConahay, J. 126
McDougall, W. 17
McKee, J.P. & Leader, F.B. 167
Meltzer, H. 135
Middleton, M.R. *et al.* 70
Miller, H.J. 201–2
Miller, N. & Bugelski, R. 27
Milner, D. 121–3, 137–9, 161–2, 200, 203, 209–12, 228
Milner, E. 166
Minard, R.D. 34, 113
minimal groups 40–2
Montague, D.O. 166
Moreno, J.L. 126
Morland, J.K. 66, 108, 109, 115, 117, 133, 136–7, 153
Morris, D. 52
Morris, M. 99
Mosher, D.L. & Scodel, A. 61, 117
Mowrer, O.H. 58
Muhyi, I. 113
Mullard, C. 224
multiracial education
    a rationale 191–95
    history 192
    vs. multiculturalism 224–8
    objectives 191–93
    and social change 191, 227–8
Murray, W. 85
Mussen, P.H. 57, 58, 140

National Association for Multiracial Education 215
National Front 176